TAKING C
YOUR VoIP PROJECT

John Q. Walker and Jeffrey T. Hicks

Cisco Press

800 East 96th Street
Indianapolis, Indiana 46240 USA

Taking Charge of Your VoIP Project

John Q. Walker and Jeffrey T. Hicks
Copyright© 2004 Cisco Systems, Inc.
Cisco Press logo is a trademark of Cisco Systems, Inc.
Published by:
Cisco Press
800 East 96th Street
Indianapolis, IN 46240 USA

Printed in the United States of America 2 3 4 5 6 7 8 9 0
Second Printing   September 2005

Library of Congress Cataloging-in-Publication Number: 2003104991
ISBN: 1-58720-092-9

Warning and Disclaimer

This book is designed to provide information about Voice over Internet Protocol. Every effort has been made to make this book as complete and as accurate as possible, but no warranty or fitness is implied.

The information is provided on an "as is" basis. The authors, Cisco Press, and Cisco Systems, Inc. shall have neither liability nor responsibility to any person or entity with respect to any loss or damages arising from the information contained in this book or from the use of the discs or programs that may accompany it.

The opinions expressed in this book belong to the author and are not necessarily those of Cisco Systems, Inc.

Corporate and Government Sales

Cisco Press offers excellent discounts on this book when ordered in quantity for bulk purchases or special sales.
For more information, please contact: **U.S. Corporate and Government Sales**
1-800-382-3419 corpsales@pearsontechgroup.com
For sales outside of the U.S. please contact: **International Sales**
international@pearsontechgroup.com

Feedback Information

At Cisco Press, our goal is to create in-depth technical books of the highest quality and value. Each book is crafted with care and precision, undergoing rigorous development that involves the unique expertise of members from the professional technical community.

Readers' feedback is a natural continuation of this process. If you have any comments regarding how we could improve the quality of this book, or otherwise alter it to better suit your needs, you can contact us through email at feedback@ciscopress.com. Please make sure to include the book title and ISBN in your message.

We greatly appreciate your assistance.

Publisher	John Wait
Editor-in-Chief	John Kane
Cisco Representative	Anthony Wolfenden
Cisco Press Program Manager	Nannette M. Noble
Production Manager	Patrick Kanouse
Development Editor	Howard A. Jones
Copy Editor	Bill McManus
Technical Editors	Mark Gallo, Mike Kisch, Branden Ritchey
Team Coordinator	Tammi Barnett
Book and Cover Designer	Louisa Adair
Composition	Mark Shirar
Indexer	Eric Schroeder

Trademark Acknowledgments

All terms mentioned in this book that are known to be trademarks or service marks have been appropriately capitalized. Cisco Press or Cisco Systems, Inc. cannot attest to the accuracy of this information. Use of a term in this book should not be regarded as affecting the validity of any trademark or service mark.

Tips in Chapter 3, pages 113-114, Copyright 2000 by Techtarget.com, 117 Kendrick Street; Suite 800; Needham, MA 02492. Reprinted with permission of TechTarget.com.

CISCO SYSTEMS

Corporate Headquarters
Cisco Systems, Inc.
170 West Tasman Drive
San Jose, CA 95134-1706
USA
www.cisco.com
Tel: 408 526-4000
    800 553-NETS (6387)
Fax: 408 526-4100

European Headquarters
Cisco Systems International BV
Haarlerbergpark
Haarlerbergweg 13-19
1101 CH Amsterdam
The Netherlands
www-europe.cisco.com
Tel: 31 0 20 357 1000
Fax: 31 0 20 357 1100

Americas Headquarters
Cisco Systems, Inc.
170 West Tasman Drive
San Jose, CA 95134-1706
USA
www.cisco.com
Tel: 408 526-7660
Fax: 408 527-0883

Asia Pacific Headquarters
Cisco Systems, Inc.
Capital Tower
168 Robinson Road
#22-01 to #29-01
Singapore 068912
www.cisco.com
Tel: +65 6317 7777
Fax: +65 6317 7799

Cisco Systems has more than 200 offices in the following countries and regions. Addresses, phone numbers, and fax numbers are listed on the
Cisco.com Web site at www.cisco.com/go/offices.

Argentina • Australia • Austria • Belgium • Brazil • Bulgaria • Canada • Chile • China PRC • Colombia • Costa Rica • Croatia • Czech Republic
Denmark • Dubai, UAE • Finland • France • Germany • Greece • Hong Kong SAR • Hungary • India • Indonesia • Ireland • Israel • Italy
Japan • Korea • Luxembourg • Malaysia • Mexico • The Netherlands • New Zealand • Norway • Peru • Philippines • Poland • Portugal
Puerto Rico • Romania • Russia • Saudi Arabia • Scotland • Singapore • Slovakia • Slovenia • South Africa • Spain • Sweden
Switzerland • Taiwan • Thailand • Turkey • Ukraine • United Kingdom • United States • Venezuela • Vietnam • Zimbabwe

About the Authors

John Q. Walker is president of Zenph Studios, Inc., creating software for high-definition audio. Before co-founding Zenph Studios, Walker was the director of Network Development at NetIQ Corporation. He was one of the four co-founders of Ganymede Software, Inc., which was acquired by NetIQ in 2000. In his 5 years as vice president of product development, Ganymede products consistently won "Best Product" and "Product of the Year" awards. For example, only two companies won *Network World* magazine's "World Class Award" *twice* in 1999: Dell Computer and Ganymede Software.

Dr. Walker has co-authored a book on portable network programming, as well as authoring dozens of technical articles, and is frequently an invited speaker on practical networking and software engineering topics. He was influential in the creation of both the IEEE 802 local-area network (LAN) and the 802.11 wireless LAN ("Wi-Fi") standards. Walker has extensive experience in the development and management of emerging technologies in engineering development organizations. At IBM, he managed teams developing high-speed networking software. Dr. Walker completed his Ph.D. in software engineering at the University of North Carolina. He holds four patents. His e-mail address is johnq@zenph.com.

Jeffrey T. Hicks is a principal software engineer/architect at NetIQ Corporation. He has recently led the development teams for the award-winning Chariot and Vivinet Assessor products. He has been active in the design and development of VoIP deployment, testing, and management solutions for the past five years. In earlier jobs, he helped develop innovative network communications software products at IBM. Mr. Hicks holds a master of engineering degree from North Carolina State University and a bachelor of science degree in computer engineering from Auburn University. His e-mail address is jeff.hicks@netiq.com.

About the Technical Reviewers

Mark Gallo is a technical manager with America Online where he leads a group of engineers responsible for the design and deployment of the domestic corporate intranet. His network certifications include Cisco CCNP and Cisco CCDP. He has led several engineering groups responsible for designing and implementing enterprise LANs and international IP networks. He has a bachelor's in electrical engineering from the University of Pittsburgh. Mark resides in northern Virginia with his wife, Betsy, and son, Paul.

Mike Kisch is a senior manager at Cisco in charge of the development of Cisco's global Business Impact program including the development of financial models, best practices, and consulting programs. Mike leads a team that is dedicated to assisting customers in determining the value of their technology investments and building a compelling business case for new IT investments. His group has been involved in the development of over 5000 ROI analysis across a variety of technologies including IP telephony, unified messaging, contact center, network security, and storage networking. He is a frequent event speaker and his work on ROI has been published in several leading technology journals. Prior to joining Cisco, Mike worked in numerous general management, marketing, marketing research, and sales positions with Information Resources, Inc. (IRI), Kraft Foods, and Anheuser Busch. Mike has an undergraduate degree from the University of Wisconsin and a master's of business administration from Washington University. He can be reached at mkisch@cisco.com.

Branden Ritchey is a network consulting engineer for Cisco Systems. He has worked in voice communications and the VoIP technology for seven years. He is currently working with customers and partners in the planning, design, and implementation of large-scale IP communications networks. He also designs and develops IPT leading practices and deployment kits to be used in the field by Cisco Advanced Services, partners, and customers. He holds the Cisco certifications CCDA, CCNA, Cisco IP Telephony Design and Support Specialist, and he has Microsoft's MCSE. He is currently working towards his CCIE Voice Certification. He can be reached at britchey@cisco.com.

Acknowledgments

Sounds of laughter make
rapid transformations to
electricity.
—James Coggins

We have had a superb editor for our work inside NetIQ: Susan M. Pearsall, Ph.D. She read every word in every chapter multiple times, at every point offering suggestions on improving readability. We received similar assistance from our editors at Cisco Press, Howard Jones and Chris Cleveland.

We cannot thank John Kane enough for his patience with us throughout this project. There was much hoop jumping at many stages of the project cycle, but John hung in there. We appreciate the many efforts of John in getting this book off the ground and into print.

The idea for this book belongs to Aimee Doyle. She coordinated the steps needed in project management to get it funded, and suggested the overall outline for the book. She was our advocate at many points in time inside NetIQ, which we appreciate. Melissa Bertone, in the office adjoining Aimee, helped us through many technical and production problems. Tammi Barnett, at Cisco Press, handled many of the behind-the-scenes matters flawlessly.

We had excellent technical reviewers. Mark Gallo, Mike Kisch, and Brian Ritchey added comments, clarified technical details, and helped make the book better in many ways.

We have had many fine reviewers inside NetIQ, who read the unfolding book a chapter at a time and provided us with excellent feedback. They're our heroes, as well. Sometimes their feedback was a fully marked-up chapter; sometimes it was simply a gem of an idea. We list them here alphabetically: Paula Acker, Jeff Aldridge, Lynne Attix, Tom Carey, James Coggins, Jeff Dozer, Peter Frame, Larry Hountz, Steve Joyce, Robby Rose, Tod Schumacher, Peter Schwaller, Chris Selvaggi, Kim Shorb, Carl Sommer, John Steigerwald, Ellen Strader, Gary Weichinger, Colleen Wood, John Wood, and Mark Zelek.

Portions of this book were originally published as an eBook on the NetIQ website. We also received great feedback from several of our eBook readers: Johnny Geypen, Dave Michels, Vivek Rana, and Matthew Trzyna.

There's a brief haiku at the start of each chapter. With a mere 17 syllables, it seems the authors have been able to summarize an entire chapter. So read each haiku, and then read our verbose chapter for the technical details and to-do lists. The authors are all on the product development team at NetIQ in Research Triangle Park, North Carolina. Daniel Wideman came up with the idea of using the haikus after returning from a week at a writers' camp.

We submitted the original version of Chapter 3, "Planning for VoIP," to the 2002 Bitpipe White Paper competition. Among more than 400 papers in our category of Networking and Communications, we won Honorable Mention. Because of our competitive nature, we were a little bummed at not winning first place—that is, until we read the awesome prize-winning paper from a team at Hitachi.

Jeff would like to thank his wonderful wife and son, Janna and Andrew, for their patience and understanding during the long process of writing this book. Without their support, it would not have been possible.

Contents at a Glance

Contents

Why We Wrote This Book

We want the chief information officers (CIOs) and information technology (IT) managers who choose to deploy VoIP in their organizations to look good. Plenty of books can provide you with technical details about VoIP, but few explain in plain language how to make it run successfully in an enterprise.

We have designed our book to start with fairly simple concepts, with each chapter building on the knowledge gained from previous chapters. We have made few assumptions about your background, other than expecting some basic understanding of the two key terms in the title: *voice* telephone conversations and *IP* data networking.

This is not a technical manual about the inner workings of industry standards such as H.323, G.711, and RTP. However, it covers the implications of these standards for implementing and managing a VoIP system.

Who Should Read this Book

We are writing for managers of enterprise IT departments—and for their managers, up to the CIO level. We are also writing for networking professionals, technology experts, and systems integrators who are embarking on the big effort to deploy voice on an IP network. And we have included material that will be useful to the folks on the other side of the big knowledge gap that we are trying to bridge; it seems few professionals in the telephony community know much about the data-networking community, and vice versa.

How This Book Is Organized

Here is what each chapter covers:

Chapter 1

- How the telephony community views this technology
- How the data networking community views this technology

Chapter 2

- The top benefits you will receive from VoIP—and which benefits are more hype than reality
- Analyzing your VoIP return on investment (ROI)
- Getting a good ROI

Chapter 3

- The planning, analysis, and assessment needed to ensure a successful deployment
- Avoiding common VoIP pitfalls through proper planning
- Why most networks are not ready for a VoIP deployment
- Pilot deployments: how big should you start, and when do you roll out?
- A roadmap for your VoIP deployment
- The critical importance of a thorough testing plan

Chapter 4

- Some options for outsourcing
- Criteria that determine whether you should roll out VoIP yourself or work with an integrator
- Selecting an integrator: important questions to ask
- A methodology for approaching outsourcing

Chapter 5

- An introduction to quality of service (QoS) and tuning concepts
- Network QoS techniques
- Tuning choices and their trade-offs
- Some QoS and tuning recommendations for VoIP

CHAPTER 1

VoIP Basics

Don't be left behind
as Voice over IP comes
into full flower.
—Jeff Aldridge

This chapter discusses basic VoIP terminology and concepts. Even the acronym *VoIP* is an example of the rampant jargon you have to master to understand and deploy VoIP. There is lots of terminology to cover, from both the telephony and data-networking communities. The proper terminology is used throughout this book, but terms are introduced and explained in plain English.

IP telephony is a phrase that is often used synonymously with VoIP. Both IP telephony and VoIP refer to the components and technology needed to place telephone calls over an IP-based network. This book uses *VoIP* as an umbrella term to cover all aspects of IP telephony.

This chapter starts with some call fundamentals. A telephone call occurs in two stages:

- Setting up the telephone connection between the person making the call (the *caller*) and the person receiving the call (the *callee*)

  - Getting from one telephone to the other, through everything that is in the middle.

  - Committing the resources to that call, so that once the callee gets it, the callee gets to keep it, and the call is not unexpectedly terminated right in the middle.

  - Ending the call when it is complete.

  - Billing someone for the call.

- The call itself

  - People or computers speak to one another for some amount of time

  - Voice (audio) is translated into a format that is sent over a network

  - The digitized audio information is transformed back into sound

Both stages involve specialized equipment and a set of rules that guides the operation of that equipment. This chapter first looks at how telephone calls work in the telephony community and then looks at how telephone calls work in the data-networking community.

In the Telephony Community

Telephony specialists approach communications technology from a background shaped by the traditional telephone network, the *Public Switched Telephone Network* (PSTN). The telephone service provided by the PSTN is called *plain old telephone service* (POTS). This plain type of telephone network that everyone takes for granted uses circuit-switched connections, which means that when you make a call, you receive a dedicated circuit from one telephone to the other, through everything that is in the middle. The typical dedicated circuit through the PSTN has evolved from a physical connection to a logical connection that involves many switches. When you speak into a phone, a microphone creates an analog transmission that is passed along the circuit.

Decades of knowledge, experience, and innovation have allowed the PSTN to achieve the quality and reliability that it has today. When you pick up a phone, you get a dial tone almost instantly. And when you dial a number, the destination phone starts ringing, usually within a few seconds. Can you even recall the last time your traditional telephone call was dropped by the network? Because the PSTN is so reliable, people are rarely willing to tolerate reduced-quality or dropped calls, and their tolerance usually comes only with additional convenience, such as the convenience provided by mobile phones.

The level of reliability that is expected from the PSTN is sometimes referred to as *five nines*. This term means that the entire network must be available and functional for 99.999 percent of the time. If you apply this principle over the period of one year:

365 days * 24 hours/day * 60 minutes/hour * 0.00001
= 5.256 minutes

Five nines means that the network can be down for a grand total of less than six minutes over the course of a year!

Telephony Standards

An international organization that is now a part of the UN, the *International Telecommunications Union* (ITU) plays a major role in standardizing the technology of the PSTN. The ITU initially provided standards and agreements for connecting telegraph links between countries starting in the nineteenth century and has evolved to oversee many areas of standards development within the global telecom industry.

The ITU includes a specific division known as the *Telecommunications Standardization Sector* or ITU-T. This division comprises many companies and organizations with interests in telecommunications standards. After the ITU-T standards have been grouped into similar functional areas, they are called *recommendations*, and they share an assigned letter of the alphabet. The following ITU-T recommendations are most relevant to this discussion:

G—Transmission systems and media, and digital systems and networks

H—Audiovisual and multimedia systems

P—Telephone transmission quality, telephone installations, and local line networks

The recommendation category letter is typically followed by a period and a number, such as G.711 or H.323. An ITU-T standard recommendation is said to be "In Force" when the standard has been approved by ITU-T membership.

Standards are crucial to the success of technologies like VoIP. Without standards, your phone call would very likely be dropped when it passed from vendor A's network to vendor B's network. Accordingly, many VoIP vendors have drawn on the expertise of the ITU-T and built VoIP products based on well-known standards.

How the PSTN Works

To talk about VoIP technology, it helps to understand a little about how the PSTN works today. The following is what has to happen when the caller makes a telephone call to the callee over the PSTN:

1   The caller picks up the telephone handset and hears a dial tone.

2   The caller enters a telephone number, specifying the address of the callee.

3   Signals are sent through the PSTN to set up a circuit for the call. The resources necessary to carry the call are reserved for it.

4   The destination phone rings, indicating to the callee that a call has arrived.

5   The callee picks up the telephone handset and begins a conversation. The audio, voice conversation is translated to digital format in the center of the network, and then back to analog at the edge.

6   The conversation ends, call billing occurs, the circuit is taken down, and resources are released.

Figure 1-1 shows the steps in a typical telephone call.

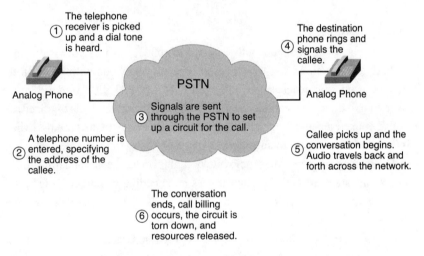

The telephone
① receiver is picked up and a dial tone is heard.

Analog Phone

A telephone number is
② entered, specifying the address of the callee.

PSTN

Signals are sent
③ through the PSTN to set up a circuit for the call.

The destination
④ phone rings and signals the callee.

Analog Phone

Callee picks up and the
⑤ conversation begins. Audio travels back and forth across the network.

The conversation ends, call billing
⑥ occurs, the circuit is torn down, and resources released.

Figure 1-1   *Six Steps in Typical Telephone Call*

These steps must happen correctly and quickly for a telephone call to succeed with high quality. When telephony professionals consider providing the same functionality and reliability on relatively new and unreliable IP networks, you can see where some doubts and skepticism can arise.

PSTN Components

Five components provide the infrastructure needed for fast and reliable calls on the PSTN. A brief introduction to these components will help you to understand what must be duplicated by VoIP technology to provide the same performance and reliability. Each of these five components is discussed in detail in the following sections:

- Voice encoding

- PSTN switches

- Private branch exchange (PBX)

- Signaling

- Telephones

Voice Encoding

When you speak into the mouthpiece of a telephone headset, your audio input is initially sent as an analog transmission over the telephone wiring. When the analog transmission reaches the entry point of the PSTN, it is *digitized,* or converted into digital format—a series of 0s and 1s. After it has been digitized, the encoded voice transmission is transported across the PSTN to the far edge, where it is converted back again to an analog signal, and finally to sound.

The method for converting audio into digital form has been standardized. The name of this standard is G.711, and it uses an encoding technique called *pulse code modulation* (PCM). Within the G.711 standard, however, there are two varieties:

- **G.711u**—Also known as μ-law encoding (the Greek letter "mu"), this is used primarily in North America.

- **G.711a**—Also known as a-law encoding, this is used primarily *outside* North America.

G.711 converts analog audio input into digital output at an output rate of 64,000 bits per second, which is commonly referred to as *64 kilobits per second* (kbps). A single G.711 voice channel is referred to as *digital signal, level 0,* or *DS0*. The fact that a DS0 takes up 64 kbps has been used in building links of the PSTN. Building a phone network link with a capacity for 24 voice channels takes 24 * 64 kbps = 1.536 megabits per second (Mbps). An additional 8 kbps is needed for framing overhead, which gives a total of 1.544 Mbps. A link with this capacity is known as a *trunk level 1,* or *T1*, link. Figure 1-2 shows the voice channels in a T1 link.

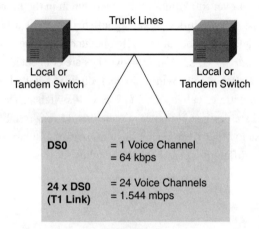

Figure 1-2   *Voice Channels in the PSTN*

You will encounter the G.711 standard again in the discussion of VoIP networks later in the chapter.

PSTN Switches

Switches are the core component of the PSTN. Switches of various types move call traffic from link to link and provide the circuits and dedicated connections necessary for PSTN calls. The links between switches are usually called *trunk lines*, and the capacity of trunk lines is usually stated in terms of the number of DS0 channels. Trunk lines use a technology called *multiplexing* to send multiple voice conversations over the same link.

PSTN switches are often categorized based on their function. However, switches that perform the same kinds of functions are often known by multiple names. If you think of connecting a phone in your house or in your company to the PSTN, the first point of entry is a switch called a *local switch* or *local office*. This type of switch is also known as a *Class 5 switch*. The local switch is usually operated by a local telephone company, which is often called a *local exchange carrier* (LEC). The local switch takes analog input from the phone connection and digitizes it for transmission through the center of the PSTN. The digitized conversation is sent over trunk lines to the next switch in the network.

The next type of switch the digital signal encounters is a tandem switch or tandem office. Tandem switches are usually operated by a long-distance company, or *interexchange carrier* (IXC). Tandem switches are connected to local switches or other tandem switches to provide a logical, circuit-switched path through the PSTN, and are sometimes called *Class 1, 2, 3,* or *4* switches. They carry massive call volumes and are designed to be very scalable and very reliable.

In VoIP systems, the IP router is analogous to the switches of the PSTN. Figure 1-3 shows different types of PSTN switches.

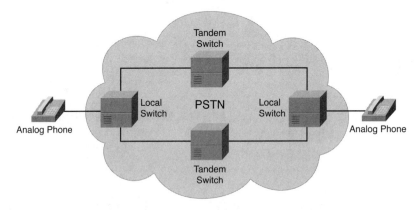

Figure 1-3 *PSTN, Showing Local and Tandem Switches*

PBXs

A *private branch exchange* (PBX) is the foundation for most corporate voice networks. Typically, a corporate telephone network is different from a residential phone system. In a corporate environment, the network has to serve multiple users who need some advanced features, such as caller ID, call transfer, and call forwarding. In addition, the typical corporation wants its phone system to act as a single network, even if it serves offices in New York, Raleigh, and London.

Whereas residential telephone systems must allocate a separate external phone line for every user, the PBX enables corporate users to share a limited number of external telephone lines, providing cost savings to the company. The

PBX also supports traditional telephone features like call waiting, call conferencing, and call forwarding. Many larger corporations connect PBXs together with "tie lines," which enable corporate users to make calls to co-workers without placing the calls on the PSTN at all. To dial another user over a tie line, you typically dial a different phone number, based on the tie line extension.

PBX systems come in all shapes and sizes. Smaller PBX systems, sometimes referred to as *key systems,* support limited numbers of users in smaller offices. Larger PBX systems may provide phone services for hundreds or thousands of users.

In VoIP systems, an IP PBX is analogous to the PBX of the PSTN, providing many of the same functions and features as a traditional PBX. Figure 1-4 shows an enterprise PBX connected to the PSTN.

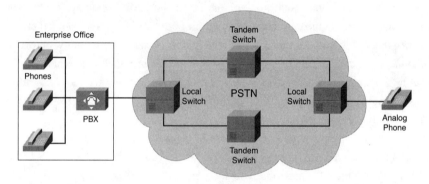

Figure 1-4 *PSTN, with an Enterprise Connected via a PBX*

In some cases a business may outsource the functionality of the PBX and engage a service provider for a solution known as *Centrex.* With a Centrex solution, the service provider owns and operates all the equipment that is needed to provide call control and phone services. The provider maintains and manages the equipment on its premises, freeing the customer from the cost and management of PBX equipment. For VoIP systems, service providers are now offering IP Centrex, which extends the traditional Centrex model to include IP-based phone calls.

Like IP Centrex solutions, many traditional PBX systems are being retrofitted in other ways to support IP telephony. Service providers have offerings that add a gateway router to your network so that PBX-based calls can be transported on your IP network. A solution like this can provide an easy first step toward a VoIP implementation, as well as a cost savings, because the PSTN is bypassed for long-distance calls. To the user, the service appears transparent, because the PBX-connected phones have all the features and functions that they had before. There is a large investment in traditional PBX systems, so don't expect them to just go away overnight and be totally replaced by VoIP.

Signaling

Establishing a telephone call requires several different types of signaling: to inform network devices that a telephone is off the hook, to supply destination information so that the call may be routed properly, and to notify both caller and callee that a call has been placed. A relatively new signaling technology, known as *Signaling System 7* (SS7), is the ITU standard that provides for signaling, call setup, and management of PSTN calls. Typically, a separate network is used for SS7 flows. Because the data transfer for SS7 does not occur on the same path as the call, it is sometimes referred to as an *out-of-band* signal.

Two key components make up an SS7 network. The *signal transfer point* (STP) provides routing through the SS7 network. You could think of STPs as the IP routers of the SS7 network. The *session control point* (SCP) provides 800-number lookup and other management features. Similarly, *Domain Name System* (DNS) and *Dymanic Host Control Protocol* (DHCP) provide address lookup and management for IP networks.

When a phone call is made, the signaling protocols find the route to the callee, establish the connections between switches, and tear down these connections after the call ends. The STPs communicate with the local and tandem switches to reserve capacity between the switches in the path between caller and callee. After the call is completed, the STPs communicate with the switches to release the reserved connections, making them available for other calls. Figure 1-5 shows an SS7 network and signaling paths.

VoIP systems have a corresponding set of rules for call signaling. The section "Call Setup Protocols" later in this chapter introduces these.

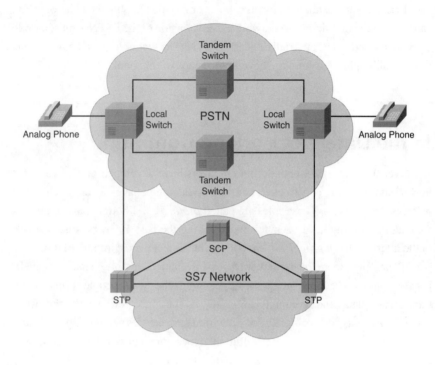

Figure 1-5 *PSTN Uses SS7 Networks for Signaling*

Telephones

Telephones that connect to the PSTN traditionally come in two flavors: analog and digital:

- **Analog telephone**—The type of phone that most people have in their homes today, it connects to the PSTN via traditional phone lines and sends an analog transmission (a waveform that varies over time).

- **Digital telephone**—The type of phone that many corporations use, it connects directly to a PBX and sends formatted digital signals.

Nowadays, specialized IP phones can connect to the PSTN as well. IP phones are discussed later in the chapter in the section "IP Phones and Softphones," which includes an explanation of how IP phone technology differs from traditional telephones.

This chapter has not mentioned cellular or mobile telephony technology. You can think of the mobile-phone network as an extension of the PSTN—most mobile calls are carried at least partially over the PSTN. The technology and components of the mobile-phone system are beyond the scope of this book.

In the Data-Networking Community

Over the years, data-networking engineers have developed precise rules for how a data packet is constructed, and how each side behaves when it sends and receives data packets. These rules are called *protocols*. Although many protocols for data networking have been developed during the past 50 years, since the rise of the Internet, the *Internet Protocol* (IP) has become the most important protocol.

IP has proved to be remarkably scalable and adaptable. That is why IP networking has become ubiquitous, changing the way people think about transferring data and communicating. Over the past few years, the word *convergence* has drawn a lot of attention to the IP-networking industry. Convergence refers to taking different types of data—voice, video, and application data—and transferring them over the same IP network.

Data-Networking Standards

Just as the ITU has been influential in the creation of standards in the telephony community, the *Internet Engineering Task Force* (IETF) has led the standardization efforts in the data-networking community.

New data-networking techniques go through a rigorous trial phase consisting of study, implementation, and review to verify their stability and robustness. Those that pass these critical examinations are known by their *Request For Comments* (RFC) number, because the RFC stage is often the last step in the transition from a draft standard to an approved standard.

Each of the components of the Internet Protocol discussed in the following sections—known by names such as *TCP*, *UDP*, and *RTP*—has one or more corresponding RFCs that describe its operation.

How VoIP Works

Voice over IP is simply the transfer of voice conversations as data over an IP network. Unlike traditional circuit-switched calls on the PSTN VoIP calls are "packet switched." In a packet-switched environment, multiple computer devices share a single data network. They communicate by sending packets of data to one another, each packet containing addressing information that specifies the source and target computers. The contents of these packets—that is, their payload—are snippets of the voice conversation. The packets within a single transmission can take different paths from end to end across a data network.

With a VoIP call, the call setup portion of the calling sequence has to be simulated—dial tone, ringing, busy signals. The audio portion of the call needs to be converted from analog to digital, cut into packets, sent across the network in packet format, reassembled, and converted from digital back to analog. Encoders and decoders at either end do the conversion from analog to digital and back. (An explanation of how they work is provided a bit later.)

Here is what happens when a VoIP call is made:

1 The caller picks up the telephone handset and hears a dial tone.

2 The caller dials a telephone number, which is mapped to the IP address of the callee.

3 Call setup protocols are invoked to locate the callee and send a signal to produce a ring.

4 The destination phone rings, indicating to the callee that a call has arrived.

5 The callee picks up the telephone handset and begins a two-way conversation. The audio transmission is encoded using a codec and travels over the IP network using a voice streaming protocol.

6 The conversation ends, call teardown occurs, and billing is performed.

VoIP Components

This chapter has already discussed the building blocks of the PSTN. To transfer voice data on the same network with e-mail and web traffic, a new set of components is required. Some of the most important components are the following:

- Codecs

- TCP/IP and VoIP protocols

- IP telephony servers and PBXs

- VoIP gateways and routers

- IP phones and softphones

Codecs

A codec (which stands for *compressor/decompressor* or *coder/decoder*) is the hardware or software that samples analog sound, converts it to digital bits, and outputs it at a predetermined data rate. Some codecs perform compression to save bandwidth. There are dozens of available codecs, each with its own characteristics.

Codecs have odd-looking names that correspond to the name of the ITU standard that describes their operation. For example, the codecs named G.711u and G.711a convert from analog to digital and back with relatively high quality. As with most things digital, higher quality implies more bits, so these two codecs use more bandwidth than lower-quality codecs.

Lower-speed codecs, such as G.726, G.729, and those in the G.723.1 family, consume less network bandwidth. However, low-speed codecs impair the quality of the audio much more than high-speed codecs because low-speed codecs apply *lossy* compression—compression that loses some of the original data. Fewer bits are sent, so the receiving side does its best to approximate what the original audio sounded like, but it is not a high-fidelity re-creation.

Table 1-1 lists some common VoIP codecs. For each codec, the codec's data rate is shown, as well as the time needed by the codec to do the analog-to-digital and digital-to-analog conversions. The middle column in the table shows the rate at which the codec generates its output. The Packetization Delay column refers to the delay a codec introduces as it converts from analog to digital and back. You will see in later chapters that this fixed amount of delay can affect the quality of the call as perceived by the listeners.

Table 1-1   *Six Common Codecs Used in VoIP*

Codec Name	Nominal Data Rate	Packetization Delay
G.711u	64.0 kbps	1.0 ms
G.711a	64.0 kbps	1.0 ms
G.726-32	32.0 kbps	1.0 ms
G.729	8.0 kbps	25.0 ms
G.723.1 MPMLQ	6.3 kbps	67.5 ms
G.723.1 ACELP	5.3 kbps	67.5 ms

Codecs use sophisticated techniques for coding and compression. You will see names that stretch the limits of your math background, like *Multi-Pulse Maximum Likelihood Quantization* (MPMLQ) and *Algebraic Code Excited Linear Predictive* (ACELP) compression. The names suggest how the codecs do their job; these topics are beyond the scope of this book.

Packet loss concealment (PLC) is an additional feature available with the G.711u or G.711a codecs. PLC techniques reduce or mask the effects of data loss during a telephone conversation. PLC does not add delay or have bad side effects, but it makes the G.711 codecs more expensive to manufacture. Codecs with PLC can provide a dramatic improvement in the voice quality when data loss occurs.

TCP/IP Protocols

The TCP/IP family of protocols forms the basis of the Internet and most current corporate networks. Computer programs send and receive data over an IP network by making program calls to the TCP/IP software, known as the *protocol stack,* in their local computer. The TCP/IP stack in the local computer exchanges information with the TCP/IP stack in the target computer to accomplish the transfer of data from one side to the other. The information they exchange includes the size of the chunks of data (the datagram size), identifies data associated with each datagram (the datagram header), and what should occur if a datagram is lost or damaged in transit.

The Internet Protocol determines how datagrams are transferred across an IP network from the sending program to the receiving program. Datagrams are the units sent and received by the two sides, and they move in hops, or segments, across a network. Each hop has its own network characteristics; for example, some hops may be Fast Ethernet hops, whereas others could be slower, broadband connections. To optimize the performance of the hops, devices on the network may perform datagram fragmentation, cutting large datagrams into smaller pieces, called *packets*, which need to be reassembled into the original datagrams by the receiving computer.

When a datagram arrives at an IP router or switch in a network, the router or switch decides where the datagram should go in its next hop and forwards it along. The section "Working on the Problem Areas" in Chapter 3, "Planning for VoIP," returns to this discussion of hops through the network, but for now, suffice it to say that too much time spent going through one or more of the hops can delay the datagrams and add variation in the delay time, making the telephone conversation sound poor.

The current version of the Internet Protocol called *IPv4* has been around since RFC 791 was published in the early 1980s. It is remarkable that despite all the changes in computer networks, the underlying protocol has not changed very much. However, IPv4 has some limitations, which have led to a new, improved version known as *IPv6*. IPv6 seeks to provide a larger address space to prevent the current Internet from running out of available IP addresses. The protocol details that are discussed in this book all apply to IPv4. IPv6 is currently being tested by the major network vendors and is being deployed in some newer networks. Look for IPv6 networks to eventually replace the current IPv4 infrastructure.

Sending and receiving application programs communicate via two related protocols when they contact their TCP/IP stack:

- **Transmission Control Protocol (TCP)**—When making calls to the TCP interface, the sending program wants to make sure that the receiving program gets everything that is sent—that is, it wants to avoid data being lost, duplicated, or out of order. TCP is known as a connection-oriented protocol because the two sides of the data exchange maintain strong tracking of everything that is sent and received. For example, your browser uses the TCP interface when fetching web pages—you don't want to see holes or out-of-order pieces of data on the screen, so your browser and the web server program work together to make sure everything is received intact.

- **User Datagram Protocol (UDP)**—When using UDP, the sending application has no assurance of delivery, and it is willing to deal with that. UDP is called a connectionless protocol, which means that when using this protocol, the two sides don't acknowledge receiving any data to make sure everything arrived intact. Think about a stock ticker running across the bottom of your computer screen. If a datagram is lost, causing one of the quotes to be lost, it is not catastrophic because another will come along shortly—a stock ticker application is a good example of a program that uses UDP to send data.

The datagrams that the application assembles contain protocol-specific information. The TCP or UDP portion of an individual datagram is nested inside an IP wrapper. For example, a UDP header describes how the payload of a UDP datagram is to be decoded. In turn, the IP header contains information such as the network addresses of the sender and the receiver. Figure 1-6 shows IP packets and their header format. (Refer to RFC 791 for more information.)

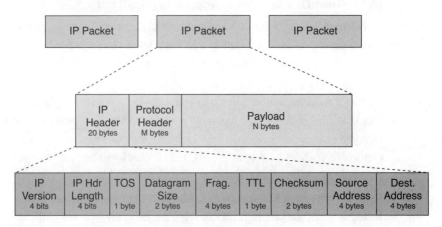

Figure 1-6 *IP Packets and Their Header Format*

Whether the protocol is TCP or UDP, the header of every IP packet contains several standard fields. You will encounter these fields throughout this book as VoIP is discussed:

- **TOS (Type Of Service)**—The TOS byte can be used to mark the priority of a packet. It is generally set to zero, which means that the devices in the network that examine the packet give their best effort in delivering it from one side of the network to the other. By setting this byte to a nonzero value, an application can request improved handling for a packet, making it less likely to be dropped or delayed. The first 6 bits of this byte are also known as the Differentiated Services (or DiffServ) field.

- **TTL (Time To Live)**—Each time a packet takes one hop in its path across a network, the number in the TTL byte is reduced by one. If a device receives a packet with a zero in its TTL byte, it discards the packet. A TTL of zero means the packet has lived too long (that is, it has taken too many hops), indicating a problem with the network or with the packet. The TTL keeps packets from circling an IP network forever.

- **Checksum**—A checksum is used to detect any changes made to the bits during transmission. The sending side feeds all the bits it is sending through a sophisticated equation and writes the final result of the equation into the Checksum field. The receiving side similarly passes all the bits it receives through the same equation. If its results match the checksum that was sent, the receiving side can be confident no bits were changed (accidentally or maliciously) during the transmission. Otherwise, it should discard the packet. This checksum is used to verify the integrity of the IP header.

- **Source Address and Destination Address**— These fields are the 4-byte IP addresses of the sending and receiving applications. These 4 bytes are traditionally written in dotted notation, like 192.168.123.158.

These definitions scratch the surface of an extremely complex subject. To obtain more detailed information, you should seek out some of the excellent books that explain TCP/IP comprehensively. A few recommended titles are provided at the end of this chapter.

VoIP Protocols

Application programs build their own families of higher-layer protocols on top of the lower-layer protocols they use for transport and other tasks. Placing a VoIP telephone call on a data network involves the call setup—the VoIP equivalent of getting a dial tone, dialing a phone number, getting a ring or a busy signal at the far end, and picking up the phone to answer the call—and then the telephone conversation. VoIP protocols are required during both phases:

- **Call setup protocols**—Several higher-layer protocols can accomplish call setup and takedown, including H.323, SIP, SCCP, MGCP, and Megaco/H.248 (these are described in the next section). The programs that implement the call setup protocol use TCP and UDP to exchange data during the call setup and takedown phases.

- **Voice streaming protocols**—The exchange of encoded voice data occurs after call setup (and before call takedown), using two data flows—one in each direction—to let both participants speak at the same time. Each of these two data flows uses a higher-layer protocol called *Real-Time Transport Protocol* (RTP), which is encapsulated in UDP as it travels through the network. Figure 1-7 illustrates the two sets of VoIP protocols.

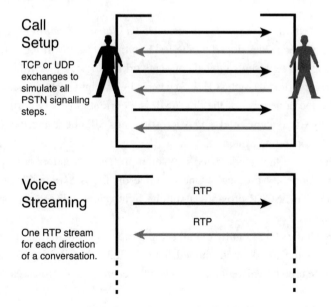

Call Setup

TCP or UDP exchanges to simulate all PSTN signalling steps.

Voice Streaming

One RTP stream for each direction of a conversation.

RTP

RTP

Figure 1-7 *Two Sets of High-Level Protocols, for Call Setup and for Conversation*

The following sections describe the call setup and voice streaming protocols in more depth.

Call Setup Protocols

Call setup protocols use TCP and UDP to transfer data during the setup and takedown phases of a telephone call. They handle functions like the mapping of phone numbers to IP addresses, generating dial tones and busy signals, ringing the callee, and hanging up. There are two families of call setup protocols: one set from the telephony community and the other from the data-networking community.

The call setup protocols H.323 and *Media Gateway Control Protocol* (MGCP) come from the telephony community by way of the ITU. H.323 is widely deployed and, among the call setup protocols, has been around the longest period of time. H.323 is actually a family of telephony-based standards for multimedia, including voice and videoconferencing. MGCP is the less flexible version, for use with inexpensive devices like home telephones.

The family of H.323 protocols has been refined for many years. As a result, it is robust and flexible, but the cost of this robustness is that it has high overhead: A calling session includes lots of handshakes and data exchanges for each function performed.

Session Initiation Protocol (SIP) and *Media Gateway Control* (Megaco) are lightweight protocols developed by the IETF in the data-networking community. SIP, in particular, represents typical data-networking logic, which asks: Why use a heavyweight protocol (such as H.323) when a lightweight protocol (such as SIP) will get the job done most of the time? SIP is a current "industry darling"—it is supported by Cisco and Nortel, and Microsoft ships SIP client interfaces with its Windows XP operating system.

In addition to the standardized call setup protocols, vendors have provided their own proprietary protocols. One example of this is *Skinny Client Control Protocol* (SCCP). SCCP provides a simple, lightweight call setup protocol for Cisco devices.

Although the H.323 family of call setup protocols is predominant today, it is likely that all the protocols discussed here (H.323, MGCP, Megaco, SIP, and SCCP) will be used by VoIP equipment in varying degrees for the foreseeable future.

Voice Streaming Protocols

Widely used for streaming audio and video, RTP is designed for applications that send data in one direction with no acknowledgments. The header of each RTP datagram contains a time stamp, so the application receiving the datagram can reconstruct the timing of the original data. It also contains a sequence number so that the receiving side can deal with missing, duplicate, or out-of-order datagrams.

The two RTP streams carrying the bidirectional conversation are the important elements in determining the quality of the voice conversations. It is helpful to understand the composition of the RTP datagrams, which transport the voice datagrams. Figure 1-8 shows the RTP header format. (Refer to RFC 1889 for more information.)

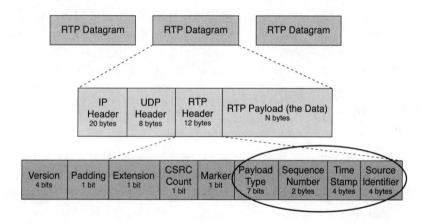

Figure 1-8   *Header Used for RTP Follows the UDP Header in Each Datagram*

All the fields related to RTP sit inside the UDP payload. So, like UDP, RTP is a connectionless protocol. The software that creates RTP datagrams is not commonly part of the TCP/IP protocol stack, so applications are written to add and recognize an additional 12-byte header in each UDP datagram. The sender fills in each header, which contains four important fields:

- **RTP Payload Type**— Indicates which codec to use. The codec conveys the type of data (such as voice, audio, or video) and how it is encoded.

- **Sequence Number**— Helps the receiving side reassemble the data and detect lost, out-of-order, and duplicate datagrams.

- **Time Stamp**— Used to reconstruct the timing of the original audio or video. It also helps the receiving side determine variations in datagram arrival times, known as *jitter.*

  It is the time stamp that brings real value to RTP. An RTP sender puts a time stamp in each datagram it sends. The receiving side of an RTP application notes when each datagram actually arrives and compares this to the time stamp. If the time between datagram arrivals is the same as when they were sent, there is no variation. However, depending on network conditions, there could be lots of variation in datagram arrival times. The receiving side can easily calculate this jitter using the time stamp.

- **Source ID**— Lets the software at the receiving side distinguish among multiple, simultaneous incoming streams.

Real bandwidth consumption by VoIP calls is higher than it first appears. The accumulation of headers can add a lot of overhead, depending on the size of the data payload. For example, a typical payload size when using the G.729 codec is 20 bytes, which means that the codec outputs 20-byte chunks of the VoIP call at a predetermined rate specific to that codec. With RTP, two-thirds of the datagram is the header, because the total header overhead consists of the following:

RTP (12 bytes) + UDP (8 bytes) + IP (20 bytes) = 40 bytes

The G.729 codec has a data rate of 8 kbps. When sent at 20-ms intervals, its payload size is 20 bytes per datagram. To this, add the 40 bytes of RTP header and any additional Layer 2 headers. For example, Ethernet drivers generally add 18 more bytes. The Bandwidth Required column in Table 1-2 shows a more accurate picture of actual bandwidth usage for some common codecs on an Ethernet network.

Some IP phones let you set the "delay between packets" or "speech packet length," which is the rate at which the sender delivers datagrams into the network. For example, at 64 kbps, a 20-ms speech datagram implies that the sending side creates a 160-byte datagram payload every 20 ms. A simple equation relates the codec speed, the delay between voice datagrams, and the datagram payload size:

Payload size (in bytes) =

$$\frac{\text{Codec speed (in bits/sec)} * \text{datagram delay (ms)}}{8 \text{ (bits/byte)} * 1000 \text{ (ms/sec)}}$$

In this example:

160 bytes = (64,000 * 20)/8000

For a given data rate, increasing the delay causes the datagrams to get larger, because the datagrams are sent less frequently to transport the same quantity of data. A delay of 30 ms at a data rate of 64 kbps would require sending 240-byte datagrams.

Table 1-2 *Common Codec Attributes*

Codec	Nominal Data Rate	Packetization Delay	Typical Datagram Spacing	Bandwidth Required
G.711u	64.0 kbps	1.0 ms	20 ms	87.2 kbps
G.711a	64.0 kbps	1.0 ms	20 ms	87.2 kbps
G.726-32	32.0 kbps	1.0 ms	20 ms	55.2 kbps
G.729	8.0 kbps	25.0 ms	20 ms	31.2 kbps
G.723.1 MPMLQ	6.3 kbps	67.5 ms	30 ms	21.9 kbps
G.723.1 ACELP	5.3 kbps	67.5 ms	30 ms	20.8 kbps

Now that you understand more about the types of protocols VoIP uses, you are ready to move on to the discussion of the next set of VoIP components.

IP Telephony Servers and PBXs

Many data-networking transactions are based on the client/server model of computing. Client computers make requests for services to server computers, which perform those services and return the results. You are probably familiar with web servers, e-mail servers, and database servers, all of which perform client/server transactions.

Adding voice data to IP networks requires yet another set of servers that are designed to provide voice services in innovative ways. An IP PBX typically serves as the core IP telephony server. On the PSTN, the PBX is often a *closed-box* system—it provides all the voice functions and features you need, but usually in a proprietary manner. Management of the closed-box platform is left up to the PBX vendor. With VoIP, an IP PBX can be built on a PC platform running on an operating system such as Microsoft Windows, Linux, or Sun Solaris. Although parts of the IP PBX are inherently proprietary, the platforms can be managed through vendor *application programming interfaces* (APIs) and through the standard APIs provided by the operating system.

An IP PBX provides functions and features similar to those that a traditional PBX provides. Although the standard PBX of the PSTN offers multiple features developed over decades, such as call transfer and call forwarding, IP PBXs are already providing the same kinds of features and more, and their development is advancing quickly. Cisco CallManager is an example of a full-featured IP PBX.

Other IP telephony servers provide new and interesting services. For example, *unified messaging*—the convergence of voice mail and e-mail—can be considered a benefit of a VoIP implementation. Unified messaging servers also run on PC platforms and talk to e-mail servers and IP PBXs to provide message access in a variety of ways.

Figure 1-9 shows key components in a VoIP deployment.

Figure 1-9 *VoIP Network and Its Typical Components*

Another new concept introduced along with IP telephony servers is *clustering,* in which several of these servers are grouped together in a cluster to offer increased scalability, reliability, and redundancy. Clustered servers function together and can be managed as a unit, providing combined processing power while logically appearing as a single server. Clustering is not available with traditional PBXs in the PSTN.

Another type of server, the *gatekeeper,* is used by the H.323 protocol to provide *call admission control* (CAC) and other management functions, such as address lookup, for multimedia services. The gatekeeper uses a set of signaling flows, RAS (*registration, admission, and status*), to work with VoIP devices. The CAC function of a gatekeeper can be especially important for networks with limited bandwidth, because the gatekeeper can track the number of calls in progress and restrict calls based on current bandwidth consumed. The goal of CAC is to limit new calls (or reroute them to the PSTN) if they may adversely impact the quality of calls that are already in progress on the VoIP network.

Video streaming and videoconferencing servers also deserve some mention here. Although not directly related to VoIP, video servers eventually take advantage of the converged network infrastructure that is needed for VoIP. Because of its higher bandwidth requirements, video over IP presents a new set of challenges that make VoIP look easy!

VoIP Gateways, Routers, and Switches

VoIP gateways and IP routers move RTP voice datagrams through an IP network. VoIP gateways provide a connection between the VoIP network and the PSTN, so these devices play a key role in the migration path toward VoIP. Although networks that have exclusively VoIP phones are growing, there are still instances when it is necessary to connect to the PSTN to place calls to PSTN users. VoIP gateways must use the SS7 protocol to signal switches in the PSTN when a phone call is originating from the VoIP network and the callee is in the PSTN. In addition, VoIP gateways may provide conversion between different codecs, which is called *transcoding*. If a codec other than G.711, say G.729, is used on the VoIP network, the voice data must be converted to G.711 before being transferred to the PSTN.

In a corporate environment, VoIP gateways can interconnect with traditional PBXs to provide a migration path and allow for staged VoIP deployments. Gateways are typically capable of speaking a large number of different protocols. These complex devices handle the variety of signaling and data protocols that are required to communicate between the VoIP network and the PSTN.

By examining the IP packet headers, IP routers make the decisions necessary to move packets to the next router and hop along the path to the destination. Tracing the route of a voice packet through the network can be useful for problem identification and diagnosis; techniques for this are discussed in later chapters. Router technology itself is well understood but is not discussed in detail in this book.

Figure 1-10 shows an expanded VoIP network with a connection to the PSTN.

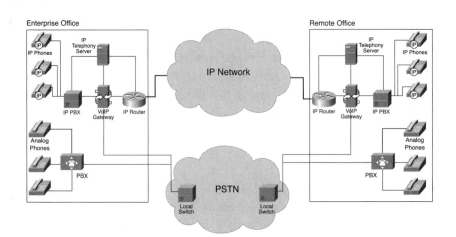

Figure 1-10 *VoIP Network with Its VoIP Gateways Connected to the PSTN*

Ethernet switches look at the link-layer header information to move packets from source to destination. These switches have become the cornerstone of many campus LANs, providing high-speed network access to the desktop. Many router-like functions are beginning to appear in switches to further blur the line between router and switch. Many VoIP implementations recommend using switch functionality to create virtual LANs (VLANs) for VoIP traffic. IP phones are typically connected directly to Ethernet switches.

IP Phones and Softphones

To make VoIP work, analog audio must be converted to digital datagrams. You know this is performed by codecs, but where does the conversion take place? Where are the codecs located?

If you are using older analog telephones, the codecs are located in the IP PBX. Incoming calls are digitized there, before being forwarded onto the IP network.

Alternatively, the codecs can be located in the telephones themselves. These new digital telephones are called *IP phones*. Rather than having a four-line telephone connector in the back, they usually have an Ethernet LAN connection. An IP phone makes data connections to an IP telephony server, which does the call setup processing.

There is yet another choice. Your computer can serve in the role of the IP phone on your desk. You plug a headset and microphone into the computer's audio card. The computer's CPU runs the software doing the codec processing, and the computer has a LAN connection into the data network. As with an IP phone, your computer, or *softphone*, probably relies on an IP telephony server to do call setup processing.

Chapter Summary

It is important to understand the terminology and concepts when dealing with a new technology. This chapter introduced and explained key VoIP components. Understanding VoIP requires knowledge of both data networking and telephony. The main PSTN components were introduced: voice encoding, switches, PBXs, signaling, and telephones. Likewise, the main VoIP components were introduced: codecs, protocols, telephony servers, IP PBXs, gateways, and IP phones.

Now that you are familiar with the basics of VoIP and its resemblances to— and distinctions from—the telephone network that you are accustomed to using, the next chapter covers the potential benefits of VoIP, and tries to separate some of the pie-in-the-sky VoIP fantasies from the real returns you can expect from your own implementation.

End Notes

The following sources provide good primers about TCP/IP:

1   Comer, D. E. *Internetworking with TCP/IP,* Volume 1: Principles, Protocols, and Architecture. Englewood Cliffs, NJ: Prentice Hall, 2000. (ISBN 0-13-018380-6.)

2   Stevens, W. R. *TCP/IP Illustrated,* Volume 1. Reading, MA: Addison-Wesley, 1994. (ISBN 0-201-63346-9.)

3   Walker II, J. Q. and J. T. Hicks. "Protocol Ensures Safer Multimedia Delivery." *Network World,* Volume 16, no. 44, November 1999: 53.

The following sources provide good overviews of VoIP:

1   Bruno, C. and Scott Hamilton. "What You Need to Know Before You Deploy VoIP." http://www.netiq.com/products/chr/whitepapers.asp. Manasquan, NJ: Tolly Research (commissioned by NetIQ Corp.), April 2, 2001.

2   Davidson, J. and J. Peters. *Voice over IP Fundamentals.* Indianapolis: Cisco Press, 2000. (ISBN 1-57870-168-6.)

3   Newton, Harry. *Newton's Telecom Dictionary.* New York: CMP Books, 2001. (ISBN 1-57820-069-5.)

4   Walker, John Q. "Checklist of VoIP Network Design Tips." http://www.netiq.com/products/chr/whitepapers.asp. San Jose, CA: NetIQ Corporation, April 2001.

CHAPTER 2

BUILDING A BUSINESS CASE FOR VOIP

To leap or to hide –
Trust evidence to decide;
Faith makes risky guide.
—James Coggins

This chapter explains how to build a business case for VoIP. It points out some of the benefits that VoIP can provide and discusses how to analyze *return on investment* (ROI) for VoIP implementation and management.

A VoIP Business Case

A business case for investing in a VoIP implementation requires evaluation of the associated ROI. VoIP offers many potential benefits, including reduced costs, new features, and converged networks. However, some of these benefits may be more hype than reality.

Planning is important for a successful VoIP implementation. The planning involves evaluating the costs and benefits associated with the implementation and anticipating possible pitfalls. Understanding the most appropriate insertion points for VoIP within an organization also plays a critical role in how significant the ROI can be. The most important questions to think about during your planning include the following:

- What kind of return should you expect from an investment in VoIP?

- What are the key factors to consider when analyzing VoIP ROI?

- What deployment scenarios (greenfield, Centrex replacement, and so on) are most likely to provide a positive ROI?

- Because management of VoIP components—networks, servers, and phones—is critical to your VoIP investment, what ongoing management resources are necessary to ensure continued success after initial deployment?

The VoIP industry has matured rapidly. The technology has advanced in less than a decade from small pilot projects and test environments to large-scale deployments in many enterprises. As new technology is adopted, it goes through a predictable process, described by Geoffrey A. Moore in his book *Crossing the Chasm*[1] and shown in Figure 2-1. There is an initial period where pioneers tend to ignore ROI because they want to deploy the technology, which gives them a real or perceived technological advantage. For example, Cisco was an innovator and early adopter of the VoIP technology that it produced. Inside Cisco, all employees have IP phones on their desks for everyday use.

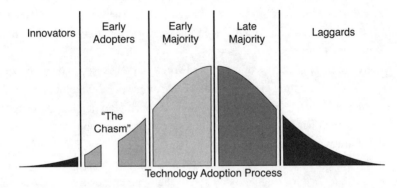

Figure 2-1 *Technology Adoption Process, from Moore's Book* Crossing the Chasm

VoIP appears to have "crossed the chasm," moving past the Early Adopters phase and into the Early Majority phase. The question of VoIP adoption has shifted from if to when. A 2001 study found that "90% of enterprises with multiple locations will start switching to IP systems for voice over the next 5 years."[2] Early Majority users are more cautious about expending capital on still-evolving technologies. They therefore prefer to wait until a technological innovation has a positive track record. In the Early Majority and all later phases of a new technology, it is difficult to ignore ROI and important to build a business case before making a purchase.

The benefits of VoIP can be measured in different ways. Bottom-line cost savings are fairly easy to quantify. Other VoIP benefits, such as productivity improvements, are more difficult to quantify in terms of ROI. These types of benefits sometimes require a leap of faith or intuition about potential results. The next section examines the potential benefits of VoIP in more detail.

VoIP Benefits and Obstacles

VoIP enthusiasts promise many benefits over the traditional PSTN. A great deal of industry excitement has been generated about the potential cost savings, the new calling features, and the reduced infrastructure of converged networks in a VoIP implementation.

There are two main types of benefits to VoIP—hard benefits and soft benefits. *Hard benefits* come with a clearly-defined cost savings. For example, replacing a PBX with a VoIP server may save a company a specific amount of money every year. On the other hand, *soft benefits* don't necessarily save money, or, if they do, they don't always save an easily calculated amount of money. But they have the potential to affect the bottom line in the future if, for example, your decision to innovate with unified messaging today means that your company is ready to make another technological leap in the future. Although both types of benefits are critical to the final ROI, most organizations focus more on the hard cost savings, because they are easier to quantify. Oftentimes it is appropriate to clearly differentiate between hard and soft benefits to improve the credibility of the business case with financial decision makers. The next section takes a closer look at three broad categories of VoIP benefits: cost savings, new features, and convergence.

Cost Savings

Expenses are almost always a driving factor in IT spending decisions. You or your boss has probably asked, "How can we do business more efficiently, with lower costs?" Cost is no less a factor if you are looking at a VoIP implementation. The cost of VoIP can be intimidating, with the need for plenty of new equipment (remember the components discussed in the introductory chapter?) and possible infrastructure upgrades. A large initial capital outlay can be cost prohibitive for some organizations.

However, these likely costs should not scare you away. Many companies are now offering equipment-leasing plans to reduce the initial capital outlay and let you spread the expense over several years. It is also a good idea to stage the deployment gradually as a means of easing the costs. Each organization generally has a variety of sites. These sites could be small branches, regional offices, or global headquarters. They could be new facilities or existing facilities that require a replacement for their current PBX. The ROI for VoIP is often different across these different site types and deployment scenarios. Many successful VoIP implementations recognize these differences and use them to guide their insertion strategy for VoIP.

The best approach to a VoIP implementation is to view it as an investment; it is intended to provide returns in capital and productivity savings. The cost savings from VoIP are likely to occur in several areas. Figure 2-2 shows a good estimate of where you can expect to gain the savings.

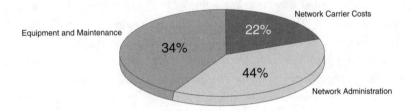

Figure 2-2   *Contribution to VoIP Cost Savings*

From "The Strategic and Financial Justifications for Convergence," Cisco Systems white paper, June 1, 2001 (http://www.cisco.com/warp/public/cc/so/neso/vvda/iptl/cnvrg_wp.htm).

The following sections consider these cost savings as they apply to capital, expenses, and productivity.

Capital and Expense Savings

When VoIP technology first appeared, a major enticement was "free phone calls." It has been said that there is no such thing as a "free lunch," but is there indeed a "free VoIP phone call?" Sort of. In the PSTN, the network is owned by the telephone provider. When you make a call, you are billed for the usage of this network. Long-distance costs can vary depending on the distance called (location of caller and callee) and the time at which the call occurs. And long-distance telephone calls can be a major line item in an organization's budget. In a VoIP implementation, the network is an IP network, and calling distance does not matter. If you own the IP network or are already paying an *Internet service provider* (ISP) for bandwidth, then VoIP employs an infrastructure that is already paid for, so VoIP calls could be considered free.

Long-Distance Service Savings

Long-distance rates on the PSTN have decreased dramatically over the same years that VoIP has matured. Assessing the cost of long-distance service is complicated because different rate structures apply to different types of calls. If you call inside your local area, one rate may apply, whereas another rate may apply to calls beyond this area. Yet a third rate may apply to calls that cross national boundaries. Throw in the myriad wireless calling plans with free long distance, and the cost savings from VoIP may be difficult to gauge.

Consider interoffice calls. Nowadays, large corporations typically find themselves with offices or supply chains spread out over many geographical locations, in countries all over the world. What is the cost of telephone communications with these offices and suppliers? To calculate this cost, you need to know how many telephone lines or how much call bandwidth you have going in and out of each office, and your typical long-distance bill. Depending on the configuration of your network and the locations of the calls you need to make, your long-distance tolls could plummet after implementing VoIP. After all, there is no distinction to be made on a data network between an international link and a regional link.

Bypassing the PSTN and making telephone calls on an IP network is referred to as *toll bypass*. Toll bypass occurs when a PBX or an IP PBX is connected to a VoIP gateway, which is then connected to an IP network, as illustrated in Figure 2-3. The call traffic goes from the PBX to the VoIP gateway instead of from the PBX to a PSTN switch, thus avoiding the toll, or cost of using the PSTN. As a result of the PSTN toll rate structure, companies with a large number of international sites are likely to see more cost savings from toll bypass than companies that make most of their calls within the United States.

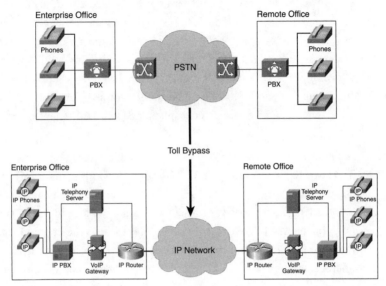

Figure 2-3   *Toll Bypass*

Savings may not be immediate or automatic, however. Many organizations should not convert to VoIP completely, or all at once. The PSTN lines may still be needed for some time during the migration phase, and some companies may want to keep the PSTN as a fallback network. But, in most cases, the long-distance costs associated with PSTN usage should decrease after a VoIP implementation.

Single Network Infrastructure Savings

The popular acronym KISS—*Keep It Simple, Stupid*—applies to your IT strategy. Maintaining separate network infrastructures is neither simple nor cheap. VoIP offers a single network infrastructure built on an IP network. How does this result in savings?

- A single network can lower the cost of network ownership. Instead of buying or leasing a PBX and network infrastructure for PSTN calls, you can spend the money on IP network infrastructure. Both voice and data traffic can take advantage of the enhancements. These savings allow VoIP to provide a lower total cost of network ownership.

- Similarly, VoIP can provide a reduced *incremental* cost of network ownership. For example, what is the current per-user cost for phone service? How does adding a new user affect this cost? Adding an additional user to a traditional PBX system may require upgrading to a new PBX with greater capacity, thus increasing the per-user cost of the system. By contrast, most campus LANs have nearly unlimited capacity, allowing a new VoIP user to be added at a reduced per-user cost. Incremental costs also extend to the addition of new corporate offices, which can often be easily and cheaply added to a VoIP-enabled data network.

- A single network is easier to expand and change. Consider this scenario: You have 10 T1 links for your PSTN traffic (supporting up to 240 calls) and a DS3 link for your data traffic. (As mentioned in Chapter 1, a DS0 link, with 64-kbps capacity, is a standard building block of the PSTN. A DS3 link has a 44.736 Mbps capacity.) The T1 links are operating at maximum capacity, but your DS3 link has plenty of bandwidth available. Your organization is growing. Instead of purchasing another T1 link for the increased call volume, moving to a VoIP implementation would let you use the available capacity on the DS3 link to carry additional voice traffic.

- A single network offers reduced wiring costs, especially in new construction. Instead of wiring for both data and voice, you pull one set of wiring. Wiring for both voice and data can be accomplished in many different ways, so proceed carefully. For example, you never want your IP phone and computer to share a hub; if you run a database query while you are on the phone, you could get reduced call quality. Such trade-offs are discussed in more detail in Chapter 5, "Quality of Service and Tuning."

- A single network can easily incorporate wireless infrastructures. Wiring a home or office for a data network can be expensive, so many organizations are turning to wireless networks using 802.11 technology. These wireless LANs support IP network applications readily, making VoIP easy to implement in this type of environment, but there are trade-offs with regard to security and potential performance issues.

- Several VoIP manufacturers offer centralized call-processing architectures. Centralized call processing enables an organization to consolidate its core call-processing equipment in one or several sites and then extend voice services to each site within the organization. For many firms, this enables them to remove PBX and key systems from each site with the enterprise while providing similar and oftentimes superior features and functionality to the branch sites. Centralized call processing is a compelling method to reduce equipment, maintenance, and support costs. It also enables many organizations to standardize the voice services that they deliver to their employees. Instead of requiring internal or outsourced resources to manage each PBX or key system, a centralized team can now manage the entire organization's voice services from a single site.

Productivity Savings

Another set of quantifiable benefits in a VoIP implementation involves savings due to productivity improvements in your IT operations. When you are thinking about moving to VoIP, be sure to consider what the new demands will mean to your IT staff, who may already be overloaded. At first glance, it may seem to be a paradox—that rolling out VoIP could offer IT savings, both for capital and staff. However, a VoIP implementation can bring IT staff savings in several areas, as discussed in detail in the following list:

- **Management and support savings**—For a traditional PBX phone system, you need one staff to manage the telephony system and another staff to manage the data network. With a VoIP system, these jobs usually merge. The convergence of infrastructure may make it feasible to reduce the internal staff required for support and management of the two separate infrastructures. However, these savings may come with a high initial cost for training. Managing a converged network requires a consolidation of skills. VoIP thus requires significant training for the data-networking group learning telecom skills, or for the telephony group learning data-networking skills. One way to try to estimate the training costs associated with VoIP is to compare a VoIP deployment to the rollout of other business-critical technologies. For example, the move from office memos and "snail mail" to an e-mail system was quite a leap technologically and required extensive training to deploy and manage. A VoIP deployment has similar characteristics.

- **Maintenance, upgrades, and additions**—Each time a new user is moved, changed, or added to the voice network, an organization incurs a cost. This cost can be as high as $150 per move, add, or change. In one estimate, these actions accounted for as much as 14 percent of an IT budget. VoIP uses IP protocols such as *Dynamic Host Control Protocol* (DHCP) to allow IP phones to automatically reconfigure themselves when moved from one location to another. Employees can move their own phones, potentially saving thousands of dollars per year. In addition, adding and changing phones become simpler, because they can often be accomplished via a software application instead of a visit by a technician. An interesting development driven by the enhanced mobility of VoIP is that many organizations are now able to move their employees more frequently to better align them with the changing dynamics of the business.

- **Enhanced mobility**—Some vendors of VoIP offer number portability. This lets individuals log in to any phone within the organization and still have their extension number (and any applications or services they use) available to them even though they are away from their desk. This enhanced mobility lets many organizations institute more flexible work environments that allow them to reduce facilities and real estate costs, while increasing employee productivity and morale.

- **Reduced site preparation time**—The need to string only one set of wires has also allowed many organizations to reduce the time it takes for them to set up new sites. In certain industries, this new capability is driving significant cost savings and even revenue growth.

When analyzing the cost savings that a VoIP implementation can provide, consider this important reality: Because end users don't see cost savings directly, they are less tolerant of reduced quality or reduced reliability. Employees in your sales department may not care that the company is saving two cents per minute on VoIP calls if their sales productivity is decreasing because of poor-quality calls or dropped calls.

New Features

New applications and features offer productivity improvements for both end users and IT staff. The benefits offered by new applications and features are not easily quantifiable, but arguably offer some of the most compelling reasons to consider a VoIP implementation.

VoIP technology vendors have been looking for the killer applications to drive the enablement and deployment of their products. Do new features imply new revenue for businesses that deploy VoIP? It is possible. Consider the following: VoIP allows for easier integration of voice with other applications. For example, web commerce applications offer voice as a means of helping customers place orders or talk to a customer service agent. Consider pithy business statistics like these: "A 5% improvement in customer loyalty can improve profitability by 40 to 95%"[3]and "Cutting customer defections by just 5% has the effect of boosting profits between 25% and 95%."[5]

Here are several examples of new applications and features that VoIP can enable:

- **Unified messaging**—This widely anticipated VoIP application is starting to pay dividends. Now that many vendors are offering voice mail, e-mail, and fax integration, users are beginning to take advantage of unified messaging systems. The ability to retrieve your messages anytime, anywhere, and in any way makes unified messaging systems an appealing productivity booster. A 2001 study found that unified messaging can provide 25 to 40 minutes of added employee productivity each day.[4] Productivity improvements come as employees reduce the time they spend retrieving messages and faxes from the home office, as well as the sometimes-lengthy search for an Internet connection to check e-mail while on the road. With expanded options for working from home, employees who once had to face a tough choice when they needed to care for a sick child can now complete more of their work without being in the office.

- **Advanced call routing**—Communicating with employees and customers in an increasingly mobile workforce and global economy can be difficult. "Phone tag" is a common inconvenience, as are time zone disparities. Advanced call routing features can help eliminate phone tag and provide better support for a remote workforce. Now employees working at home can have their business calls routed to a home telephone. And call routing can also include integration with *customer relationship management* (CRM) systems to look up customer information and route support calls to the appropriate technical support group.

- **Integration into business applications** — The ability to chat directly from one computer to another has widespread appeal, as statistics indicating the popularity of *instant messaging* (IM) applications reveal. Instant messaging provides some of the immediacy of a telephone conversation, an immediacy that is lacking in e-mail communications. *InformationWeek* found the following: "The total minutes U.S. workers spent using the top three instant-messaging applications — from AOL, MSN, and Yahoo — increased 110% from 2.3 billion minutes in September 2000 to 4.9 billion in September 2001."[6] It also noted: "The number of unique users of instant-messaging applications in the workplace also jumped 34%, from 10 million in September 2000 to 13.4 million in September 2001."[6] Microsoft Windows Messenger, which enables instant messaging, also has VoIP capabilities. The possibility is enticing: chatting with someone in an IM session, then clicking a button and calling that person with voice, video, and text communications all integrated into a single application.

- **Easier to add new features** — New features can be added to a VoIP implementation much more quickly and easily than to a traditional PBX. Traditional PBX systems, being proprietary in nature, tend to leave the addition of new features to the discretion of the PBX vendor. VoIP systems are built from common "off-the-shelf" subsystems. They can take advantage of client/server architecture, open development platforms, and well-known standards to speed deployment of new applications and features.

Many experts believe that more productivity applications are just around the corner. For example, Kevin Tolly of The Tolly Group, Inc. observes, "The infrastructure needs to be in place before software and application developers have any incentive to be inventive. Voice-over-IP application development will no doubt rise steeply as the number of converged networks increases."[7]

Convergence

The consolidation of different types of application traffic on the same IP network is known as *convergence*. Putting voice, video, and data on the same network is a common example of convergence. Earlier in the chapter some of the tangible returns from convergence were examined—single network infrastructure and management savings. Does convergence offer any other benefits that are not as easily seen?

Convergence just makes too much sense not to happen. A single scalable network infrastructure that provides for all of your business communication needs offers cost and management savings. It is not going to happen overnight, but it is best to at least start thinking about it now. The question of convergence is no longer "if it will happen" but "when it will happen." Within the next few years, look for a majority of enterprises to be in the middle of converged network projects. Figure 2-4 shows the percentage of companies that are implementing converged network projects.

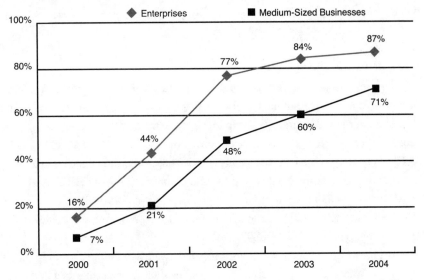

Figure 2-4 *Percentage of Companies Implementing Converged Network IP Telephony Projects*

From "The Strategic and Financial Justifications for Convergence," Cisco Systems white paper, June 1, 2001 (http://www.cisco.com/warp/public/cc/so/neso/vvda/iptl/cnvrg_wp.htm).

Voice is the easiest step in convergence because of its relatively low bandwidth requirements. After a VoIP implementation, the next step toward convergence would be to put video on the network. In many corporations today, video represents a third network infrastructure beyond voice and data. This third network infrastructure consists of dedicated ISDN lines that link conference rooms together for videoconferencing. Video streaming is also growing in acceptance for uses such as corporate training and distance learning. Adding video traffic to an IP network can reduce the need for an additional video network infrastructure and provide further benefits in a converged network.

Obstacles

A discussion of VoIP benefits would not be complete without consideration of the downsides or potential obstacles in a VoIP implementation. The major downsides for VoIP are cost and business risk. As mentioned earlier, the cost has to be considered as an investment. And, as you see in this section, the business risk can be reduced with proper planning and good management.

Cost and Capital Investment

The initial cost of VoIP can be high, if you start with a large project. You have to buy new network equipment, servers, IP phones, management software, and diagnostic tools. In addition, a complex network infrastructure upgrade may be required, because your current network infrastructure may not be tuned to handle VoIP adequately. Good voice quality places strict requirements on the VoIP network traffic, in terms of latency, jitter, and number of lost packets. These topics are discussed in more detail in later chapters, but for now, you should recognize that a complex network infrastructure upgrade may be required to provide quality levels comparable to those of PSTN calls.

Training also has a cost, and VoIP requires extensive training for the IT staff and users. The necessary consolidation of skill sets between the telephony and data-networking groups has already been mentioned; staff may require a whole series of costly coursework. VoIP is a relatively new technology, and personnel with the skills required for successful deployment and management may be difficult to find and expensive to hire.

Business Risk

Quality and reliability pose potentially the biggest obstacles to VoIP. This book was written to help you find ways to reduce the risks, but quality and reliability have been a concern since the introduction of VoIP. With the PSTN, you rarely have to worry about these issues. You and the rest of your organization are used to "five nines" of reliability. A converged IP network consolidates voice and data traffic onto one complex subsystem (which probably includes PSTN fallback). Today, if your data network goes down, you can at least call the IT group and report the failure. Although it is unlikely that an entire network will fail, you need to consider what happens if elements of a converged network go down.

There is also the concern about stepping into the unknown. When you begin a VoIP implementation, you won't necessarily have all the answers in place. To some extent, you will be learning as you go. However, VoIP implementations have been done thousands of times before. Although the specific details for your organization might not be known, established IT project principles, such as proper planning, assessment, and management, will carry you through. Treating VoIP as an IT project is discussed extensively in the next section.

Analyzing VoIP ROI

Managers considering VoIP in their organizations are often asked to "show their numbers." What is the cost of successfully deploying VoIP, and what is the likely return on that investment?

Two examples of VoIP deployments and their positive ROIs were related by Cisco to *Unified Communications Alert*, which reports as follows:

- "H.B. Fuller Company, a worldwide manufacturer and marketer of specialty chemicals, expects to save approximately $2 million over five years from a roll out of 3000 IP phones along with Cisco Unity unified messaging. H.B. Fuller says the primary ROI drivers are the reduction of $60,000 in annual network administration and training costs, significant annual savings in inter office calling charges, a $52,000 reduction in wiring costs at one site alone, and the elimination of 85% of costs associated with PBX upgrades. In addition, H.B. Fuller expects to save $37,000 annually in moves, adds and changes costs."

- "[F]or Cray Inc., the global market leader in supercomputers, a deployment of 650 IP phones is said to have generated a seven-month payback on investment and a 33% productivity increase in network support. Cray says it was able to save $30,000 in the first year in costs it would have absorbed due to moves, adds and changes with its previous PBX system. In addition, it is saving $25,000 annually in inter-office calling costs now that it has converged voice onto its enterprise network. Cray notes that when it compared the cost of Cisco's telephony and data gear to the cost of selecting a PBX, the up front costs were equal. But it was when factoring in additional operating costs and productivity benefits that Cray made the purchase decision to go with an IP/PBX."[8]

A VoIP deployment should be addressed through the same decision-making process as any major IT project. The steps involved in putting together such a project are reviewed in this section. The final section of this chapter circles back to show you where to start your first VoIP projects—in situations where your ROI is likely to be good.

Treating VoIP as a Major IT Project

Consider a VoIP deployment a major IT project. Good IT managers are familiar with what is involved in pulling off a successful, staged IT project. Like any such project, VoIP involves rolling out a major new data-networking application, along with the hardware and infrastructure to support it. The project should be staged and budgeted throughout its life cycle.

IT project life cycles are typically illustrated using a PERT or Gantt chart. These charts are common in project scheduling; they show tasks and the resources assigned to the tasks over time. Every IT project goes through similar stages during its life cycle. The stages have different durations, different costs, and probably use different tools and personnel. Figure 2-5 shows a high-level view of the chart for a major IT project.

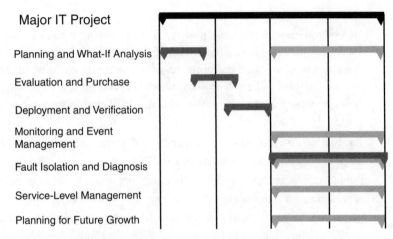

Major IT Project

Planning and What-If Analysis

Evaluation and Purchase

Deployment and Verification

Monitoring and Event
Management

Fault Isolation and Diagnosis

Service-Level Management

Planning for Future Growth

Figure 2-5 *IT Project Life Cycle*

To deliver and maintain excellent application service, you need to be involved from the beginning of the life cycle of a project. For each major project you undertake, you will likely find several different tasks that you need to address, tasks similar to the ones discussed in the following sections.

Getting It Going

The first steps in a major project entail upfront planning—deciding what you need and what you are going to buy to meet that need. Then it is time to get everything installed, running, and integrated.

- **Planning and what-if analysis**—Any time you embark on a major project, it is important to know where you are starting from. That way, you will have a better idea of what is involved in reaching your target. And you don't want to make a change that will result in an overall reduction in the quality of the services you have been providing. With VoIP, you are probably deploying new software, using new network devices, and generating new network traffic. You should therefore consider the following questions: Is the existing network ready? What might happen to the applications currently running on the network? How well will the VoIP traffic perform? What happens if the network goes down?

Before you get started, assess how ready your network is in its present state. That way, you have a better idea of what you have to purchase, and you know what to expect performance-wise when you have finished. And it is a good thing to be able to show your users and management what they can expect, along with the benefits they will receive from the new project.

- **Evaluation and purchase of equipment, software, and services**—This stage is sometimes known as the bake-off. When you are evaluating products from multiple vendors, it is vitally important to run consistent, repeatable tests—to compare apples to apples. Vendors often cite performance statistics using different metrics. For example, a network device's throughput might be measured as the maximum data rate attainable with zero percent data loss, or as the average data rate realistically achieved by an application. When you are making purchasing decisions on which a significant portion of your budget is riding, testing is also vital to verify that each vendor's products will interoperate in your network with your current equipment.

- **Deployment and verification**—A networking team that is familiar with transaction-oriented applications will be challenged as it deploys multimedia applications like VoIP. The team may discover that its IP routers are not configured properly only after verification testing points out slowdowns or failures. It may discover bandwidth limitations only after users complain. And it may discover impacts on other applications only after it has to field new help desk complaints. You'd like to replace this thankless firefighting with the kind of proactive management that leads to user satisfaction, right from the start of a staged roll out. Proactive management is discussed in the next section and in much more detail in Chapter 6, "Ongoing VoIP Management."

Keeping It Running Well

VoIP management involves ensuring the reliability of telephone calls (how well you are reaching your "five nines" uptime target) and the quality of the telephone calls (whether phone calls sound as good over the IP network as they do when using the PSTN). The two goals may encompass hundreds or thousands of components, including the following:

- The contents of the data network along the path between the parties in a conversation, including routers, switches, *network interface cards* (NICs), and cabling
- The range of telephony components, including the VoIP servers and their hardware and software
- Whatever the users come in contact with, including IP phones, desktop computers, and their software and configuration

In the past, managing telephone systems has been relatively straightforward, compared to managing VoIP. Those in the telephony community are accustomed to managing costly, high-quality devices that use dedicated telephone wiring. Their management activities were more like expensive insurance—having a specialist to call if something ever went wrong, someone who visited the key hardware a few times a year to install the latest updates.

With VoIP, the management activities need to be proactive, as they must be with other IT applications. These management activities can be categorized as follows:

- **Monitoring and event management**—With the complexity of today's applications and networks, many products let you monitor the performance of specific devices, LAN segments, or applications. Many of these products, however, cannot tell you the level of quality or performance your users are experiencing. For most enterprises, network performance is vital to the success of the business as a whole. And, of course, telephone service is perhaps the most vital application of them all.
- **Fault isolation and diagnosis**—When applications and networks consisted of terminals accessing mainframes, problem determination was much easier. Now, with a mix of protocols, applications, and dispersed intelligence, your job is much more difficult. If a user is unable to get a dial tone, is the server or the network at fault? You need to make this top-level decision quickly, because you often have different teams who specialize in either network or application troubleshooting.

- **Service-level management**—Users need to be as happy as you are with the level of service being offered. *Service-level agreements* (SLAs) provide a standard for the actual performance you are delivering.

- **Planning for future growth**—Establish trends showing the network behavior and performance over time, so you can tune your existing infrastructure and plan future investments. As you need to grow or change your existing system, you return to the top of the life cycle chart again, doing planning and analysis for the improvements.

To keep the VoIP system running well, you want to report on what is happening across the many components involved. You want to evaluate their performance and capacity, and see what the trends indicate. The trends can change quickly: Adding more users may result in many more calls on the network. A new business plan for your sales team also can change traffic patterns. The call volume during peak periods can rise dramatically, beyond original expectations. These kinds of changes drive the need to include good benchmarking and ongoing assessment as part of day-to-day VoIP management.

Project Dependencies

Your VoIP project may have dependencies on other IT projects. *Quality of service* (QoS) is a requirement for VoIP, and a network infrastructure upgrade to support QoS may be a prerequisite for a VoIP deployment. Different teams could be handling the network upgrade and the VoIP roll out. Careful planning and coordination will be a necessity to keep the projects on track.

Try to keep things simple. Take each high-level task in the project and break it down into subtasks. If you can reduce the dependencies, then do so. A VoIP deployment is complicated enough by itself.

Now that you have seen how to apply IT project principles to your VoIP project, it is time to discuss how to estimate the ROI for this project.

Estimating Investments and Returns

A return on investment is calculated by taking the expected returns from a project, subtracting the cost of implementing the project, and dividing by the amount of time required. The divisor is usually given in years, so that the resulting units are measured in annual ROI.

An economical way to begin calculating ROI is with a spreadsheet. Start by roughing in the costs and the expected returns. The savings and returns are often spread out over many months or years. Most fields contain "guesstimates" initially, but they give you a place to start and a set of questions to ask vendors and service providers. Figure 2-6 shows an initial spreadsheet for calculating ROI. The contents of the "Total Costs per Year" row are broken down in Figure 2-7; the "Total Returns Per Year" are described in Figure 2-10.

Accountants understand that money spent on a VoIP project might have been spent elsewhere, with a different potential return. The simple approach illustrated here does not itemize the time value of money; consider adding rows for it, as necessary.

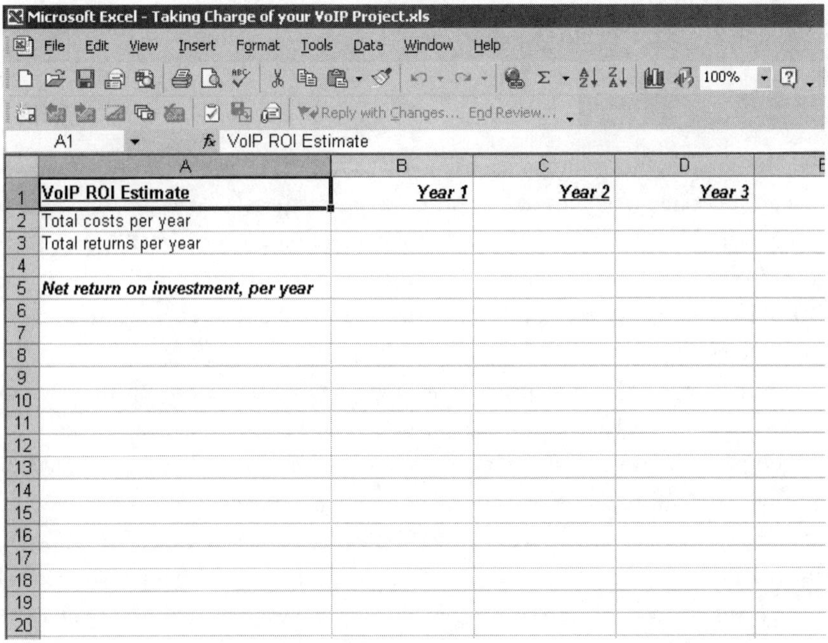

	A	B	C	D	E
1	**VoIP ROI Estimate**	***Year 1***	***Year 2***	***Year 3***	
2	Total costs per year				
3	Total returns per year				
4					
5	***Net return on investment, per year***				
6					
7					
8					
9					
10					
11					
12					
13					
14					
15					
16					
17					
18					
19					
20					

Figure 2-6 *A Basic ROI Model: Total Costs Subtracted from Total Savings, from Year to Year.*

Don't assume that you are starting on your ROI estimate blindly. Draw on your past IT project experience. Look at other, similar IT projects where you have rolled out major applications. For example, look at your first staged e-mail deployments or review the implementation of your *customer relationship management* (CRM) system. The seven project stages discussed previously will have occurred during these previous projects. Using these past projects for guidance, do your ROI analysis with your own internal data. Be careful of drawing numbers from industry averages, because your company may be different.

Incidentally, depending on the vendors you are evaluating, there are mature software tools available to help you calculate VoIP ROI. For example, Cisco customers can work with their account representative to use the Cisco *Converged Network Investment Calculator* (CNIC).[9] Customers of Infonet's *Global Multimedia Service* (GMS) have access to a similar tool.[10]

Investments

Recent literature on implementing VoIP often provides information about the savings, but rarely includes details on the associated costs. That is a symptom of being in the early stages of the technology-adoption process. VoIP has matured considerably, and the staging of a VoIP project is now well understood. Calculating costs is therefore amenable to a detailed breakdown that shows budgeted costs.

A first pass at such a breakdown might simply be to add up the costs of hardware, software, bandwidth, and personnel. That is the right idea, but those can be complex numbers to just type right into a calculator. Instead, construct a spreadsheet in which the rows represent the major stages of the project and the columns represent time periods. On the first page of the "Cost" section, show the time periods by years, as shown in Figure 2-7. On the underlying pages, which make up the individual cells, it is a good idea to show the breakdown by quarters, because that time frame may more closely correspond to your budgeting process.

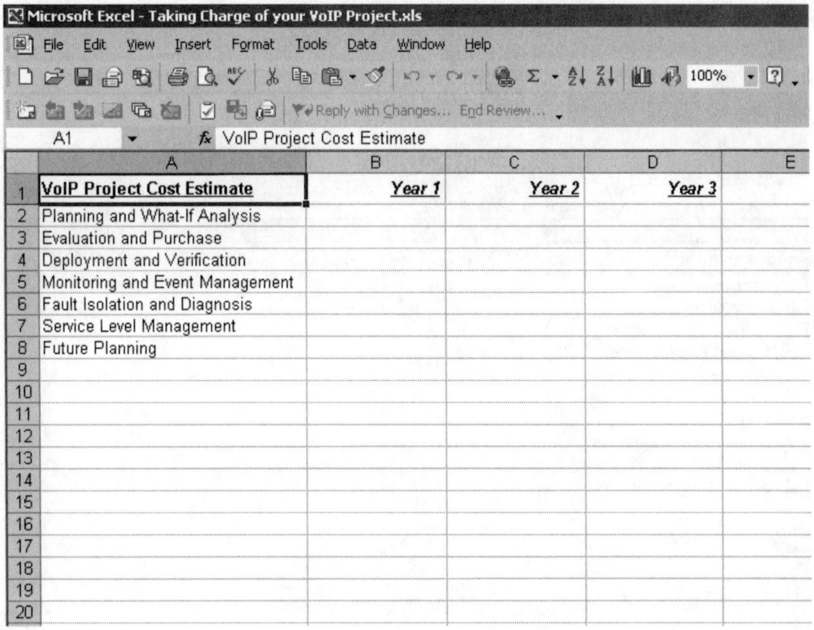

Figure 2-7 *First Step in Reviewing Costs of the VoIP Project Stages over Time*

Behind each cell in Figure 2-7, you will have essentially another spreadsheet, broken down quarter by quarter. For example, consider the first row, the "Planning and What-If Analysis" stage. This is clearly the first set of items to consider.

What-if analysis first involves training the key members of your IT and telephony teams about the technology and implications of VoIP. Second, it involves decisions affecting the scope and additional costs of the project, including the questions "Where do you want to deploy VoIP?" and "What new features do you plan to take advantage of?" Third, it involves some testing and evaluation. For example, when you assess the current state of your data network, you need to determine what changes are necessary to accommodate VoIP traffic. Doing an assessment has a cost in terms of the time and material needed to do it. And you will have many meetings and many assignments for those attending the meetings; how is their time accounted for? Finally, this is probably a good time to get outside, expert assistance from folks who have done this before, so you need to include a budget for consulting. An example of the costs for this first stage is shown in Figure 2-8.

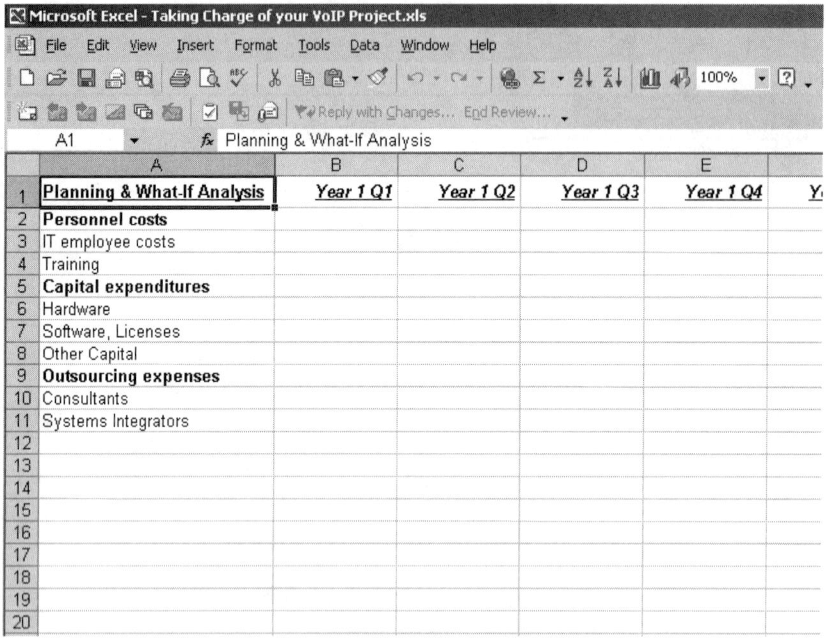
Microsoft Excel - Taking Charge of your VoIP Project.xls

File Edit View Insert Format Tools Data Window Help

A1 Planning & What-If Analysis

	A	B	C	D	E	
1	**Planning & What-If Analysis**	***Year 1 Q1***	***Year 1 Q2***	***Year 1 Q3***	***Year 1 Q4***	***Y***
2	**Personnel costs**					
3	IT employee costs					
4	Training					
5	**Capital expenditures**					
6	Hardware					
7	Software, Licenses					
8	Other Capital					
9	**Outsourcing expenses**					
10	Consultants					
11	Systems Integrators					
12						
13						
14						
15						
16						
17						
18						
19						
20						

Figure 2-8 *For Each Stage, Look at the Costs for Each Component per Quarter. Roll This Information Up into the Annual Costs*

The next stage, after you have envisioned the outlines of your first VoIP deployment, is where you decide what equipment to acquire and how it might best be configured. Figure 2-9 shows the "Evaluation and Purchase" stage. In this stage, the budget for hardware and software will probably be considerably higher than for other IT projects. This is also the project stage where you initiate a small pilot deployment, which introduces training for end users and the help desk team. Again, you need to consider any pilot deployments in the budget.

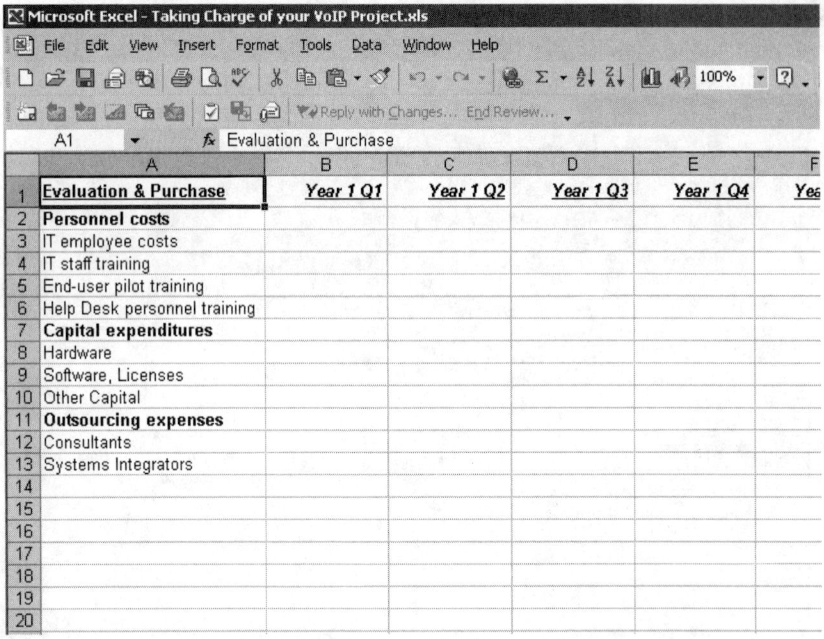
Microsoft Excel - Taking Charge of your VoIP Project.xls

	A	B	C	D	E	F
1	Evaluation & Purchase	Year 1 Q1	Year 1 Q2	Year 1 Q3	Year 1 Q4	Yea
2	**Personnel costs**					
3	IT employee costs					
4	IT staff training					
5	End-user pilot training					
6	Help Desk personnel training					
7	**Capital expenditures**					
8	Hardware					
9	Software, Licenses					
10	Other Capital					
11	**Outsourcing expenses**					
12	Consultants					
13	Systems Integrators					
14						
15						
16						
17						
18						
19						
20						

Figure 2-9 *The "Evaluation and Purchase" Stage Probably Involves a Pilot Program, Which May Be the First Time End Users and the Help Desk Get Directly Involved*

Continue planning for these kinds of steps for each stage of the project. Following the "Deployment and Verification" stage, you will surely need some new tools to help you monitor, manage, and verify the health of your new system. You also need to invest in training your IT crew to use these new tools. But remember that some or all of these steps in your project may be completed by a systems integrator or VoIP consultant, and you need to understand their initial and ongoing costs.

Returns

On the other side of the ROI formula for VoIP are the returns you expect to realize. As discussed at the beginning of this chapter, these may well consist of productivity improvements for your end users, improved profit due to improved customer satisfaction and increased sales, and expense reductions for the teams maintaining the telephony and data-networking infrastructure. Figure 2-10 shows the opening page of the "Returns" section of your spreadsheet.

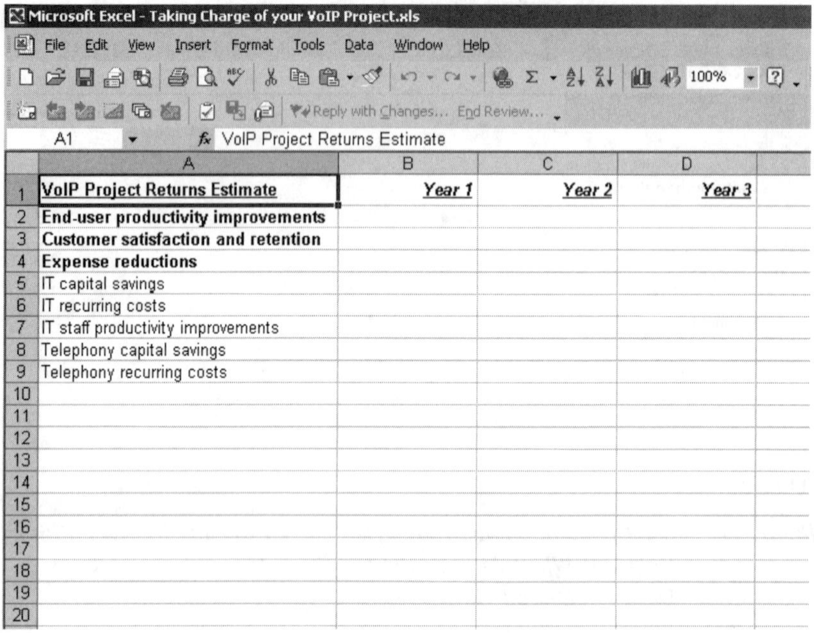

Figure 2-10 *Returns from Investment in VoIP Are Found in Several Areas of Organization*

Be sure to separate the returns experienced by the end users—who are actually conducting your business better or faster—from those experienced by the IT and telephony staffs—who are reducing their costs or supporting your end users better or faster.

End-user productivity improvements were discussed in detail in the "New Features" section of this chapter. These include the use of unified messaging or advanced call routing, the integration of telephony into end users' day-to-day business applications, and the fact that end users can become more mobile more quickly.

A separate consideration is how your organization's end users might respond to your customers better. VoIP is often driven by a business unit wanting to improve levels of customer satisfaction. Plenty of evidence suggests that high customer retention positively influences profit. Strong, fast interconnection between the telephone system and the CRM, which VoIP can offer, positively influences customer retention. And any time customers find it easier to contact a representative, who may be on the road or working from home, they experience a more positive interaction with your company and your brand. VoIP's easy call-forwarding mechanisms can make a representative's physical location completely transparent to a customer.

Savings realized from improved productivity might be difficult to calculate in advance of a VoIP implementation. In that case, you might want to focus initially on cost savings, which are easier to predict. There are extensive savings to be achieved by the IT and telephony staff, as discussed in detail earlier in the "Cost Savings" section of this chapter. The savings relate to getting down to a single common infrastructure, constructed from low-cost, industry-standard components and managed by a single team.

Finally, consider how to factor in the advantage of taking the first step toward network convergence. Data networks serve the applications that use them. New applications are making the design and management of networks much more complex. More and more, the different kinds of traditional networks—in particular, telephone, radio, television, and computers—are converging onto packet-switched IP networks. The original networks arose because users and applications had very specific requirements. For example, two-way telephone conversations take little bandwidth but must have low latency, simulating face-to-face speech. By contrast, television requires a great deal of bandwidth, but because it is a one-way broadcast, it has no concerns about latency. These conflicting requirements must be honored in the new converged networks.

VoIP is probably the simplest step on the path to convergence. It brings with it the hard network-tuning lessons required by multimedia applications (such as low latency and low packet loss), but it has relatively meager bandwidth requirements. It is time to get started, and VoIP is the place to begin.

Getting a Good ROI

Implementing a VoIP system is not a "forklift upgrade," meaning it is unlikely that you'll come in with a forklift, remove all the old equipment, and replace it with shiny, new stuff. VoIP deployments are best done iteratively, picking some candidate sites or locations where the success is likely—places where the ROI will be good. You want to win big the first few times, and build on your successes.

Take advantage of the easy opportunities. Pick your battles. The following are some candidates where the ROI for your first steps toward a full implementation is likely to be good:

- **Outfitting new offices or sites**—Some say that remodeling an old house is three times the work of building similar rooms from scratch. Similarly, gutting an existing infrastructure, trying to fit new infrastructure into something for which it was not designed, is both difficult and expensive. A new branch office or a new wing of a building still in the planning stage is a good place to consider an early VoIP implementation. Spec it out right, planning for future growth, and make sure the new network equipment and wiring have suitable capacity.

- **Planning a data network upgrade**—A network upgrade means changing the network's architecture and installing devices, such as IP routers and switches, with much higher capacity. Include VoIP requirements in the planning, and make sure the new devices support the VoIP characteristics you will use.

- **Sitting on excess capacity**—You may be in the enviable position of having significantly upgraded your data networks already. You have replaced the hubs in your LANs with high-speed switches and given your users fast computers with fast LAN cards. Your WAN backbones use high-capacity fiber and optical switches. Bandwidth truly has been in excess after the dot-com bubble. Go for it!

- **Reconsidering an expiring PBX lease or service contract**—Don't consider a forklift upgrade when you are renegotiating your current PSTN contracts. However, this is a good time to bring in a secondary set of potential providers and to consider converting a portion of the organization to VoIP. You may get surprising negotiation leverage, and your existing provider may be very interested in being on your short list of VoIP providers, thus giving you some great assistance in getting started with VoIP.

- **Upgrading the current voice network**—If your voice network is currently constrained, you know improvements are necessary, soon. This may mean an architectural reworking; does it make sense to convert some of your telephony backbone to VoIP, without changing end-user phones? As an alternative, if you are at the point where you need to add new phones, can they be VoIP phones, added a few at a time? Such an approach will help you to gain experience with VoIP in small steps while gathering feedback on user satisfaction with the new phones. Such feedback can help build momentum and gain a buy-in from those controlling your budget.

- **Supporting remote users with an excellent VPN**—VoIP can be an excellent way to provide telephone support to remote workers, such as those providing help desk support for your organization from their offices at home. The keys to making this work well are high-speed network connections to their remote locations and high-speed, high-capacity VPN support. These workers are good candidates for IP phones or softphones.

- **Converging technologies after a company merger or acquisition**— Mergers or acquisitions often bring together different network technologies and phone systems. In these situations, it often makes sense to begin the process of convergence. It may be the case that a company that you have acquired has already implemented VoIP. Leverage its experience and apply it within the new merged company. Or maybe you have implemented VoIP and have acquired a company with a traditional PBX system. Instead of trying to manage and merge both types of systems, consider extending your VoIP system to the acquired company.

Chapter Summary

This chapter looked at building a business case for VoIP and introduced the wide range of potential benefits, as well as the obstacles you may encounter during the project. It showed the elements of a simple spreadsheet, to help with the calculation of VoIP's return on investments. The last section discussed where to start—situations where your ROI is likely to be good.

The next chapter discusses how to start—what you should consider in the planning, analysis, and evaluation stages of a VoIP implementation:

- A roadmap for your VoIP deployment

- How to avoid common VoIP pitfalls through proper planning

- Why most networks are not ready for a VoIP deployment

- Pilot deployments: how big should you start, and when should you roll them out?

- The importance of a thorough testing plan

- Why VoIP management is critically important

End Notes

1   Moore, Geoffrey A., *Crossing the Chasm*. New York: HarperBusiness, 1991. (ISBN 0-88730-519-9.)

2   "The IP Contact Center," Aspect Communications white paper, May 2001.

3   "Customer Loyalty," Bain & Co., http://www.bain.com/bainweb/consulting_expertise/capabilities_detail.asp?capID=55. See also "CRM & Call Center Statistics," *CommWeb.com*, September 30, 2001, http://www.commweb.com/article/COM20010822S0005.

4   "The Strategic and Financial Justifications for Convergence," Cisco Systems white paper, June 1, 2001, http://www.cisco.com/warp/public/cc/so/neso/vvda/iptl/cnvrg_wp.htm

5 "Library Research Factoids," Customer Care Institute, http://www.customercare.com/library/research/studies.htm. See also "CRM & Call Center Statistics," *CommWeb.com*, September 30, 2001, http://www.commweb.com/article/COM20010822S0005.

6 "IM Usage in Workplace Rising," *InformationWeek*, November 14, 2001, http://www.informationweek.com/story/IWK20011114S0002.

7 Tolly, Kevin, "VoIP: Neither Panacea nor Pariah," *NetworkWorld*, February 18, 2002, p. 24, http://www.nwfusion.com/columnists/2002/0218tolly.html.

8 "Cisco: 12 New IP-Based Telephony Products," *Unified Communications Alert*, http://www.ucalert.com/2001_issues/11016.html#Cisco:%2012%20New%20IP-Based%20Telephony%20Products.

9 "Over the Hurdles," *Packet Magazine*, First Quarter 2002, http://www.cisco.com/warp/public/784/packet/jan02/p35-cover.html.

10 "Infonet Introduces Software Tool to Demonstrate ROI for Converged Networks," Infonet press release, November 13, 2001, http://www.infonet.com/about/newsroom/press_release.asp?month=1113&year=2001.

CHAPTER 3

PLANNING FOR VOIP

*A plan for success
needs absolute attention.
Do not use duct tape.*
—Scott Kavanagh

This chapter explains what you need to consider when planning a VoIP deployment. Continuing with the IT project plan introduced in Chapter 2, "Building a Business Case for VoIP," this chapter covers the first three stages in depth:

- Planning, analysis, and assessment.
- Evaluation and purchase.
- Initial deployment.

Tuning and VoIP management are discussed in later chapters.

Planning, Analysis, and Assessment

If you are packing your bags for an extended adventure, you try to anticipate everything you might need. You make a list of the items you need to have with you and when you might need them. To make your list, you start with the things you have already and then add the things you need but must acquire.

A VoIP deployment is analogous to such an extended adventure. Even before you pack your bags, you need to decide what you want to accomplish and settle on an accompanying schedule and budget. You need to determine where you are today so that you know how far you have to travel to reach your target.

Planning is the most important phase of a successful VoIP deployment. If you complete the upfront work and set the right expectations, every other step should be a matter of checking to make sure that expectations are being met.

Like most large IT projects, a VoIP deployment may face schedule and time constraints. Because shortcuts during the planning and evaluation process can have negative effects on the final implementation, start by estimating the time required to complete these stages. The Tolly Group, Inc. estimates that 8 to 12 months are needed to complete the planning and evaluation stages of a major VoIP project, as shown in Figure 3-1.

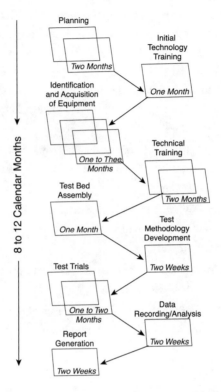

Figure 3-1   *The Tolly Group, Inc. estimate for a major VoIP project*
    From The Tolly Group, Inc. ITclarity ad, 2000.

This may seem like a large amount of time just for planning and evaluation. This amount of time will probably decrease as more deployments occur and processes are refined. Tools can help automate the planning process, thus yielding further productivity improvements. However, the planning phase can still take a significant portion of the project life cycle. The time is well spent: Many questions are answered, and a large amount of data is collected during this stage. During planning there are two broad sets of questions to answer:

- **Where are you currently?** What do you need to know to initiate your planning—the information related to your current environment?

- **Where are you headed?** What are the things you need to decide—the scope of your deployment and the components that comprise it?

When you embark on the planning phase of a VoIP deployment, you start by collecting information about your current data network and its usage. Compile this information with a view toward understanding what must be done to reach your final goal—a successful VoIP deployment. This information is broken down into four categories of questions:

- **Telephony usage**—What is the current call volume? What is the profile of these calls, including their typical frequency, duration, location, and call flow?

- **Reliability**—What is the current data network/system reliability? What is your target reliability? What will it take to get from the current state of reliability to your target?

- **Call quality**—What is the current estimated call quality? What is your target call quality? What will it take to get from the current level of call quality to your target?

- **VoIP readiness**—How do you assess VoIP readiness? What is needed to perform a readiness assessment?

For each category of questions, there is an established methodology for finding the most useful answers. These methods are discussed in detail in the following sections.

Understanding Current Telephony Usage

Key characteristics of the telephone calls that travel over your existing phone system are well known; the data has been captured somewhere, ever since your telephones were first used. To understand how many users and how many calls your VoIP system must support, look at how many your current telephone system supports. A team somewhere within your organization, or under contract by your organization, knows this information intimately and has been tracking it for years. Here is what you can find out from them, or from their records:

- Number of calls

- Number of users (number of distinct phone numbers)

- Duration of calls

- Number of concurrent calls

- Call volume profiles—peak and average usage statistics
  - When do they occur?
  - How long are they?
- Location and call flow—What percentage of the calls occurs within each site? What percentage occurs within the organization, from site to site? How many calls go to and from the outside world?

All of this information helps you to plan your VoIP deployment because it enables you to understand the requirements and expectations that your deployment must fulfill.

Call Detail Records

Telephone records and the current *private branch exchange* (PBX) call volume reports are a good source of data about the likely call volume a network will have to handle. Your current phone supplier or the system itself captures information about telephone calls in *call detail records* (CDRs). You have seen simple examples of these, in your monthly itemized long-distance bill. CDRs include information such as the date and time of each call, the number that was called, the duration of the call, and its cost. Actually, lots more information is captured internally, including information about incoming calls, whether an attempted call was completed or not, the account to which a call should be billed, and so on.

Softcopy CDRs can be easily processed. Many PBXs can sort them or export them as *comma-separated value* (CSV) files, which you can load into spreadsheet programs, such as Microsoft Excel. A useful statistic often calculated from CDRs is the *busy hour*—the clock hour in a day when the most calls occur—and the *busy day*. Calls during the busy hour are usually broken into two categories: the *busy hour calls attempted* (BHCA) and the *busy hour calls completed* (BHCC). These two numbers, BHCA and BHCC, describe the peak call volume. (For the *Public Switched Telephone Network* (PSTN) in the U.S., the busiest hour on the busiest day is usually after lunchtime on Mother's Day.)

Call Volume Statistics

In the telephony industry, the busy hour traffic is often calculated in erlangs. An *erlang* is a number that represents the busyness of a particular telephone line. An erlang value of 1 means that the telephone line is 100 percent busy. Similarly, telephony statistics may include an Erlang B calculation, which is used to tabulate one of the following factors, given the other two:

- **Busy hour traffic (BHT)**—The number of hours of call traffic during the busiest hour of operation

- **Blocking**—The percentage of calls that are blocked because not enough lines are available

- **Lines**—The number of lines in a trunk group

Simple calculators are available that implement the Erlang B calculation and allow for some quick modeling scenarios of the different statistics. To find them, enter "erlang calculator" in a web search engine.

Call Flow Analysis

When it comes to determining where to stage a VoIP deployment, the flow of call traffic is an especially useful statistic. If a large percentage of calls occurs within a particular site (intrasite traffic), that location may be ideal for VoIP on the LAN. If a high volume of call traffic passes between two sites (intersite traffic), those sites may be candidates for VoIP because they can take advantage of toll bypass.

In addition to examining call flow within the corporate network, it is a good idea to determine how many calls travel to and from the PSTN. Analyzing the data using the busy-hour calculations can allow for capacity planning when VoIP traffic is added to the data network.

The current telephony usage information that you gather will serve as valuable input for the later planning stages of your deployment. The next section looks at the next category of questions to ask as you are gathering data about your current network: reliability.

Understanding Reliability

Users have come to expect a high level of reliability from their phone system. Decades of knowledge, experience, and innovation have raised PSTN reliability very high. When you pick up a phone, you get a dial tone almost instantly. Can you even recall the last time a telephone call was dropped by the PSTN? Typical user expectations of unavailability for the phone system are about 5 minutes, cumulatively, per year. The level of availability the PSTN delivers in the U.S. is sometimes referred to as "five nines," which means that a dial tone is available 99.999 percent of the time. Table 3-1 shows the amount of downtime for different availability percentages.

Table 3-1 *Nines of Availability and Corresponding Downtime*

Availability	Cumulative Downtime per Year
99.000%	3 days, 15 hours, 36 minutes
99.500%	1 day, 19 hours, 48 minutes
99.900%	8 hours, 46 minutes
99.950%	4 hours, 23 minutes
99.990%	53 minutes
99.999%	5 minutes
99.9999%	30 seconds

To determine the reliability of a system, you need to know the availability percentage. Availability is defined as follows:

Availability = Mean time between failures / total time

where:

Mean time between failures = Average time between each outage or failure

Total time = Mean time between failures + Mean time to repair the failures

Another way to look at availability is to compare the total downtime with the total elapsed time:

Availability = 1 − (System outage time)/(System elapsed time)

Sometimes the key measure is unavailability, which is easily derived from availability:

Unavailability = 1 − Availability

So in Table 3-1, the availability of "five nines," 99.999 percent, was calculated as follows:

$$.99999 = 1 - (5 \,/\, 365 * 24 * 60)$$
$$= 1 - (5 \,/\, 525{,}600)$$

Contrast the PSTN's level of reliability with what is achieved by most data networks today and you will recognize the challenge that a VoIP deployment faces. Data networks just have not reached the reliability found in the PSTN yet. Instead, they are plagued by periodic outages. Network outages are caused by a variety of events, such as user errors, software failures, and other technology failures, as shown in Figure 3-2.

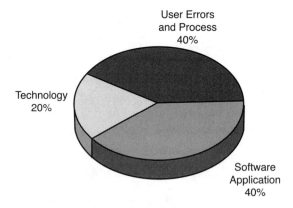

Figure 3-2   *Reasons for System Unavailability*

From "Getting Ready for Voice over Data," Cisco presentation, 2000.

As shown in the figure, the causes of systems unavailability include the following:

- **User errors and process**—Change management, process consistency
- **Technology**—Hardware, network links, environmental issues, natural disasters
- **Software application**—Software issues, performance and load, scaling

So, by now you may be thinking, "Wow, my e-mail server goes down a lot. What will happen when my phone and e-mail are on the same network?" On average, computer system reliability is estimated at around 98.5 percent.[1] This number, which works out to 5 days and 11.4 hours of downtime each year, includes not only the data networks and their components, but also all the core business applications, servers, and mainframes.

Although the core business applications, servers, and mainframes are certainly important to your business, their high availability is not required to reach five nines of VoIP reliability. For VoIP, you should instead focus specifically on two areas:

- The reliability of the network and its components

- The reliability of the VoIP components (VoIP server, gateways, IP PBXs)

First, consider network reliability. A survey by the Merit Project shows that most network outages stem from performance issues, such as peak load and insufficient bandwidth.[1] Most often, the problem is too much traffic and too little capacity. Security intrusions, particularly denial-of-service (DoS) attacks, only add to the network outage problem.

Second, your key VoIP components really are server boxes, running complex operating systems and complex applications on off-the-shelf computers. They are susceptible to the three categories of problems discussed previously: The software can fail in various ways; users, attackers, and the IT team can cause problems; and every piece of hardware technology has many failure modes. These server boxes need to be made highly reliable, and kept highly reliable, to achieve high VoIP availability.

Therefore, consider two strong recommendations for ensuring high VoIP reliability:

- **Get a strong handle on your network traffic**—Understand the network's current capacity and traffic mix, including applications, flows, and priorities. Understand where the traffic should be when the VoIP deployment is complete. Control tightly what is flowing in and out of the network (by using firewalls, for example). Use network policy management to control the priority of each type of traffic. Apply firm user management, to police what each user can do and to control which resources users can access.

- **Get high-quality VoIP server, gateway, and IP PBX boxes, and secure them well**—Install their required software, then put change management and access controls on the box. Control tightly what changes are made and who can make them. Lock them down, to avoid physical or network intrusions. Put them on an *uninterruptible power supply* (UPS) to avoid downtime due to power outages.

After following these guidelines, the individual components that make up the network should be examined as well. Cisco Systems identifies the key availability items as those that follow.[2] All are discussed in detail in the following sections:

- Hardware reliability
- Software reliability and features
- Network link and carrier reliability
- Environment and electrical power
- Network design
- User errors and process management

Hardware Reliability

Inevitably hardware fails, so plan in advance to purchase hardware that is resilient—resistant to failure. In many instances, network equipment vendors have included features to help make their hardware more resilient. For example, devices may have multiple CPUs, power supplies, and cooling fans. If one of these components fails, the device can still operate. The duplication of components to make the system more resilient is referred to as *redundancy.*

Load balancing also provides resiliency and scalability. In a load-balanced scenario, multiple devices are configured to share the network or server load. For example, a group of web servers may be configured to alternate when responding to requests for the same website content. Load balancing of web servers is commonplace and provides resiliency in the case where a single server in the group fails.

Clustering, a third technique for achieving resiliency, enables multiple devices to behave as a single entity. Within a cluster of devices, typically one device serves as the primary device or publisher. Other devices act as the backups or subscribers. If the primary device fails, a backup takes over in a seamless manner that is transparent to users. In addition to resiliency, clustering also provides for easier management and scalability. The entire group of devices can be managed as a single unit and, when combined, can support more users than a single device. Clustering is a good way to improve the reliability of VoIP servers. Figure 3-3 shows an example of clustering.

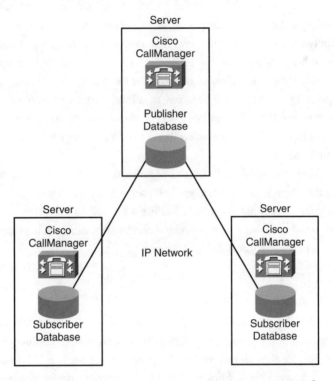

Figure 3-3   *Cisco CallManager in a Typical Cluster Configuration[3]*

Software Reliability and Features

To improve reliability, don't install lots of other programs or applications on your VoIP servers. Even though server operating systems generally try to minimize the impact that one application can have on another, ill-behaved programs can use large amounts of CPU and memory, creating server-performance problems. Worse yet, programs that provide device drivers, or operate in kernel mode, can potentially cause the server to crash. Limit the applications installed on critical VoIP servers to what is needed to operate and manage the server. Many vendors offer certification programs to ensure that programs installed on their servers won't adversely affect server performance. Likewise, shop around for management tools that are vendor-certified.

Test software patches carefully and apply them in stages. For example, you might apply patches to a limited number of servers and wait to see the effects before applying them to all your servers. Unfortunately, fixes for software often introduce other problems, so it is best to test them out before widespread deployment. Check to see if you can apply the fix "hot," without a server reboot. Some operating systems have features to allow fixes to be applied while the system is running. If the fix requires a server reboot, plan to do the updates during off-hours, or have a backup server available to bring online while the other server is being updated.

Lock VoIP servers down with the tightest intrusion security available. You want to make sure that your critical VoIP servers are not vulnerable to attack. Securing your servers may require installing a firewall to protect or an intrusion detection system to warn you of any security violations. Chapter 8, "VoIP Security," is devoted entirely to VoIP security.

Link and Carrier Reliability

Network link resiliency is an important consideration when you are shopping around for an *Internet service provider* (ISP). Investigate the reliability record for the ISP. A *service level agreement* (SLA) generally requires an ISP to provide to its customer certain levels of link availability and network performance. Talk with other customers; thorough SLA contracts and tight adherence to them are strong indicators of ISP reliability. Be sure to include reliability details in your contracts with the ISP. Finally, consider what happens when a failure does occur. How quickly does the ISP restore service? When a link goes down, what is the process for opening a "trouble ticket"? All of these questions should be answered in a properly structured contract with your provider. Chapter 7, "Establishing VoIP SLAs," covers VoIP SLAs in greater depth.

Environmental and Electrical Power

The environment surrounding your network is a factor that is easy to ignore. However, environmental factors should be included in any reliability assessment.

Temperature extremes can lead to system failure. Flood damage can wipe out your system and require extensive repairs. Proper air conditioning may be lacking in server locations. Whenever possible, raised floors or rooms that are protected against environmental hazards should be considered.

With *plain old telephone service* (POTS), the phones are powered by the phone line, which may be independent of the local electrical system. Observe that you can call the electrical company from your wired phone at home when the power goes out there. Ethernet switches are now available that provide power to IP phones over the standard Ethernet wiring. It is a good idea to look at the current capacity and reliability level of the power system for key components in your network. UPS boxes can reduce the risk of a power failure affecting these key systems.

Network Design

Good network design can eliminate problems that stem from a single point of failure, which can arise when all traffic must go through one device. (For example, an office has a single firewall that must filter all incoming network traffic.) Single points of failure can also create performance bottlenecks if a device is overburdened. Look for these points in your network design and seek to eliminate them.

Even if you use redundant components, make sure that if one device fails, its redundant partner(s) can handle the load sufficiently. For example, if you have two DS-3s, where each DS-3 carries 30 Mbps of traffic, the failure of one DS-3 can result in heavy congestion on the remaining DS-3.

Figure 3-4 shows an example of a single point of failure in a network.

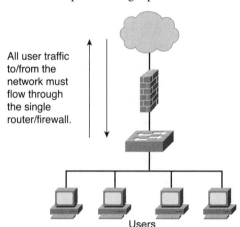

All user traffic
to/from the
network must
flow through
the single
router/firewall.

Users

Figure 3-4 *When All Traffic Flows Through a Single Device, It Can Create a Single Point of Failure*

When a failure occurs, operator intervention is not always required because good network design can make the network self-healing. Self-healing networks can reroute data over different paths in the case of a link failure along the primary path. Take advantage of dynamic routing protocols to take some pressure off your network operator. Advanced routing protocols, such as *Hot Standby Router Protocol* (HSRP), can provide increased resiliency by allowing multiple IP routers to be deployed and act as a single default gateway. Consider the case in which a single router serves as your default gateway. If it fails, you may not be able to access the rest of the network.

A dynamic routing protocol, such as *Open Shortest Path First* (OSPF), is preferable to the use of static routes, because dynamic protocols can adapt to network changes. Be sure to work through possible failure scenarios to ensure that traffic is not "black-holed"—that is, consumed by a router and not forwarded—while the network converges.

A good network design also considers security. Firewalls and intrusion detection systems should be used to protect the enterprise network from outside intrusions. *Network address translation* (NAT) devices can keep computer addresses hidden from hackers. However, be careful where you place the NAT devices, because it can be difficult to configure VoIP to work correctly across a NAT device.

As you design your network, don't neglect other crucial network services such as *Domain Name Service* (DNS) or *Dynamic Host Configuration Protocol* (DHCP). Most IP phones use DHCP to minimize the configuration necessary to obtain an IP address. If the DHCP service is down, the IP phone is unable to join the network. DNS and DHCP services run on server computers, so primary and backup servers may be necessary.

User Errors and IT Process Management

User error and IT processes are the final contributors to availability issues. To prevent both sources of network disruptions, you need good IT processes in place to support VoIP well. Look to eliminate error-prone processes; in doing so, you will be able to reduce or avoid user errors. Here are some tips to help your IT staff avoid user errors:

- **Thorough training**—Give the IT staff the training needed to support and manage a VoIP deployment.

- **Intuitive user interfaces**—Look for configuration and management tools that are intuitive and easy to use.

- **Redesign or automate tricky tasks**—Automation is a good way to handle error-prone tasks.

Your goals in maintaining a reliable VoIP deployment occur in stages:

- **Prevent**—If you prevent and avoid problems altogether, you increase availability.

- **Detect**—When prevention fails, you want to spot problems as soon as possible, to shorten the time that elapses before isolation and repair.

- **React**—When a problem is encountered, you want a timely and appropriate reaction to shorten the isolation and repair time. Having reacted well, close the loop by making the necessary long-term fixes and responses to prevent and avoid the same problems in the future.

These are the goals in the IT project stages introduced in Chapter 2:

- **Management and monitoring**—VoIP management is required to ensure the reliability and availability of the components and high call quality. Management is critical if you are going to be proactive in dealing with problems. When a problem occurs, how long does it take you to detect it?

Ideally, you would like to know about the problem *before* users start calling it in. Management software tools should let you set thresholds for key reliability and call-quality measurements and then receive notifications when the thresholds are crossed.

- **Fault isolation, diagnosis, and repair speed**—Once you do detect a problem, the key to maintaining a reliable VoIP network is how quickly you can isolate, diagnose, and fix it. You need to quickly pinpoint the component in the VoIP system—server, phone, router, or network link—that is causing the problem.

Once you reach a point where the system is very reliable and you can resolve any availability problems quickly, then it is time to take a look at network performance as it relates to call quality.

Understanding Call Quality

Traditional networked applications and VoIP applications have different network performance requirements. For example, while file-transfer applications consume large amounts of bandwidth by sending data as quickly as possible, *enterprise resource planning* (ERP) applications send small amounts of data, but use frequent flows between sender and receiver. By contrast, VoIP applications consume relatively little bandwidth, but can't tolerate large delays or variations.

Even when they are carried on the same network, voice traffic and data traffic can't be handled the same way, for the following reasons:

- They have different packet sizes.

- They are sent at different rates.

- They are buffered and delivered to the destination differently.

- They must fulfill very different user expectations.

Although an e-mail message or a file transfer can be delayed by half an hour without exciting anyone's notice, delays of a few hundred milliseconds can impair a VoIP telephone call. (A millisecond, abbreviated ms, is one thousandth of a second, so 1000 ms equal 1 second.) And when you start to run VoIP across any given enterprise network, delays caused by other applications, overloaded routers, or faulty switches may be inevitable.

Most data networks are not ready to provide the performance needed for PSTN-level call quality or reliability. You might argue that the quality is great on a campus LAN with underutilized capacity, but how many enterprise networks consist of a single campus LAN? This section looks at the network performance issues before and after a VoIP deployment.

Network Performance Before VoIP

Data networks have customarily been tuned to make network applications, such as web transactions, e-mail, and ERP, run really well. Two characteristics of these types of applications affect their performance requirements on the network:

- **They send data using the TCP protocol** — TCP is a connection-oriented protocol, which means that the two sides of the data exchange maintain strong tracking about everything that is sent and received. For example, your browser uses the TCP interface when fetching web pages — you don't want to see holes or out-of-order pieces of data on the screen, so your browser and the web server program work together to make sure everything is received intact. TCP also provides congestion control so that when a sender is sending too fast, the receiver sends a "slow down" message. TCP applications are usually elastic, consuming as much bandwidth as is available to them.

- **They are transaction-oriented** — Application transactions consist of requests and responses. A transaction can be as simple as a single request and response: a credit card number is sent and an authorization is received. Or a transaction can contain many short request and response flows, or even, in the case of a file transfer, a single transmission of a large amount of data. In a typical application transaction, a client requests a web page, and the server responds by sending the information. Similarly, an application might request a set of records from a *Structured Query Language* (SQL) query on the server. The amount of time it takes to perform a transaction gives the user an indicator for how responsive the application feels. The back-and-forth nature of these transactions means the application demands certain performance provisions from the network.

How do you know when one of these transaction-oriented applications is not performing well? The key performance measurements are throughput and response time.

Throughput numbers tell the rate at which traffic can flow through a network. This is the key measurement for applications such as FTP, which need to transfer large amounts of data. Networks with higher throughput can deliver data in a shorter period of time. A measurement reflecting a network's capacity, throughput is usually measured in bytes or bits per second.

Response time is a measurement that indicates how long it takes to send a request and receive a reply over a network. The response-time metric is key for network transactions, because the longer an operation takes, the more impatient a user gets. Usually described in milliseconds or seconds, the response time measurement for a transaction reflects the user's experience with a network.

A network that consistently provides high throughput and low response time lets TCP-based transactional applications perform well.

Network Performance with VoIP

Because of additional requirements to provide good call quality, voice traffic places a new set of demands on data networks. Even a network that is tuned to provide the high throughput and low response time needed to make other applications perform well may perform poorly when voice traffic is added. Voice has real-time characteristics, which have very strict requirements for network performance. Voice applications have two characteristics that require real-time network performance:

- **They send data using the Real-time Transport Protocol** — RTP is an application-layer protocol that rides on the connectionless User Datagram Protocol. UDP is said to be connectionless because it provides for no acknowledgments or tracking of the data sent and received. Nor does UDP provide for retransmission of data that has been lost by the network. In contrast to TCP applications, RTP does not provide congestion control directly, so a sender could overwhelm a receiver by sending too much data, too quickly. To help prevent this problem, RTP applications usually send data at a fixed data rate.

- **Interactive conversations can't tolerate large delays**—A typical telephone conversation usually depends on a certain amount of interaction between the caller and the callee. The higher the level of interaction, the less you can tolerate delays in the conversation. If the delay is too high, the conversation is burdened by a "walkie-talkie" effect—the talkers feel they must complete each sentence with some keyword like *over* to let the receiver know that they have finished talking. This can become very tedious, and gives both parties in the conversation a perception of poor call quality.

When a converged network is tuned correctly, many types of applications can coexist and perform well. But the converse is also true. How do you know if the voice call quality is poor? Call quality is discussed in depth later in the sections where several underlying network performance measurements that play a key role in determining call quality are introduced. The fundamental network performance measurements for voice traffic are delay, jitter, and packet loss. These issues and their impact on call quality are discussed in detail in the next section.

After this brief introduction to some of the network performance issues that come into play when you deploy VoIP, the next portion of this chapter examines the reality that call quality equals network performance.

Standards for Measuring Call Quality

The quality goal for a VoIP call is the same level of quality that the PSTN consistently delivers, and it is a lofty goal. PSTN-level quality is sometimes referred to as "toll" quality, and it is excellent. Some companies have even advertised PSTN quality so good that "you can hear a pin drop." Getting good call quality day in and day out with a VoIP deployment is possible, but it implies that you know what level of call quality you are getting. That is why it helps to understand some of the different measurement standards for voice quality.

Ever since the telephone was invented, call-quality testing has usually been *subjective*: picking up a telephone and listening to the quality of the voice. The leading subjective measurement of voice quality is the *mean opinion score,* or MOS, as described in the *International Telecommunications Union* (ITU) recommendation P.800.[4]

NOTE   All ITU publications can be accessed from http://www.itu.int/publications/main_publ/itut.html.

To determine a MOS for a telephone call by using human listeners, lots of people listen to a call. A sentence is read aloud. After hearing the sentence, the listeners give their opinion of how good it sounded. (A sentence commonly used in MOS testing is "Nowadays, a chicken leg is a rare dish.")

This certainly works well, but it is pretty expensive to hire a bunch of people to assign a score to your calls each time you make a tuning adjustment or network configuration change. The good news is that the human behavioral patterns have been heavily researched and quantified. The research describes how humans would most likely react—what MOS they would give—as they hear audio with different levels of delay or packet loss. This mapping between audio performance characteristics and a quality score makes the MOS standard valuable for network assessments, benchmarking, tuning, and monitoring.

The MOS described in ITU P.800 is a subjective measurement of call quality as perceived by the receiver. A MOS can range from 5 down to 1, using the rating scale in Table 3-2.

Table 3-2   *Mean Opinion Score Scale*

MOS	Quality Rating
5	Excellent
4	Good
3	Fair
2	Poor
1	Bad

A MOS of 4 or higher is generally considered toll quality. A MOS below 3.6 results in many users who are not satisfied with the call quality.

Although MOS is a subjective measurement, considerable progress has been made in establishing objective measurements of call quality. Various standards have been developed:

- **PSQM (ITU P.861)/PSQM+**—Perceptual Speech Quality Measure
- **PESQ (ITU P.862)**—Perceptual Evaluation of Speech Quality

- **PAMS (British Telecom)**—Perceptual Analysis Measurement System
- **The E-Model (ITU G.107)**

PSQM, PSQM+, and PESQ are part of a succession of algorithm modifications starting in ITU recommendation P.861.[5] PESQ is the latest algorithm. British Telecom developed PAMS, which is similar to PSQM. Each of these measurements—PSQM, PAMS, and PESQ—sends a reference signal through the telephony network and then uses *digital signal processor* (DSP) algorithms to compare the reference signal with the signal that is received on the other end of the network. Initially, these objective measurements were used in testing with codecs, but now several voice testing and measurement tools have implemented them as ways of testing VoIP systems. However, MOS is the widely accepted criterion for call quality, and the vendors that implement these scoring algorithms all map their scores to MOS.

All of these measurement methods are good in test labs for analyzing the clarity of individual devices. For example, it makes sense to use PSQM or PESQ to describe the quality of a telephone handset. However, these approaches are not very well suited to assessing call quality on a data network, because they don't know about data networking—they are based on older telephony approaches:

- The underlying models are not based on data network issues, so they can't map back to the network issues of delay, jitter, and packet loss. Their output does not direct the network staff how to tune the data network.

- They don't factor in the end-to-end delay between the telephone speaker and listener. Excessive delay adversely affects MOS.

- They show quality in one direction at a time, rather than the two-way flow used in a real telephone conversation.

- They don't scale to let you see the effect of multiple, simultaneous calls between a pair of locations.

- They require invasive hardware probes, which you need to purchase and deploy before beginning VoIP measurements.

To address these shortcomings, ITU recommendation G.107[6] introduced the E-model.[7] The E-model is better suited for use in data-network call-quality assessment because it takes into account impairments specific to data networks. As the E-model was developed, many subjective tests were performed—each time with varying degrees of network impairments. The resulting data was used to obtain a model for an objective calculation. The output of an E-model calculation is a single scalar, called an *R-value,* derived from delays and equipment impairment factors. Once an R-value is obtained, it can be mapped to an estimated MOS.

Figure 3-5 shows the mapping between R-values and estimated MOS. R-values from the E-model are shown on the X-axis, with MOS values on the Y-axis. The S-curve shows the mapping between R-values and an estimated MOS.

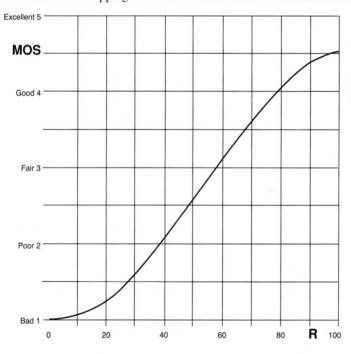

Figure 3-5 *Mapping Between R-values and Estimated MOS*
From the ITU-T G.107 Recommendation

The E-model makes particular sense for use in a VoIP-readiness assessment of a data network. Assessment tools generate RTP streams to simulate VoIP calls running between software agents in a data network. Each time a simulated VoIP call is run, measurements are collected for the delay, packet loss, and the amount of variability in the arrival time of the datagrams (known as *jitter*). These measurements capture the network performance metrics that underlie voice quality: how the two people on the two telephones perceive the quality of their conversation.

How exactly does the E-model come up with a MOS, given the data-network statistics? The first step is to calculate an R-value.

Calculating an R-Value

The R-value, the output from the E-model, ranges from 100 down to 0, where 100 is excellent and 0 is poor. The calculation of an R-value starts with the unadulterated signal. With no network and no equipment, quality is perfect. In equation form:

$R = R_0$

But, the network and the equipment impair the signal, reducing its quality as it travels from end to end:

$R = R_0 - I_s - I_d - I_e + A$

where:

- I_s—Simultaneous impairments to the signal.

- I_d—Delays introduced from end to end.

- I_e—Impairment introduced by the equipment, including packet loss.

- A—The advantage factor. For example, mobile users may tolerate lower quality because of the convenience. Set to 0 in most models and assessments.

(Source: ITU-T G.107 Recommendation)

The three data-network measurements that are key to call quality have already been mentioned: delay, jitter, and packet loss. In the R-value calculation, these measurements become impairment factors, which are influenced by the implicit delay and impairment of the codec. An E-model calculation considers all of the following factors: network delay, percentage of packet loss, packet loss burstiness, delay introduced by the jitter buffer, data lost due to jitter buffer overruns, and the behavior of the codec. Once the R-value is calculated from these factors, an estimate of the MOS can be directly calculated from the R-value.

Figure 3-6 shows the input to the E-model calculation and resulting output. The E-model calculation takes as its input network statistics. Its output is an R-value, which is straightforwardly converted to a MOS estimate.

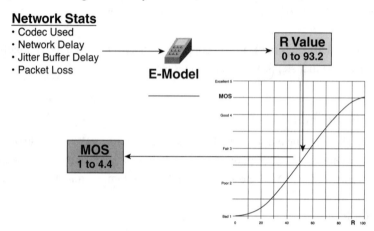

Figure 3-6 *The E-Model Calculation*

The inherent degradation that occurs when converting an actual voice conversation to a network signal and back reduces the theoretical maximum R-value (a value with no impairments) to 93.2, so the highest possible MOS is 4.4. The R-value range from 0 to 93.2 maps to a MOS range of 1.0 to 4.4.

Figure 3-7 shows user satisfaction with different MOS values. R-values from the E-model are shown on the left, with MOS values on the right. The likely opinion of human listeners is shown in the middle.

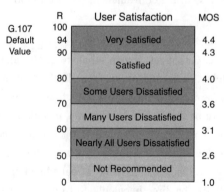

Figure 3-7 *Correspondence of User Satisfaction to MOS Values*

Now that you have been introduced to the basics of the E-model calculation, you are ready to look in detail at each of the input components: codecs, delay, jitter, and loss.

Codec Selection

Codecs were introduced in Chapter 1, "VoIP Basics," in the section "VoIP Components." In audio processing, a codec (which stands for *compressor/ decompressor* or *coder/decoder*) is the hardware or software that samples the sound and determines the data rate. There are dozens of available codecs, each with different characteristics.

The names of codecs correspond to the name of the ITU standard that describes their operation. The codecs named G.711u and G.711a convert from analog to digital and back with high quality and no compression. To do this, however, takes a fair amount of bandwidth. The G.711 codec, also called *pulse code modulation* (PCM), was designed based on several fundamental signaling characteristics:

- It uses a frequency range of 4 kHz for voice information. Although the human voice covers a broader range of possible frequencies, this range is broad enough to make human conversation quite intelligible.

- To capture the proper degree of resolution, the voice information is sampled at double the frequency range, or 8000 times per second. Thus, PCM grabs a chunk of data every 0.125 ms (1 second / 8000 = 0.000125 seconds).

- Each sample occupies 8 bits of data, so the overall bandwidth required is 8000 * 8, or 64,000 bps.

When G.711 was developed, modern DSP technology was not available. But new compression algorithms make it possible to provide intelligible voice communications with reduced bandwidth consumption.[8]

The lower-speed codecs, G.726-32, G.729, and those in the G.723.1 family, consume less network bandwidth. Low-speed codecs impair the quality of the audio signal much more than high-speed codecs, however, because they compress the signal with lossy compression. Fewer bits are sent, so the receiving side does its best to approximate what the original signal sounded like. The fact that they use less bandwidth is good, because you can run more concurrent calls over the same links, but the compression they use reduces the clarity, introduces delay, and makes the voice quality very sensitive to lost data.

The way that the codec impairs the audio can reduce the R-value significantly. Codec impairments are added directly into the I_e portion of the R-value equation. For example, using the G.723.1a codec causes 19 points to be subtracted directly from the 93.2 points available in the theoretical maximum R-value.

Table 3-3 lists some of the most commonly used VoIP codecs and their default values. The Packetization Delay column refers to the delay a codec introduces as it converts a signal from analog to digital. Packetization delay is included in the MOS estimate, as is the jitter buffer delay, the delay introduced by the effects of buffering to reduce interarrival delay variations.

Table 3-3   *Default Attributes for Six Common Codecs*

Codec	Data Rate	Typical Datagram Size	Packetization Delay	Bandwidth Required	Typical Jitter Buffer Delay	Theoretical Maximum MOS
G.711u	64.0 kbps	20 ms	1.0 ms	87.2 kbps	2 datagrams (40 ms)	4.41
G.711a	64.0 kbps	20 ms	1.0 ms	87.2 kbps	2 datagrams (40 ms)	4.41
G.726-32	32.0 kbps	20 ms	1.0 ms	55.2 kbps	2 datagrams (40 ms)	4.22
G.729	8.0 kbps	20 ms	25.0 ms	31.2 kbps	2 datagrams (40 ms)	4.07
G.723.1 MPMLQ	6.3 kbps	30 ms	67.5 ms	21.9 kbps	2 datagrams (60 ms)	3.87
G.723.1 ACELP	5.3 kbps	30 ms	67.5 ms	20.8 kbps	2 datagrams (60 ms)	3.69

The Bandwidth Required column shows that the real bandwidth consumption by VoIP calls is actually higher than it first appears. The G.729 codec, for example, has a data payload rate of 8 kbps, but its actual bandwidth usage is higher than this; when sent at 20-ms intervals, the payload size is 20 bytes per datagram. To this add the 40 bytes of RTP header (yes, the header is bigger than the payload) and any additional Layer 2 headers. For example, Ethernet adds 18 more bytes.

It is worth observing in the table that both G.723.1 codecs result in calls of only Acceptable quality at best. Their theoretical maximum MOS is below the 4.0 value needed to be considered Good.

Packet loss concealment (PLC) is an additional option if you are using the G.711u or G.711a codecs. PLC techniques reduce or mask the effects of data loss during a VoIP conversation. When PLC is enabled, it is assumed that the quality of the conversation will be improved; this improvement is factored into the MOS estimate calculation if any data is lost. PLC makes the codec itself more expensive to manufacture, but does not otherwise add delay or have other bad side effects.

Delay

The time it takes a conversation to travel from the speaker to the listener is the end-to-end delay, or *latency*. Latency introduces into a conversation blank spaces that are annoying at best. At worst, they can even cause the listener to misunderstand you, because so much of the meaning in speech is carried nonverbally, by such things as inflection and tone and pauses in the conversation.

End-to-end delay is actually made up of four components:

- **Propagation delay**—The time to travel across the network from end to end. It is based on the speed of light and the distance the signal must travel. For example, the propagation delay between Singapore and Boston is much longer than the propagation delay between New York and Boston.

- **Transport delay**—The time to get through the network devices along the path. Networks with many firewalls, many routers, congestion, or slow WANs introduce more delay than an overprovisioned LAN on one floor of a building.

- **Packetization delay**—The time for the codec to digitize the analog signal and build frames—and undo it at the other end. The G.729 codec has a higher packetization delay than the G.711 codecs because it takes longer to compress and decompress the signal.

- **Jitter buffer delay**—The delay introduced by the receiver as it holds one or more datagrams to reduce variations in arrival times.

The combined value of propagation delay and transport delay is typically termed "network delay" or "one-way delay." The packetization delay is a fixed value and depends on the codec being used. Dynamic jitter buffers add varying amounts of delay, depending on network conditions and queuing. Likewise, you can readily experience transport delay as a result of network traffic congestion, particularly if you have deep queues.

Many VoIP engineers don't know how much latency is too much. A simple answer is 150 ms. The ITU has conducted studies on the impact that delay has on quality. These studies are published as ITU Recommendation G.114.[9] Delays greater than 150 ms cause a conversation to become uncomfortable. This level of delay is usually the point at which both parties begin to speak at the same time and can't recover gracefully—by the time they realize the other party is also talking, they are too far into their own words.

The end-to-end delay affects the MOS for each codec differently. Codecs that use little or no compression, such as G.711, can tolerate larger delays before the MOS begins to degrade.

Figure 3-8 shows the effect of end-to-end delay on MOS. If there is no jitter and no packet loss, the MOS is influenced only by the end-to-end delay and choice of VoIP codec. This graph shows the effect on the MOS of just end-to-end delay for four example codecs.

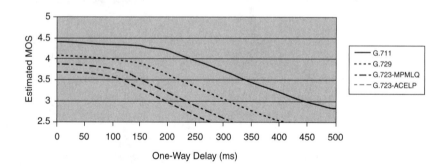

Figure 3-8   Four Example Codecs

One-way delay is measured in various ways. One simple approach measures response time (round-trip delay) and divides the resulting value by two. This is not always a good approximation of one-way delay. The round-trip response time hides assumptions about the symmetry of the paths between two locations. In fact, the two RTP streams in a VoIP call can take different paths through an IP network.

Figure 3-9 shows one-way delay measurements for a bidirectional call. There's quite a difference between the one-way delay values in the two directions of this conversation. At about 130 ms, the one-way delay slightly affects the MOS.

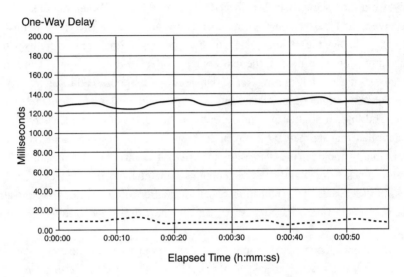

One-Way Delay

Figure 3-9   One-Way Delay Values in Two Directions of a Conversation

The most accurate approach to measuring one-way delay is to synchronize the clocks of the sender and receiver. However, synchronizing clocks in a network is a nontrivial undertaking. Recommended methods of clock synchronization, such as the *Global Positioning System* (GPS) and other high-resolution protocols, have an accuracy of about ±1 ms; contrast this with the *Network Time Protocol* (NTP),[10] which is accurate to about ±200 ms—not good enough for MOS calculations. After the clocks are synchronized, the one-way delay measurement for each RTP datagram is calculated as follows:

One-way delay = Receiver time stamp – Sender time stamp

Jitter

Jitter, also called *delay variation,* indicates the differences in arrival times among all datagrams sent during a VoIP call. When a datagram is sent, the sender gives it a time stamp, which is placed in the RTP header. When the datagram is received, the receiver generates another time stamp. These two time stamps are used to calculate the packet's transit time. If the transit times for datagrams within the same call are different, the call contains jitter. In a video application, jitter manifests itself as a flickering image, whereas in a telephone call its effect may be similar to the effect of lost data: Some words may be missing or garbled.

The amount of jitter in a call depends on the degree of difference between the datagrams' transit times. If the transit time for all datagrams is the same (no matter how long it took for the datagrams to arrive), the call contains no jitter. If the transit times differ slightly, the call contains some jitter. As jitter values exceed 40 ms, the MOS declines, indicating poor call quality. Jitter provides a short-term measurement of network congestion and can show the effects of queuing within the network.

IP phones send voice datagrams at a constant rate based on the codec's default speech frame size. The speech frame size is the amount of time that the codec takes to build a datagram with voice data for transmission. For example, G.711 typically has a default speech frame size of 20 ms. Every 20 ms, the G.711 codec outputs a datagram for transmission.

The receiving side is expecting to receive datagrams at a constant rate—in the preceding example, every 20 ms. To lessen the impact of jitter, VoIP phones usually have a jitter buffer. The jitter buffer can usually hold one or two datagrams at a time and may adjust itself dynamically based on the perceived jitter. As datagrams arrive, they are placed in the jitter buffer, which holds them long enough to supply them to the codec at a more constant rate. If a datagram arrives too early or too late, it may not fit in the jitter buffer and is discarded. You would like to make the jitter buffer just large enough to handle any variation due to the data network. However, for every millisecond that you increase the jitter buffer, you add a millisecond of delay.

The datagrams that are discarded because they do not fit in the jitter buffer come across as lost data to the listener. As you will see next, lost data has a noticeable impact on call quality.

Lost Data

VoIP datagrams are sent using RTP. Although every RTP datagram contains a sequence number to help applications detect data loss and datagrams received out of order, there is not enough time to retransmit lost or out-of-order datagrams.

Any lost datagram impairs the quality of the audio signal, because when a datagram is lost during a VoIP transmission, you can lose an entire syllable or word in a conversation. Obviously, data loss can severely impair call quality. Data loss is thus a key call-quality impairment factor in calculating the MOS.

To measure data loss, each side keeps track of how many bytes of data it sent. The sender tells the receiver how many bytes it sent, and the receiver compares that value to the number of bytes it received to determine lost data.

A few different profiles describe datagram loss. The simplest describes a more-or-less random loss. That occurs when there is general, consistent congestion in the network, so one or two datagrams are lost occasionally. But it is bursts of loss that degrade quality most significantly. A *burst* is generally considered to be more than one consecutive lost datagram. Human listeners don't readily notice lower quality if loss is randomly distributed, with just a few datagrams at a time dropped. This type of loss pattern has some effect, but the quality decline mostly stems from a combination of loss and delay. Bursts of loss, however, can have a devastating effect, and are weighted heavily in the E-model calculation.

Take, for example, the following comparison charts in Figures 3-10 and 3-11.

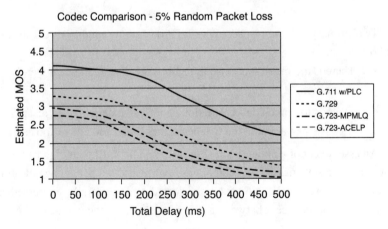

Figure 3-10 *Effect on MOS of 5 Percent Randomized Packet Loss on Four Codecs, as Delay Increases*

At 5 percent random packet loss, the MOS starts at around 4 for the G.711 codec with PLC and declines as the delay increases. Contrast this with 5 percent bursty packet loss in Figure 3-11, and you see that the MOS starts at around 3.5 for the same codec. The effect of bursty packet loss is even greater on the other codecs with high compression. For example, G.729 starts with a MOS of around 3.4 for 5 percent random packet loss. However, with 5 percent bursty packet loss, G.729 drops to a MOS below 2.

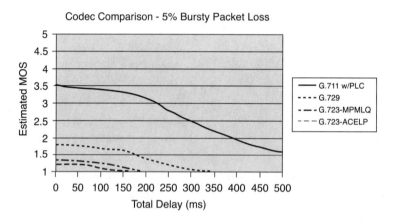

Figure 3-11   *Effect on MOS of 5 Percent Bursty Packet Loss on Four Codecs, as Delay Increases*

Two primary reasons explain why RTP datagrams might be lost in a data network:

- There is too much traffic, so datagrams are discarded when there's congestion.

- There is too much delay variation (jitter), so datagrams are discarded because they arrive at the listener's jitter buffer too late or too early.

An assessment of a network's readiness to handle VoIP with high call quality should include statistics on lost datagrams, expressed as a percentage of all data sent in the relevant calls. For example, lost data is generally expressed as a percentage of all data sent between a pair of agents over the course of the entire assessment. Other charts might show data loss as a percentage of data sent at a certain time of day, averaged over the course of all days in the assessment.

Good call quality is essential to the success of a VoIP deployment—especially when you recall that your users are accustomed to toll-quality calls. The concepts, tips, and trade-offs that follow should allow you to establish good call quality in your VoIP network.

VoIP-Readiness Assessment

We started this chapter by asking the question, "Where are you currently?" Answering it tells you how close you are to being ready for a successful VoIP deployment. After analyzing your current telephony usage, reliability, and call quality, the final piece of information needed to answer this question is in the form of a VoIP-readiness assessment.

You are probably uncertain whether your existing data network is ready to carry high-quality voice transmissions. A VoIP-readiness assessment should systematically analyze data-network configuration, monitor utilization of key components, and assess call quality by generating traffic loads that imitate a VoIP system's traffic across the network. Such measurements provide information that can't be gleaned from a pilot implementation that simply uses an IP PBX and a few dozen IP phones.[11] A VoIP-readiness assessment is designed to do the following:

- Evaluate VoIP call quality over several days, running hundreds or even thousands of simulated calls over the network and taking measurements

- Determine whether an existing data network is ready to deliver quality VoIP calls in its current configuration

A VoIP-readiness assessment should comprise several approaches to network readiness, which is why this section begins with a discussion of network configuration.

Configuration Assessment

A configuration assessment looks at the current state of your network equipment to see if it is ready for VoIP. An estimate is made of what equipment needs to be upgraded to continue with a VoIP deployment. For example, *quality of service* (QoS) is a requirement for a VoIP deployment. Do your switches and routers support QoS mechanisms? If not, does the software or hardware need to be upgraded? These recommended upgrades should be aimed at increased functionality, capacity, reliability, and call quality.

Start by taking an inventory of your network equipment. Software tools can discover the network devices using the *Simple Network Management Protocol* (SNMP). SNMP agents running on network devices provide management information in standardized and proprietary formats called *Management Information Base* (MIB) objects. Network discovery tools can collect configuration information from the MIB objects on IP routers and switches. Some of the tools, such as Microsoft Visio, can also help you draw a diagram of the network.

Figure 3-12 shows network discovery using SNMP.

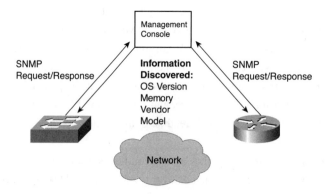

Figure 3-12 *Network Discovery Tools Gather Router and Switch Information Using SNMP Requests and Responses*

Having collected the device information, look at how the configuration matches the specifications recommended by the VoIP vendor. Does the current configuration meet the criteria needed to support VoIP? The following parameters should be included in a configuration assessment:

- **Operating system**—What version of operating system is running on the routers, switches, firewalls, and other devices? Is it a version that can support VoIP traffic? Does it have the proper functionality to support VoIP?

- **Memory**—How much memory (RAM) is installed in the network devices? Is there enough memory to support VoIP functions well? Is there enough memory to support the number of calls that will be added to the network? Additional Flash memory may be needed if an operating system upgrade is required.

- **QoS**—Most vendors recommend some QoS mechanism. Do the network devices support those QoS mechanisms? Is QoS already configured on the IP routers? What QoS mechanism is in use? How is VoIP traffic to be prioritized?

- **VLANs**—A *virtual LAN* (VLAN) is used to group or segregate LAN traffic by users. VLANs enable different data classes to be prioritized by the switches using the 802.1p standard. Do the switches support VLANs and 802.1p? Do the switches have VLANs already configured?

- **Shared LAN hubs**—Shared hubs offer no QoS guarantees. Any device attached to the hub, even an IP phone, can end up competing with any other attached devices for bandwidth. Consider upgrading all shared hubs in the network to switches.

- **Interface speed**—The interfaces in the routers operate at various speeds. Are the interfaces 56 kbps, 1.544 Mbps, 10 Mbps, 100 Mbps, or 1000 Mbps (gigabit)? For Ethernet interfaces, do they support full-duplex mode of operation? Do the interface speeds support the number of VoIP calls that will be added to the network?

- **Power to the phone**—If you are about to upgrade your switches, ask your vendor if the specific platform supports providing power to IP telephone handsets via high-speed Ethernet (Cat 5) cable.

After you have analyzed the configuration of key network components, it is time to look at how they are currently being used.

Utilization Assessment

In addition to the configuration information, you should also collect utilization statistics for the network devices and links. Once you have discovered the hardware devices and links, monitor them for a period of time—a reasonable start is to monitor for 24 hours a day, for 7 days. Collect enough data to see whether there are any problematic time periods—certain days or certain hours within a day when utilization is high. What you want to see is whether the devices have sufficient capacity to support VoIP well. If they are already operating near 100 percent capacity, adding VoIP traffic is not a good idea. Consider monitoring these metrics:

- **CPU utilization**—A device's processor utilization is a good indication of its workload. If the CPU utilization is consistently high, a processor upgrade may be in order. Look at the average and the peak CPU utilization. The average CPU utilization may be low, but the peaks during busy times may indicate problems when VoIP traffic is added.

- **Memory utilization**—To reduce jitter in a network, there should be plenty of available buffers. If buffers are highly utilized, there may be more delay associated with buffering packets and thus jitter can increase. Look at the average and peak buffer utilization.

- **Backplane utilization**—A key utilization metric for switches. Provides a good indication of how much network traffic is flowing through the switch.

- **Dropped packets**—When congestion occurs at a bottleneck, packets get dropped. Dropped packets are detrimental to VoIP call quality, so a high number for this statistic indicates frequent or prolonged congestion. This statistic may be correlated to high CPU utilization numbers.

- **Buffer errors**—Failures that occur when allocating router memory buffers result in discarded or delayed packets. If you are seeing these types of failures, then it is a good indication that the device needs more physical memory.

- **Interface errors**—Errors such as *cyclic redundancy check* (CRC) errors can indicate a physical media problem, such as a bad Ethernet cable. These types of errors will result in discarded packets.

- **Bandwidth utilization**—What percentage of your bandwidth is already being used? A sure way to achieve excellent voice quality is to be sincerely overprovisioned. The bandwidth utilization should give a good indication of capacity available for VoIP. Pay close attention to bandwidth utilization on WAN links that will carry VoIP traffic. These links typically have less capacity and are usually highly utilized even before VoIP traffic is added.

When analyzing the utilization of the network components, be sure to look at average and peak values.

After you have collected the configuration and utilization information, you have some good indications of problem areas that need to be addressed or areas where VoIP should perform well. Combine these statistics with your current telephony usage statistics that were discussed previously, and plan ahead for potential problem areas before the VoIP traffic is added.

Call-Quality Assessment

The call-quality portion of a VoIP-readiness assessment determines how well VoIP will sound on a network by assessing the quality of simulated VoIP calls. To assess call quality, realistic VoIP traffic is sent across the network and the resulting flows are measured. Measurements for delay, jitter, and packet loss are collected and input to the E-model to obtain a MOS.

There are several characteristics of the simulated VoIP traffic to consider before running a call-quality assessment:

- The codecs that are used. Compression algorithms, data rates, and datagram sizes that are used.

- Whether PLC is enabled for G.711 codecs.

- Voice datagram sizes.

- The ability to use silence suppression. Silence suppression can be used by some IP phones to reduce the amount of bandwidth consumed. With silence suppression, if no one is talking, the phone sends much smaller packets.

- Jitter buffers and their sizes.

- QoS.

You can use preconfigured defaults for system parameters, or you can tune them to see how various technical choices affect call quality and bandwidth consumption. For example, you can examine the effects of a half-dozen codecs representing various compression algorithms; you also can tinker with jitter buffers, datagram size, and silence suppression.

Call-quality testing simulates VoIP traffic between preselected points on a network for a chosen period of time. While the simulated calls are running, measurements are taken and call-quality scores are calculated. Reports quantify what is collected over the course of an assessment to ascertain a network's readiness and capacity for handling real VoIP traffic.

Assessment software measures delay, jitter, and lost data, and produces a report showing call quality by day of week, location, network cause, and so on. You end up being able to tell what technical factors affect call quality. What is wonderful is that you can get all of these answers before you have spent a lot of money, time, and energy on actually deploying VoIP equipment. You can work through all the data-network issues so that by the time you actually start running the real VoIP piece of it, you have a data network that is going to work well. You also can make cost-effective decisions about network infrastructure and application traffic after you know how VoIP is performing.

When running a call-quality assessment, try to model the expected VoIP traffic. For example, we have eight major sites in NetIQ. From our development site in Raleigh, we rarely call our sales offices in Japan and Europe. It makes sense to set up just one simulated call from Raleigh to Japan and from Raleigh to Europe. An assessment generates several calls an hour, although we probably make less than one call a day between these sites. Part of an assessment is to make sure that you can get a connection and make a toll-quality call any time you want, so testing throughout the day is fine. We call infrequently from Raleigh to Portland, so we would probably define two calls between those sites. Finally, we make many calls to our Houston and San Jose sites, so we would define 10 simultaneous calls.

A call-quality assessment is not a stress test; remember, you are running simulated traffic on a production network. Test with an approximation of the average call volume during work hours, as opposed to the peak call volume. There is a nice "weakest component mode," though, that is easily observed. If the data network is already heavily loaded with existing application traffic and you then add VoIP traffic, it is the VoIP traffic that breaks "first"—it shows high delay, jitter, packet loss, or some combination. Points of weakness are readily seen during preliminary test runs. If initial runs show a high MOS, the additional VoIP traffic will probably have no adverse effect on the other application traffic. However, if initial runs quickly show a low MOS, you may or may not be affecting the other traffic—but you know immediately that the network resources are stretched too thin.

Predicting call quality before investing in VoIP equipment is a valuable step in the VoIP-readiness assessment. The call-quality assessment can be difficult without the proper tools. John Walker cowrote a white paper[12] that details how to do a call-quality assessment with one such tool, NetIQ's Vivinet Assessor.[13]

Bandwidth Modeling

In previous phases of the planning process, you have collected current telephony usage statistics and hardware configuration information. Now it is time to use some of that information for modeling purposes. The goal of modeling is to look at existing telephony usage and existing data-network utilization and try to determine if the current network infrastructure can support the future VoIP traffic. This is the time to ask all the "what if" questions concerning call volume and link capacity. The simplest case for modeling uses the projected call volumes, codec selections, and bandwidth requirements. Calculate the bandwidth required by the new VoIP traffic and see whether its additional bandwidth requirements overload the network. Modeling can require a lot of math to calculate different values for different input variables. You may need to redo the calculations over and over, changing a different variable each time.

Modeling is often done for critical network links. As you are looking at initial VoIP deployments, ask the "what if" questions before the voice traffic is placed on the network. Take a look at the different links that need to support VoIP traffic. Then, take the following parameters as input for a model of that traffic:

- **Codec**—What codecs are used for the calls? As discussed earlier, different codecs have different bandwidth requirements. For example, G.711 requires 64 kbps (without protocol header overhead), but G.729 requires only 8 kbps. Selecting a codec with a lower bandwidth may allow more calls, but the resulting MOS will be lower.

- **Number of calls**—What is the number of simultaneous voice calls that could be supported? This number may be represented in erlangs to represent the number of hours of call traffic that occurs during the peak call volume.

- **Current bandwidth utilization**—What is the current bandwidth utilization? This is usually expressed as a percentage of the total bandwidth available.

- **Bandwidth capacity**—What is the maximum bandwidth capacity for the link? This is usually expressed in kilobits per second or megabits per second.

A Modeling Example

Suppose that there is a T1 link between the NetIQ offices in Raleigh and Houston. Based on hardware analysis and assessment, you know that the link has a speed of 1.544 Mbps, average utilization of 35 percent, and a peak utilization of 75 percent (occurring at various times throughout the week). To handle peak usage scenarios you need to keep the total utilization, including the additional VoIP traffic, to 75 percent of the link capacity. Because the T1 link is full duplex (you can send and receive data at the same time), you will use the single-direction call bandwidth for the calculations.

The call volume data says that you need to support, on average, 20 simultaneous calls between Raleigh and Houston. Your first choice is to use G.711 as the codec because it has the highest theoretical maximum MOS.

What if you add 20 G.711 calls to this link?

20 calls * 87.2 kbps per call = 1744 kbps = 1.744 Mbps

The resulting call volume for 20 G.711 calls alone would exceed the capacity for the link. So try changing the codec.

What if you switch to a G.729 codec?

20 calls * 31.2 kbps per call = 624 kbps

The link has, on average, bandwidth usage of 1.544 Mbps * 35% = 540 kbps. This leaves 1544 kbps – 540 kbps = 1004 kbps of bandwidth, on average, available for VoIP calls. So the 20 simultaneous calls using the G.729 codec could be sustained over the link. However, you are right at, or in some cases above, your target utilization goal, which is 75 percent of the link capacity. In addition, during peak utilization periods, only 1.544 Mbps * 25% = 386 kbps would be available. Thus, some of the calls would be dropped or would suffer reduced call quality. So on average, this link might be okay, but when it comes to call quality, you want to be better than average.

Figure 3-13 shows a graphical example of the link utilization using this scenario. The bandwidth utilization after the VoIP calls are added to the link is dangerously close, or in some cases above, the target utilization.

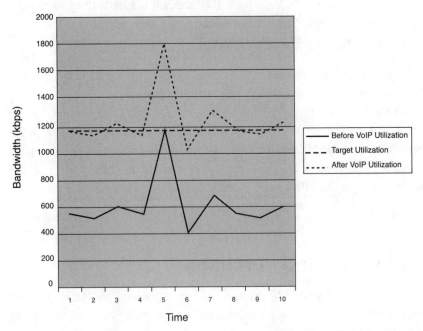

Figure 3-13 *Link Bandwidth Utilization Before and After VoIP Traffic Is Added*

What if you enable RTP header compression on this link? IP routers support RTP header compression in an effort to reduce the bandwidth required by VoIP traffic. The IP, UDP, and RTP headers are compressed from 40 bytes to between 2 and 4 bytes. Although RTP header compression can dramatically reduce the bandwidth requirements for some codecs, you need to be careful because there is a trade-off. The compression and decompression that occurs on each end of the link can add delay and severely degrade CPU performance, which may show up as reduced call quality.

For bandwidth modeling purposes, assume that there is no delay problem on the T1 link, but you know that there is a capacity problem with the additional VoIP call traffic. Assume that you enable RTP header compression on both ends of the link and the header compresses from 40 to 4 bytes. Now the bandwidth requirements for each G.729 call are as follows:

20 bytes G.729 payload + 4 bytes RTP/UDP/IP header + 18 bytes Layer 2 header * 8 bits/byte * 50 packets/second = 16.8 kbps per call

20 calls * 16.8 kbps per call = 336 kbps

Now, call traffic is consuming 336 kbps, which fits in the 386 kbps that you have available in the worst case during peak utilization.

Modeling can get very complicated, very quickly. There are many other questions that you can ask: What if QoS mechanisms are applied? What if silence suppression is enabled? Start simple. Look at the bandwidth considerations related to your VoIP deployment and go from there, performing the calculations again for each variable you consider.

Evaluation and Purchase

At this stage of your VoIP deployment, you begin to act on the information you collected during planning, analysis, and assessment. First, you rectify any problems that were identified; in particular, you make the network improvements necessary for good call quality and upgrade the equipment gaps. Second, you set up a pilot deployment, to gain firsthand experience taking the steps necessary to perform a full-blown deployment. During the pilot deployment, you evaluate and purchase your first round of new VoIP equipment.

Start with a realistic budget. Make some initial estimates about what the deployment and its ongoing management will cost. What devices and services do you need to purchase and how much will they probably cost? Are these estimates close to what you expect to spend?

Table 3-4 shows another chart from The Tolly Group, Inc., with their estimate of the cost of completing the planning and evaluation stages of a major VoIP deployment. Its numbers include the purchase of equipment for a small pilot deployment and the related test equipment and personnel training. The Tolly Group estimates that the process costs at least $250,000 when done in a structured manner. The chart is part of an advertisement promoting The Tolly Group's services. It is a good itemization, although the costs have changed somewhat since it was originally created.

Table 3-4 *Estimates to Get Through the Planning and Evaluation Stages for a VoIP Deployment*

Equipment Description	Estimated Cost in 2000
IP PBXs (2)	$80,000
IP Telephony Gateways (2)	$16,000
IP Phones	$3,000 to $6,000
Fast Ethernet/Gigabit Ethernet Switches	$3,000 to $30,000
Test Bed Wiring Infrastructure	$2,000 to $4,000
PCs and Servers	$30,000 to $50,000
Voice Quality Tester	$39,000
Data Traffic Simulator	$12,000 to $20,000
Application Traffic Simulator	$14,000
WAN Simulators	$20,000
QoS Appliances	$15,000 to $30,000
VPN/Firewall Appliances	$1,500 to $5,000
Fast Ethernet/Gigabit Ethernet Analyzers	$1,500 to $5,000
Training	$10,000 to $20,000
Test Racks	$2,000 to $4,000
Total	$252,500 to $343,000

From The Tolly Group, Inc. ITclarity ad, 2000.

Working on the Problem Areas

Before you begin the pilot deployment, resolve any problems identified during planning, analysis, and assessment. The changes to the network that you will make at this stage fall into two main categories:

* Upgrading the network for good call quality

* Eliminating the equipment gaps

The sections that follow offer some pointers for making the necessary adjustments.

Upgrading the Data Network for Good Call Quality

By now, you have presumably completed an initial VoIP readiness assessment, from a single call to the maximum number of expected calls at peak network usage, and you understand the mean opinion scores you have seen. You have also compared call quality across a range of locations.

If the call quality is good and the other traffic is relatively unaffected, that is a great start—your next tasks are simpler. Move to the next step of eliminating equipment gaps, as discussed in the upcoming section "Eliminating Equipment Gaps."

If the call quality is not acceptable, determine what the problems are and where they are located. What factor influenced the poor quality the most: end-to-end delay, jitter, lost data, or a combination of all three? Can a simple change in the VoIP configuration options, such as the choice of codec, improve the call quality sufficiently? Where are the most likely bottlenecks?

Begin remedying poor call quality by cleaning up the existing network traffic. It has been estimated that 20 to 50 percent of network traffic is unnecessary traffic that is produced by unneeded network services that are turned on by the default settings of modern operating systems. End users and even administrators are usually unaware that this traffic even exists.[14] A good way to detect this traffic is with a network protocol analyzer. Sometimes, older systems still generate unused traffic. Common examples are the NetBEUI and IPX protocols. Reducing network traffic not only frees up bandwidth, it also reduces processor and memory utilization on your PCs and servers.[14]

Now, look at the costs of making the required network improvements. Choices include adding more bandwidth, upgrading or replacing existing network equipment, laying out your network architecture in a more efficient configuration, reconfiguring or tuning the network for QoS, or a combination of these.

These choices are only the start of a decision tree for a network administrator, because the costs of these different choices are not equal. For example, adding more bandwidth may be a recurring expense if bandwidth is leased; upgrading the hardware may be a capital expense; and QoS tuning may appear to be free, but it usually has a high cost in personnel time.

Analyze the costs in as much depth as you can and decide whether you want to proceed with network changes. Readying the network is an iterative process of making the most cost-effective improvements a step at a time, then repeating the VoIP-readiness assessment to see if you are reaching your call-quality goals.

If your cost estimates for preparing the data network for VoIP appear to be too high, it is a good time to take another look at your VoIP deployment plan. By this point, you understand better what the deployment will require, so you have some choices:

- You can decide how to budget costs intelligently at the right time in the future.

- You can increase your current budget and proceed—considering this a suitable long-term investment.

- You can approach VoIP as a staged deployment, taking some steps now and saving some steps for later.

Obtaining More Bandwidth

Here are four tuning techniques worth exploring to conserve and ration bandwidth:

- **RTP header compression**—Saves bandwidth by reducing the number of bytes in RTP datagrams. VoIP traffic uses RTP to encapsulate the speech frames. RTP header compression (called *cRTP*) is used among IP routers in the network backbone. It can reduce the 40-byte RTP headers to a tenth of their original size, halving the bandwidth consumed when using low-speed codec. In streaming video, by contrast, the payload is often 10 times the size of the header, so compression may not be noticeable. Enable it when there is a link along the route with bandwidth lower than 500 kbps. So, why not always use cRTP? It adds latency, increasing the transport delay component of the end-to-end delay.

- **Silence suppression**—Saves bandwidth by making the payload smaller. In most telephone conversations, there are times when one speaker or the other (or both) are silent. During silence, it is not necessary to send full packets; a much smaller packet can be sent, indicating silence during the period. Enabling silence suppression at each end of the conversation can typically reduce overall payloads by 50 percent, although call quality may be affected.

- **RTP multiplexing**—Can save bandwidth by putting multiple packets of audio information into one datagram. This means that only one IP/UDP/RTP header is necessary, instead of one for each audio packet. Delay is increased, though, because the datagram can't be sent until multiple packets have been generated. Another downside is that the loss of a single datagram can mean the loss of multiple audio packets, further eroding the call quality.

- **Call admission control**—Lets you avoid having too many concurrent VoIP conversations. If your WAN bandwidth only supports two VoIP calls well, you want to avoid a third call. VoIP server software can limit the number of concurrent conversations to a predefined number, to avoid overloading slow links. Excess calls can then be automatically routed to the PSTN.

These four techniques may help, but ultimately you may need bigger pipes. Look for the slowest links, or the links where the contention for bandwidth is greatest. Many delay and data-loss problems can be solved by having lots of available bandwidth to accommodate the VoIP conversations and the other concurrent network transactions effortlessly.

Upgrading or Replacing Existing Equipment

Upgrading or replacing your data-network equipment may give you the boost you need, without buying additional bandwidth from your service provider. The latest, fastest equipment often can increase bandwidth, decrease latency, and increase capacity. Here are some upgrades to consider:

- **Hubs often create bottlenecks in a heavily used LAN**—Consider replacing hubs with *Layer 3 switches*. Recent switches are also much better at handling IP multicast traffic than those of a few years ago; check to see if the combination of old switches and IP multicast is massively throttling your available LAN capacity. Also, aside from being orders of magnitude faster than traditional IP routers, high-speed switches have become more reasonable in price. Purchasing these is an especially good move if your older routers don't support the QoS schemes that you plan to implement, because you have to replace them anyway.

- **Routers operate using queues for the arriving and departing traffic**—Routers always seem to function better with lots of RAM. Doubling or tripling a router's RAM is frequently a cost-effective upgrade.

- **Modern hardware-based firewalls have much higher capacities than some older, software-based models**—Firewalls are often bottlenecks, greatly increasing transport delay as they reach their limits.

- **In the WAN, look for ways to reduce delay**—A change from satellite links to terrestrial links for VoIP traffic flows can significantly reduce the fixed propagation delay.

- **Network backbones can become the bottlenecks over time**—Is the backbone now the place where traffic slows down during peak usage periods? Is it time to consider gigabit switches and routers?

Changing the Network Design

Will laying out the network and arranging the users differently help improve the key VoIP measurements? Network redesign is obviously a big step. Consider changing the layout of your data network with alternatives like these:

- Could VoIP conversations take *shorter, more direct routes,* reducing their propagation and transport delays? For example, do you have traffic going from New York City through San Diego back to Florida?

- Fewer hops can reduce the cumulative transport delay. VoIP traffic is much more sensitive to the number of hops than traditional TCP transactions. Do some VoIP flows take 30 or 40 hops from end to end? Could the number of hops be reduced by re-engineering the network?

- Clustering of traffic patterns means finding out which users are using which network applications, and where they are located. Does unnecessary data traffic flow on the same links as critical VoIP traffic? Could servers be positioned closer to clients, reducing backbone traffic? Could firewalls be placed differently?

- Look for bottlenecks or other congestion points. If they can't be eliminated, can the voice traffic be routed around them?

- Consider a layered architecture. QoS increases the load on your network devices. A layered architecture means that you push CPU-intensive work, such as classifying packets with access-control lists, out to the edge of your network. This lets the core of the network focus on high-speed switching, which is critical to delay-sensitive voice traffic.

Reconfiguring or Tuning the Network for QoS

Network devices and applications have powerful techniques available for dealing with the sharing of network resources, collectively referred to as QoS. QoS is most useful in VoIP deployments to help with consistency. At times when overall congestion rises, you would like VoIP traffic to maintain consistently low levels of delay, jitter, and packet loss. As with having lots of available bandwidth, QoS also can give you breathing room.

QoS is a large topic with lots of technical details, so tuning choices are discussed in detail Chapter 5, "Quality of Service and Tuning." At this point, though, plan on using QoS to make a good situation better—don't plan on using it to move you from a marginal situation to "good enough." QoS is most useful to mitigate the effects of occasional congestion; it is not designed to alleviate chronic congestion. If a link is frequently congested, additional bandwidth is probably the right solution, rather than a QoS strategy.

Eliminating Equipment Gaps

An outline of equipment configuration items to analyze was supplied earlier in the chapter, in the section "Configuration Assessment." Begin making the upgrades, starting with those that are the most cost effective. Make changes or upgrades one device at a time to start with, verifying proper operation after each change. Do all of this before adding any VoIP traffic to the mix; your intention is to make sure that you are doing what is necessary for VoIP without degrading the existing data-network traffic.

For example, before updating the operating system of an IP router, build a small acceptance test, in which a variety of representative traffic is generated among several places in a network, to see that it is routed correctly. For example, the test should contain flows consisting of TCP, UDP, ICMP, IP multicast, and router-table-update traffic. Run the acceptance test before making the upgrade, noting both proper operation and the traffic's performance. (An application-traffic generator can be especially helpful for this type of testing.[15]) Make the equipment changes, then run the acceptance test again, checking to see that everything is operating as before and that performance meets or exceeds the previous measurements.

Building a Pilot Deployment

A pilot deployment is the place for your entire team to get firsthand experience with VoIP systems and their behavior. And, during the pilot deployment, you evaluate and purchase your first round of new VoIP equipment.

Learning New Lessons Well

The reason to perform a pilot deployment is to learn. Your test lab is the place for everyone on your team to get their hands dirty with VoIP configuration details. Schedule times for unstructured use of the new equipment. Connect the equipment in many different combinations. Make mistakes; get into situations where nothing seems to work, and spend the time required to debug the situation. Start printing pages for your notebook of troubleshooting guides and hex-dump decodes. For example, see "Troubleshooting and Debugging VoIP Call Basics" for the Cisco basic guide to troubleshooting and debugging VoIP calls.[16]

Your test lab is where the whole team needs to get very comfortable with how VoIP behaves, including how it mixes with other traffic and how it behaves when something is wrong, how to debug VoIP, and how to isolate and fix a problem.

Take equipment out of the boxes, get it up and running, read the manual, and play with all the configuration choices. Do benchmark testing. Build a mini-representation of your data-network traffic, such as a mix of e-mail, ERP, web browsing, streaming video, database queries, and so on. How does the application traffic perform with no VoIP? How does it perform when VoIP is added?

Be sure to include representative firewalls, DNS and DHCP servers, VPN servers, traffic shapers, and other specialized networking gear in the test lab.

Configure the firewalls to mimic the settings in your production firewalls, then make sure all the VoIP traffic—both setup and call traffic—passes through the firewalls and traffic shapers as intended. These devices are most likely to be sources of configuration errors or omissions. Learn all you can in the test lab, and learn more in the pilot to assure it is right when you do the full deployment.

Interoperability of equipment is a topic to tackle thoroughly during a pilot. If you are using equipment from multiple vendors, does it work together as expected? Can your management system (which is probably built by yet a different vendor than your other VoIP equipment) see deeply enough into the data collected by each component?

The pilot also is the time to work through a range of tuning choices. For example, some QoS techniques require that the devices at each of the hops through the IP network be reconfigured. Making these changes may be tedious when done by hand, but you will find that by doing things manually, you learn where great productivity gains can be made. Your team members need to be experts at tuning data networks for VoIP—such tuning is done not just once (at the initial deployment), but whenever a new device is added or topology changes are made.

Extensive education of the IT and support teams should take place during the pilot. To many people who are experienced in the data-networking community, the VoIP concepts discussed so far may be new, alien, and confusing. Send them to classes, let them read detailed articles on the web, devour the documentation from the vendors, read the weekly and monthly journals, and let them play in the lab.

How much should you spend on VoIP education? About US$10,000 for each technical staff member is a rough estimate. This includes salary time; those in the lower end of the salary range probably require more training than those at the higher end, so this estimate holds across a range of job titles.

Finally, your team needs to become experts at monitoring and managing the VoIP system. Install the server and agent management components and start gathering reports. You need to learn which events in your environment should be routed to you as alerts, and which should be handled automatically. What does it look like at the management console when a break occurs in the network? What does congestion look like? What happens when call quality declines?

Starting the Pilot

The locations where you choose to roll out VoIP for a pilot program have a noticeable influence on what you can learn from the pilot. First of all, pick places where the ROI is high, the potential for disruption is low, and the users' cooperation and feedback level is high. Refer to Chapter 2 for some good candidates.

You want to pick two locations so that you can run VoIP both within a single location and between a pair of locations. One of the best places to start a VoIP pilot is between a pair of branch offices. This is true for several reasons:

- From a cost perspective, it is usually prohibitively expensive to put full-featured telephony equipment in small branch offices, even though the users in these offices may need the same features as the central office.

- From a project-management standpoint, it is much simpler to coordinate the roll out of a new technology in small groups. Because branch offices conveniently organize small groups geographically (where they share the same infrastructure), but are separate from other groups, a branch office is an ideal place to start with VoIP.

- Starting with small groups of users means less risk. Even though IP telephony products are maturing rapidly, few businesses have the confidence to forklift the rock-solid equipment they have been using the past 20 years and replace it with "converged" equipment.

- To get deployments started, VoIP vendors have some nice "branch office" packages with fairly attractive pricing.

Evaluating Equipment and Systems

Your test lab and your pilot deployment are the places to evaluate the new VoIP hardware and software equipment you plan to acquire. The question you are attempting to answer in an evaluation is whether the components and their vendors meet your expectations.

Review how you make evaluation and purchase decisions. Presumably, your goal is to obtain equipment that gets you where you are headed. You would like your purchases to be cost effective, scalable, and reliable. VoIP equipment may have a range of expected lifetimes; do the purchases satisfy the life cycle expectations that you have for them?

New purchases are commonly evaluated in a setting that represents typical usage in your environment. When measurements and comparisons are done by professional testing labs or at shows, they are sometimes known as *bake-offs* or *shoot-outs*. A representative bake-off requires some planning, though, to make sure that you are testing what is important for your environment. Effective analysis skills and thorough testing tools are not necessarily common, which is why many people rely on the evaluations and comparisons done by professional testing labs. So, you face a trade-off: Do a bake-off in house, tailored to your environment, or depend on the results done by professional testing labs.

Network performance questions are easy to pursue as you evaluate network equipment for VoIP:

- What is the user throughput through the device for one application session?

- How many sessions can you run concurrently? When you reach that number, what is the user throughput?

- What is a recommended maximum number of sessions to configure, by CPU or RAM?

- How many locations (address pairs) can you have in concurrent sessions?

- Ask the same questions as the preceding four, but with regard to response time rather than throughput—what is the latency through the device with one session? When you reach the maximum, how bad does the latency get? What is the recommended maximum?

- Ask similar questions, but in the context of end-to-end delay, packet loss, and jitter—what are the key network performance metrics for VoIP and multimedia traffic?

- What happens as you add IP multicast traffic?

- Put together a realistic traffic mix in the test lab. Suppose your network is 60 percent TCP, 30 percent RTP, and 10 percent UDP, with a mix of transactions, file transfers, and streaming. What are the representative throughput, response time, delay, lost data, and jitter values for the corresponding application traffic?

- What happens when you leave traffic mixes like this going for days or weeks at a time?

In the end, you may determine that the devices you are evaluating have similar measurements. But the process of purchasing and using the equipment has brought you closer to what is probably the most important element of the evaluation: your relationship with the vendor.

A common question when converting telephones to VoIP is which vendor to choose. It is best to consider 3 or 4 vendors, and to build pilots with a size of about 10 IP phones each. The vendors will know you have your eye on a larger rollout than just 10—how do they treat you during the pilot? How is their product reliability? How is their technical support?

The quality of the relationship you build with the equipment vendors, and the quality and price of their products, should guide you in deciding what to buy. It takes performing a pilot to give you the confidence to know what to select.

Watching for VoIP Gotchas

Tom Lancaster, in his excellent VoIP tips on searchNetworking.com, has called attention to some gotchas you are likely to encounter in your pilot: echo[17] and full-duplex capability[18] in softphones. This advice is supplied in the following sections.

Dealing with Echo Problems

Echo sounds like a speaker's words are being repeated as soon as they reach the receiving end of a call. As long as the echo is reasonably quiet and short, most people can tolerate it, if they notice it at all. However, as the time between your speech and the echo grows, the echo becomes irritating.

The first step in getting rid of echo is to isolate its source. Usually only one party hears the echo. If that is the case, the echo source is on the far end. This is fairly logical if you think about standing in a canyon shouting "echo echo echo." If you stand right next to a wall and shout "echo," you are not going to hear one. To hear the echo, you have to stand far enough away that the sound has time to travel from you to the reflection and bounce back to you. When you shout "echo" into a nearby wall, more sound bounces back to you, but the delay is so short that you can't hear it. For this reason, if your local gateway is causing an echo, you won't hear it because you are too close.

After you figure out which end of the circuit is causing the echo, look for the usual suspects. The easy bet is cheap headsets or conference phones. These devices are notorious for allowing the output from the speaker back into the input (the microphone). In this case, an echo problem is easy to diagnose because you can swap out the equipment immediately and note whether the echo disappears. If it does not, the next guess is any place where different telephony technologies meet. For instance, a two-wire to four-wire conversion and a digital-to-analog gateway are common causes of noticeable echo. Troubleshooting these components takes a little more effort, and usually some testing instruments are needed to measure things such as decibel loss and impedance.

Determining Full-Duplex Capability in Softphones

The audio hardware in PCs that are being used as softphones needs to be able to record and play back at the same time. This is called *full-duplex audio*; without it, you can speak or listen, but not both at the same time. Unfortunately, many PCs have hardware that does not support full-duplex audio. For these computers, you may have to use an external device, such as an IP phone, instead of your PC's sound card and microphone. Upgrading sound cards in a few PCs in a small office may be pretty annoying, but it can be a budget-buster if you order 200 softphones for your corporation and find out your desktops all require upgrades before you can use them.

Checking whether your PCs support full-duplex audio is a fairly simple matter. Start by making sure your microphone and speakers are plugged in and turned on. Open a program that you can use to record and play back sound from your microphone. Microsoft Sound Recorder is a free package that ships with Windows (Accessories/Entertainment/Sound Recorder). If you don't already have a favorite third-party application, use the Microsoft program.

Next, make a recording. Do this by clicking the Record icon and speaking into your microphone for a minute. After you have finished, open a second instance of Sound Recorder (or your favorite application). On the first Sound Recorder, rewind your recording and play it back. After it starts to play back, quickly switch to the second instance of Sound Recorder. On the second instance, begin recording again for a few seconds. If you can play back the second recording, you know the PC supports full-duplex audio.

Transcoding

Transcoding is the process that converts between different codecs. Transcoding can be problematic for VoIP, but you never had to worry about it in the PSTN. In a VoIP deployment, you may be using a mix of different codecs such as G.711, G.726, and G.729. All PSTN calls use the G.711 encoding. Consider the example where a call originates from an IP phone using the G.729 codec. The destination is a phone in the PSTN. The VoIP gateway must transcode the G.729 data stream to G.711 and vice versa.

The conversion process between codecs is costly. It increases delay and lowers the call quality. Try to avoid data conversions between codecs whenever possible.

Deployment, Tuning, and Testing

Presumably you have planned your VoIP deployment well, understood your user requirements, and understood the existing data network. You have put together a shopping list of upgrades and new equipment, and have completed their evaluation and purchase. You have made the upgrades necessary in the network, and are sure everything is working well without VoIP.

Now it is a matter of making the VoIP deployment work as you planned.

Deploy the new components one at a time, starting in the places in the network where the new components are most likely to work well the first time. Most breakage in a network occurs when changes are made. If possible, make one change at a time and be ready to withdraw the change if something breaks.

Be sure to plan for service provider changes that may be required. There will probably be a phased migration for your PSTN access and you may need more bandwidth for your current WAN links. You may be moving from separate voice and data links to integrated connections. These kinds of changes that are outside of your control need to be scheduled well in advance.

It is unlikely everything will work as desired without some tuning. Chapter 5, describes the many techniques available for tuning network traffic.

Testing is an absolutely vital part of the deployment phase. Testing helps you to get unequivocal answers to questions like these: Does the deployment work as you planned? Do all the features work? Can everyone be reached? Does the deployment behave well under stress? To answer these questions, you need to construct a test plan; your team should be able to confirm that every aspect of the project is working as desired. An outline for constructing a VoIP test plan is described in this section.

Assembling a Test Plan

Getting your VoIP deployment deployed well means making sure it is working as designed. Deployment teams put together test plans to verify that the specifications have been met. Here are some of the key elements of a VoIP deployment test plan:

- **Is the deployment operational and functionally complete?** Does the end-user equipment work right (microphones, handsets, headphones, sound cards, dialing interfaces)? Does each of the VoIP functions work? For every user? At every interface?

  If you have PSTN failover, does a break in the VoIP system cause the PSTN failover to occur quickly?

- **Is the deployment easy to use?** You want the system to be easy to use for each of your end users, to avoid a long series of help desk calls. Put together a list of representative tasks that each user should be able to accomplish. Observe some controlled user interface testing to ensure that they can do all the tasks, quickly and without errors.

  You want your IT team to be able to do their jobs easily and without errors. Can they add, modify, and remove users easily? Can they quickly and correctly find and isolate faults when they occur?

- **Is network performance good for the networked applications?** Do telephone conversations sound good? With VoIP, network performance is synonymous with call quality. This chapter places great importance on the need for adequate bandwidth, low delay, and low jitter. The proof is in the measurement of these variables on the deployed network.

- **Do the transaction-oriented applications on the network perform well?** The quality of the experience using traditional applications is measured by response time or throughput. For each critical application on the network, is the response time or throughput still meeting expectations?

  This second set of measurements requires you to do benchmarking. Treat it like a high school chemistry experiment. Collect a representative set of timing samples before making any changes, make the changes, and then rerun the exact same set of measurements.

- **Do the settings interact well with other equipment and applications?** Setting up VoIP involves many changes to your existing data-network equipment. Are the routers still routing correctly? Are the firewalls still permitting and constraining the right traffic? Does IP multicast traffic still get routed correctly?

- **Is the deployment stable under stress?** You designed the VoIP system to support a given number of calls simultaneously, along with all your other network traffic. When that limit is reached, is the call quality still good? Are you using call admission, so that the number of calls can't be exceeded? What happens as the volume of background data-network traffic increases, or if a new video-streaming application is added?

- **Is there extraneous traffic?** You have asked the question of whether the system is doing what you want it to do. Now ask whether it is doing anything you don't expect. Are there excess or redundant network flows, possibly caused by configuration options you did not understand? You may need a network protocol analyzer to help in this assessment—take some snapshots of the network before and after VoIP, and see if there are any unexpected flows.

- **Does the deployment report on problems well?** Activate the VoIP management system and make sure that it is operating correctly. Baseline its operation for a few days, then purposely cause faults in the system. Are the faults diagnosed promptly and correctly? Are the faulty components isolated? Do the alerts go to the right network management console? Are any automatic recovery operations performed right?

Chapter Summary

Getting VoIP working well is not about "what to do if it does not work." You can make it work well the first time. The steps to deploy VoIP successfully are part of classic IT project management: Plan thoroughly, evaluate and experiment with the designs and devices you plan to use, and then roll out the deployment incrementally, building upon your successes and learning as you proceed.

This chapter has described these project steps thoroughly, with lots of questions and bulleted lists. You may have discovered that there are more tasks here than you are prepared to take on with your current team. If that is your situation, you will find the next chapter helpful, which discusses outsourcing alternatives.

End Notes

1   "MERIT Project Results," IT Resource Survey Results, Computer Associates International, 1997, www.meritproject.com/ it_survey_results.htm.

2   "Getting Ready for Voice over Data," Hank Lambert, Cisco Systems, VoiceCon 2001, Washington, D.C., February 26, 2001.

3   "Cisco CallManager Clustering," Cisco Systems, http://www.cisco.com/ en/US/products/sw/voicesw/ps556/products_administration_guide_ chapter09186a00800c4ca9.html#14862.

4   ITU-T Recommendation P.800, "Methods for Subjective Determination of Transmission Quality," http://www.itu.int/publications/main_publ/ itut.html.

5   ITU-T Recommendation P.861, "Objective Quality Measurement of Telephone-Band (300-3400 Hz) Speech Codecs," http://www.itu.int/ publications/main_publ/itut.html.

6   ITU-T Recommendation G.107, "The E-Model, a Computational Model for Use in Transmission Planning," http://www.itu.int/publications/main_publ/ itut.html.

7   ITU-T Recommendation G.108, "Application of the E-Model: A Planning Guide," http://www.itu.int/publications/main_publ/itut.html.

8   "VoIP Voice Quality Often Best," Tom Lancaster, SearchNetworking.com *Networking Tips and Newsletters*, December 20, 2001, http:// searchnetworking.techtarget.com/tip 1,289483,sid7_gci783354,00.html.

NOTE   You must be a registered member of SearchNetworking.com or another site in the TechTarget network to log in to these sites.

---

9   ITU-T Recommendation G.114, "One-Way Transmission Time," http:// www.itu.int/publications/main_publ/itut.html.

10   Network Time Protocol Version 3, RFC 1305, http://www.ietf.org/rfc/ rfc1305.txt.

11   "Assess Your Network," Tom Lancaster, SearchNetworking.com *Networking Tips and Newsletters*, December 6, 2001, http://searchnetworking.techtarget.com/ tip 0,289483,sid7_gci784 599,00.html.

12   "Doing a VoIP Assessment with Vivinet Assessor," Susan Pearsall and John Q. Walker, NetIQ Corporation white paper, March 2002, http://www.netiq.com/products/va/whitepapers.asp.

13   For more information on Vivinet Assessor, see the NetIQ Corporation website: http://www.netiq.com/products/va/.

14 "VoIP in the Enterprise: Preparing Your Network," Tom Lancaster, SearchNetworking.com *Networking Tips and Newsletters*, January 31, 2002, http://searchnetworking.techtarget.com/tip/ 1,289483,sid7_gci8010 18,00.html.

15 For more information on Chariot, see the NetIQ Corporation website: http://www.netiq.com/products/chr/.

16 "Troubleshooting and Debugging VoIP Call Basics," Cisco Systems website, http://www.cisco.com/warp/public/788/voip voip_debugcalls.html.

17 "Troubleshooting VoIP Echo Problems," Tom Lancaster, SearchNetworking.com *Networking Tips and Newsletters*, November 29, 2001, http://searchnetworking.techtarget.com/ tip1,289483,sid7_gci783354,00.html.

18 "Check for Full Duplex Capability," Tom Lancaster, SearchNetworking.com *Networking Tips and Newsletters*, December 13, 2001, http://searchnetworking.techtarget.com/tip/ 1,289483,sid7_gci785861,00.html.

CHAPTER 4

DO IT YOURSELF, OR OUTSOURCE?

VoIP makes new demands;
lack the skills or resources?
Outsourcing may help.
—Mark Zelek

This chapter explains how to decide whether to outsource VoIP deployment and management or do it yourself. The previous chapter detailed a step-by-step process for deploying VoIP successfully using classic IT project management: plan thoroughly, evaluate and experiment with the designs and devices you plan to use, and then roll out the deployment incrementally, building on your successes and learning as you proceed.

However, initial deployment and ongoing management of VoIP may entail more tasks than you are prepared to take on with your current team. This chapter discusses outsourcing alternatives to help you fill in the gaps and ensure a successful VoIP project.

Why Outsource?

Outsourcing means that you pay specialists to do some or all of the tasks you need to accomplish during the course of a project. This may be a one-time task, such as assessing what the voice quality would be on your current data network, or it may be an ongoing task, such as managing your WAN or managing and monitoring your VoIP applications. The advantages of VoIP outsourcing lie in the areas of cost, quality, speed, and innovation.

One area of cost savings stems from opportunity costs. Small businesses should be the world-class specialists in what they do. Because they don't have access to the know-how, technologies, capital, economies of scale, and other resources of large companies, they must increase their leverage in their area of expertise. The managers in a small organization should not get so bogged down in running the network and the telephone system that they are unable to focus on building the business. Herb Kelleher, CEO of Southwest Airlines, observes that "People who are in the business full time can do it better and cheaper."[1] You should be able to do your job better than anyone else; VoIP outsourcers should be expert in their chosen field. It may be worthwhile to seriously consider outsourcing all the things that are really keeping you from growing your organization profitably.

Another area of potential cost savings opens up when you avoid the in-house costs of mastering the skills necessary to deploy and manage a VoIP system well. The potential costs for even a modest pilot were described in the previous chapter. Can some of those costs be borne by specialists in those topics?

A team already experienced in VoIP deployment and management should perform these tasks much faster and with higher quality than could your team if it is performing these tasks for the first time. VoIP is a business-critical network application. Do you want experienced professionals, bound by a contractual obligation, to get it right, doing it for you—or do you think you can get it right the first time? Although this book has already provided a significant amount of advice for doing it yourself, every installation is unique.

Presumably, a team that is already expert in VoIP will have seen many different network topologies and deployment variations, which should help it to quickly find creative solutions to any obstacles encountered in your network. When you outsource, you are more likely to benefit from the latest innovations in the field.

Some Options for Outsourcing

Does your team have the resources and skills necessary to make your VoIP deployment a success? If not, which resources and skills should be outsourced, and to whom? Each of the project phases outlined in previous chapters will be examined in this section as the second question is considered. Because the planning phase may be somewhat lengthy and may require various different skill sets, it is a logical place to start when considering outsourcing part or all of a VoIP deployment.

Planning, Assessment, and Pilots

You may not be fully sold on the idea that VoIP can work successfully in your enterprise. Perhaps you would like to collect more information and do some additional planning, but don't have the time or skills needed. There are companies that you can call on to outsource the services that you need for a VoIP deployment. They are known as *system integrators* because they integrate a variety of products and services to create the solution that you need. System integrators offer a great wealth of knowledge and experience when it comes to planning for VoIP. Consider outsourcing VoIP-readiness assessments, network improvements, and pilot deployments to a system integrator. Outsourcing each topic is discussed in detail in the following sections.

VoIP-Readiness Assessment

The first planning step that a system integrator can complete for you is a *VoIP-readiness assessment*. This assessment analyzes your current telephony and data networks and determines whether the data network is ready for VoIP. Such an assessment is cost-effective, kind of like a pop quiz—with little preparation, you get a good idea of where you stand and what you must do to be successful.

A good readiness assessment provides an executive summary report with a "go, no-go" indication, as well as detailed reports to help you deal with problem areas. The assessment reports should provide you with the following information:

- Hardware configuration assessment

- Link and device utilization and capacity for VoIP

- Call-quality estimation

By using the reports, you can determine what your network needs before you continue with a VoIP deployment. One advantage of outsourcing a VoIP-readiness assessment is that you get all of this information before you have to make an investment in costly VoIP equipment or training. The assessment reports pinpoint likely network problems that could lead to failures or poor call quality. Network improvements may be necessary before going to the next phase. Therefore, you should consider engaging a system integrator who can provide both assessment services and help with network improvements.

Network Improvements

After you have had a readiness assessment performed, you should have reports showing what needs to be upgraded in the data network to support toll-quality calls. You may choose to outsource some or all of the following:

- **Upgrades of equipment and links**—The routers may need a higher level of operating system to support VoIP, and they may need more memory to support the new operating system and increased network traffic. Switches and routers may need to have VLANs configured. Certain links may need upgrades for capacity purposes. (These are just a few of the improvements that can be outsourced.)

- **Implementing QoS**—Some level of quality of service is required for a successful VoIP deployment. Trying out and tuning different mechanisms enables you to find what works before you roll it out widely. There are many different QoS mechanisms, with a bewildering array of trade-offs, so choosing an outside expert to come in may be cost-effective. Don't underestimate the impact that VoIP can have on your current network traffic, and vice versa.

- **New network service contracts and SLAs**—From the readiness assessment, you may have learned that some of your existing network links need more capacity to better support the additional VoIP traffic. As an alternative, you may have sufficient capacity, but the current tuning may be biased toward high throughput for file transfers rather than low delay and jitter. You may have to create new SLAs for VoIP and also update existing SLAs to take into account the real-time performance requirements of VoIP.

After you have finished the network upgrades and improvements, it is time to start a pilot deployment.

VoIP Pilot Deployments

A system integrator can provide the know-how to get the pilot deployment up and running quickly. The pilot is the time to learn about VoIP's technical intricacies—and there is a lot to learn! You may want to outsource this step as a training exercise for your staff. Experts can walk you through a small deployment, modeling the necessary steps and working through the initial problems while training your staff to do it the next time. During the pilot, you have to install, configure, and test new equipment. This is also a good time to gain experience managing the ongoing operation of a deployed VoIP system, and an expert can walk you through it as you learn.

Begin the pilot in a test lab, then roll it out to a small group of users. A pilot deployment can also serve as a decision point for saying "Yes," "No," or "Not now" to a larger VoIP deployment. When outsourcing a VoIP pilot, look for an integrator who can provide services such as the following:

- **Install, configure, and test VoIP equipment**—You may need call servers, IP PBXs, and VoIP phones—softphones and IP phones have their own unique setup issues. You probably need a VoIP gateway to provide for calls coming from and going to the PSTN. However, it can be difficult to configure a VoIP gateway that provides seamless integration between the IP network and the PSTN.

- **Train and educate**—One goal of the pilot deployment is to learn as much as you can about VoIP. If you plan to take over the operation of the VoIP implementation after the pilot, you need a skills transfer from the integrator.

- **Verify**—How do you know the pilot is working? What kind of call quality can you expect from the full-scale deployment? The integrator needs to verify that the pilot is up and running successfully.

After you have finished an initial VoIP pilot deployment, you have a wealth of information to consider. Did the pilot go smoothly? Are you ready for the next step? If so, you may want to begin a larger deployment.

VoIP Deployment

A VoIP deployment is really just a pilot on a larger scale. Whereas a pilot may take place in a lab under controlled conditions, the VoIP deployment takes place in the real world, with real users. You have several options for outsourcing a VoIP deployment:

- **Toll bypass using VoIP gateways**—Your current phone-service carrier may be able to provide one of the least disruptive toll-bypass services. Some carriers can provide VoIP gateways that connect to your traditional PBXs. PSTN traffic can pass through the PBX, to the VoIP gateway, and over an IP network backbone, also provided by the carrier. This option can mean reduced costs for calls between corporate sites, and it offers a first step in the migration to a larger VoIP deployment. Figure 4-1 shows a toll-bypass scenario using VoIP gateways.

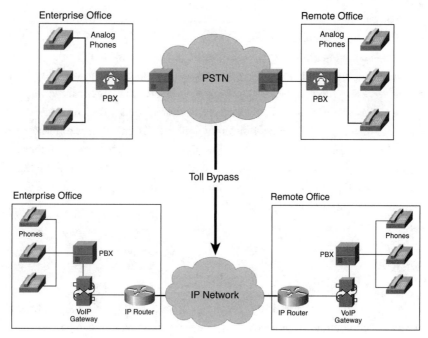

Figure 4-1   *Toll Bypass Using VoIP Gateways*

- **VoIP deployment with IP PBXs**—Post-pilot, you may be ready to
  invest in more VoIP equipment and take a further step toward a converged
  network. Integrators offer services to install, configure, and test a VoIP
  deployment using IP PBXs in conjunction with, or as a replacement for,
  traditional PBXs. The service may be bundled with tuning, management,
  and training.

A VoIP deployment can and probably should be staged. Don't try to do more
than you are capable of doing. After you have a VoIP system deployed, it still takes
a good bit of tuning to make it all work well together.

Application Integration

You are moving to VoIP because of the new features it offers. You are integrating these features into new voice-enabled applications. However, you probably need some assistance with making the whole system work together. System integrators can help make your unified messaging system work with your e-mail servers to provide the new features that you are expecting from VoIP.

Application integration is a relatively new area for VoIP. It is an area that requires knowledge of a range of different applications, including complex web-based applications and ERP applications that may need to work together. In addition, new VoIP application servers may need to be installed, configured, and tested. Integrating a new technology with new or existing applications is an area that you may want to leave to experts.

Tuning

Tuning a VoIP network for optimal performance requires skills that are hard to come by. When you are dealing with a system that has a virtually unlimited number of configuration choices, getting the right combinations can be a daunting task. Consider letting someone else master the various permutations of QoS and tuning. The many possible combinations make this phase of a VoIP deployment a step that you may not want to tackle. After you have read Chapter 5, "Quality of Service and Tuning," you will have a better sense for how to tackle it—and whether to outsource it.

Good network tuning involves analyzing the network design and traffic flow. Many of the criteria for a good network design were touched upon in Chapter 3, "Planning for VoIP." System integrators can analyze both your network design and network traffic flow and suggest ways to make the network run more efficiently. Because many network equipment vendors offer certification programs for network design and deployment, you should look for system integrators who have vendor certifications.

Management and Monitoring

After the VoIP deployment is up and running, you need to manage and monitor it to ensure that it continues to perform well. A new type of service has emerged to provide network management and monitoring solutions. If you are interested in outsourcing at this stage, *managed service providers* (MSPs) are companies that offer network management services for a monthly fee. An MSP can manage your VoIP deployment for you. Generally, MSPs offer two types of services:

- **Self service**—The MSP leases to you a management application and handles the installation, configuration, and maintenance of the application, but you manage your network by using the application. Your staff handles the day-to-day management and monitoring with the tools provided by the MSP.

- **Full service**—The MSP provides all the resources that are needed to fully manage and monitor your network. You don't have to provide any staff for management purposes, and you pay a predictable cost for the service.

Enterprise Management Associates (http://www.enterprisemanagement.com/) provides lots of information about management software and services.

If you choose an MSP for either type of VoIP management service, you need to consider what kinds of thresholds and SLAs will be used. Management is not an option for a successful VoIP deployment, it is a requirement. The question is: Who provides the service?

Problem Isolation and Diagnosis

This used to be easy in the PSTN—if something broke, you called in the POTS specialist to fix it as soon as possible, and had an expensive agreement to do so. It is still a good idea to outsource if your team does not have the skills to isolate and fix problems quickly.

On the other hand, outsourcing maintenance and problem diagnosis can leave some companies feeling out of control. If you do choose to outsource troubleshooting, you have to depend on the service provider to react to and resolve the problem in a timely manner.

Training

Proper training is a necessary requirement for a VoIP deployment. In addition to IT staff, your end users will need to be trained how to use new IP phones. The IP phones may have different options and function keys. Access to voice mail may be different in a unified messaging system. You don't want to have frustrated end users on day one of your VoIP deployment.

High-tech training companies with excellent teachers continually refine their material, making it more pertinent and useful in real-world situations. And to remain competitive, they keep it up-to-date. Rely on them to train your IT staff for VoIP deployment and management, and to train your end users for phone and messaging features.

Consider having your team members get technical certifications. Technical certifications are gained through focused programs that train your staff to be experts in various technical areas. New VoIP certifications are available from a number of companies.

Whether to Outsource—And to Whom?

The previous sections have described a range of potential VoIP outsourcing choices, from which you can choose any or all. But before you sign a contract with an integrator or MSP, think carefully about the resources you already have that make your situation unique. Look internally to make the decisions about outsourcing; look externally to find the right integrator or provider with whom you can work.

Determining Whether to Outsource

The following sections provide some criteria to help with the internal decisions; for instance, whether you should roll out and manage VoIP yourself or work with an integrator.

Skills

Is VoIP going to be an area of core expertise for your team? VoIP should be treated as another IP network application, which, like others, needs excellent availability, performance, and security. And perhaps you have decided that such converged IP application expertise is part of a core skill set that your team needs.

What skills does your team have, and which skills is it lacking? Can team members be trained in the areas where their skills are weaker? Does the training fit into your schedule and budget?

In 2001, the city of Dallas, Texas, replaced six separate networks with a single, 8500-site IP network, supporting both data and VoIP applications. Looking back on the project, their IT managers recommend "using an integrator in these early days of VoIP deployment." They reason that, "as with any new technology, staff skill sets are hard to come by until deployments become mainstream." After relying on integrators to provide expertise for many of the planning and deployment tasks, they observe that "while finding VoIP skill sets is difficult, at least we are now training people on one technology, not 10."[2]

Schedule

Just as it may take many months to plan and deploy a VoIP system, it may take many months to interview and decide upon the right integrator. In addition, the integrators themselves may have their own schedule conflicts because of commitments to other projects; so they, too, can delay your deployment.

On the other hand, you may be ready to start the VoIP implementation as soon as possible, but you may not have the time and personnel readily available to gain the necessary skills. An integrator might be able to get started much sooner than your resources permit.

Conflicts

Other commitments for your skilled team members may be the gating factor in deciding whether to outsource. If you have to start implementing VoIP right away, but your team is committed to other IT projects, choose an integrator.

Budget

Like most IT projects, a VoIP project comes with two costs: the initial cost to get it running well the first time, and the ongoing cost to keep it running well. Include both elements in your budgets. Some sample budget spreadsheets were examined in Chapter 2, "Building a Business Case for VoIP," which included salaries and capital expenses, among other items. Using an integrator may be more or less expensive in certain areas than doing it yourself. Look at each item in your budget and decide whether you are spending wisely.

Package Deals

Don't overlook the economics of the package deals that may be available. For example, if another division or location in your enterprise is already using an integrator for a VoIP project, could your group be included for a small additional cost?

Some packages couple deployment and management. You may have the skills and resources to complete a VoIP deployment, but can't take on its ongoing management and troubleshooting. After all, you may have to tackle other, unrelated IT projects in the coming months. Some providers and integrators offer low package prices to handle the entire project.

Finding the Right Integrator

Having decided to consider external outsourcing, whom do you employ? The following sections offer suggestions and questions to help drive your decision-making process.

Quality and Expertise

You should do some research to determine whether the integrator is capable of doing the job you that you need to have completed. Carefully examine his or her expertise and track record. Each VoIP installation is a little different from every other. How many VoIP outsourcing projects has he or she done before? Ask to look at his or her portfolio. Does it meet your quality expectations?

If their staff is well qualified, they are probably certified on the products and equipment they are installing or maintaining. Request copies of the vendor certifications their team has earned, and, in particular, of those who will be working on your project.

A system integrator's customer service team is in place to respond to requests from your team and your employees after the VoIP project is up and running. Look at the process followed by the customer service team. Inquire about its availability, how many calls it receives per day, what the wait time is for calls, how many issues are dispatched each day (by severity and amount of time open), and so on. Observe the customer service team firsthand—would you be comfortable having your team call members of that team?

Chapter 7, "Establishing VoIP SLAs," discusses service-level agreements. What SLAs do other customers have with this integrator? How often are the SLAs met, and what is the penalty when they are not met? Ask to see some real SLAs from other customers, as well as the integrator's track record in meeting them.

Demand excellence—providing services is what integrators and providers do for a living. The way they do it should constantly amaze you—you should be continually pleased at how they do their job so much better than you could.[3]

Capability

Is the integrator a good match for your organization in size and capability? Consider the size of the integrator's team, relative to the size of your VoIP deployment. The size of the projects they completed at their other customers' sites is a good way to gauge their ability to complete your project. If you have multiple branches spread out geographically, the integrator may have to travel. Are they international, nationwide, or regional?

And, finally, you need to judge whether they will indeed be attentive to your project. If it is too small for them, they may not take as active an interest in your needs as you prefer.

Integrity

After you have examined the quality of the integrator's work, examine the quality of their company. What is the company's reputation in the industry? What is its reputation among your peers? The integrator should be happy to supply a list of the company's customers; talk to the customers. Who else has used the company for similar projects, and what was their experience like? Would they recommend the company for the type of work you are planning?

You also might want to explore the integrity issue from a negative perspective. Has the company had complaints filed against it? If so, how were they resolved? The Better Business Bureau may be a good source of information. (In the U.S., contact the office that is located in or near the integrator's city.) Also, examine the company's financial reports—you want to be reassured that the company will be strong and viable far into the future.

One more thing to probe is the integrator's security policies. If you outsource your VoIP deployment or management to a third party, that party will end up collecting a lot of information about your organization and your employees. Ask to see the company's information-security policies. How does it protect your information in its databases? Who has access to your information?

Relationship

One of the reasons to evaluate the integrator firsthand is to get a sense of the relationship you will have with them. Personalities and cultures differ. Were you to evaluate five integrators, there is probably one with whom you would have an excellent relationship, and one with whom the relationship would be poor. Rank the quality of the relationship in addition to ranking the quality of their work. Ask yourself if you want to work with them.

You have a responsibility here, too. Once you outsource, your integrator or provider is part of your company; treat him or her as you would a colleague.

Cost

And, finally, there is the question of cost. You have a budget for your VoIP project, and some portion will be spent on outsourcing. Does the integrator meet your budget expectations? Can the integrator meet your schedules, without going over budget?

Often, an integrator's or provider's services are available on a fixed-fee or per-transaction-fee basis. When you agree to a billing and payment schedule, plan ahead for post-deployment needs. Take the time to work out a business relationship that both organizations will be comfortable with—one in which both can succeed.

The most desirable goal is a long-term relationship supported by a continually renewable, short-term contract. This gives both parties the ability to adjust things as business conditions change. But be sure to make provisions for a relatively quick and well-defined exit process if things change. Obviously, consult an attorney before you sign any contract.

To simplify, when outsourcing, pick great partners. Where do you go to find such providers? Speak with your current data network and PSTN providers, as well as the potential vendors of VoIP equipment. Their firms may well offer comprehensive outsourcing services. Many will take on direct management of the entire system. If they can't do all that is required, ask them for recommendations for companies that can.

Ask for recommendations from the consultants that your enterprise has worked with successfully in the past. However, if you can't get a recommendation from your provider or your network of contacts, the Internet is always a great way to find candidates for outsourcing just about every aspect of the venture.

A Methodology for Approaching Outsourcing

Previous chapters extensively discussed the six steps that should comprise an IT project. Outsourcing of a VoIP project can be undertaken through a similar process. You plan what needs to be outsourced and why, evaluate candidates and choose one, and let them start their work. Parts of their work may be ongoing, so you need to monitor them and give them feedback on whether they are meeting your expectations. If the process goes well, will the VoIP deployment expand? Will you involve them in future projects? This section outlines a methodology for creating a partnership with the individuals to whom you will outsource part or all of your VoIP project.

Starting the Partnership

Just as with the VoIP deployment itself, the first steps in outsourcing a major project involve upfront planning—deciding what you need and how you are going to meet those needs. Before you outsource, analyze your situation to make sure outsourcing is appropriate and is likely to succeed.

Planning and Analysis

One way to start is by drawing up a list of the most difficult problems you face in VoIP deployment and management. For each problem, write down the things that would have to be done to fix them. Then, ask, "Do we have the personnel and expertise to successfully resolve all of these issues?" If the answer is no due to lack of time, lack of organizational expertise, lack of money, or the potential ongoing operational cost, then outsourcing is a possible solution.

Above all, don't make a change that will result in an overall reduction in the quality of the services you have been providing. With VoIP, you are probably deploying new software, using new network devices, generating new network traffic, and doing new types of management, monitoring, and troubleshooting. The section "Some Options for Outsourcing," earlier in the chapter, has a pretty thorough list. Determine which of these tasks should be outsourced, make sure you are aware of the budget and schedule for each, and make a list of your—and your users'—quality expectations.

Evaluation of Potential Providers

This stage is your individualized "bake-off," where you compare the likely candidates for your outsourcing contracts. You may wonder how best to choose an integrator. The previous section provided a list of questions to consider. Pare down your list of candidates, and then invite a handful of candidates to participate in a discussion with you and your team. Evaluate them based on the criteria that are important to you and rank them. The vendors will be doing everything they can in the bidding process to differentiate themselves from the other candidates. When you are evaluating offerings from multiple vendors, it is important to ask for the same thing, consistently, from each of them—to compare apples to apples.

Your organizational or corporate policies may dictate which vendor to select based upon its bid. If a bid seems too low or too high, though, you may want to investigate to find out why. It is quite possible that the vendor is omitting something from or adding something to your spec that you should be aware of. In some situations, rather than choosing vendors based upon lowest price, the winning vendor is selected as the bid that is closest to the average of all the bid proposals.

The most important consideration may be the long-term relationship you will develop with a provider or systems integrator. VoIP is business-critical; having interviewed your potential partners, whom do you trust most?

Project Management

Manage the transition from inside operations to an outside provider carefully. As a project manager, by outsourcing, you are not abdicating responsibility for the results; you are simply achieving the same or improved results in a more effective way. Work with the people both inside and outside your organization to help ensure a smooth transition. Think about how the change will affect all of your employees—especially those who are now doing the soon-to-be-outsourced work—and help them to make the transition. And don't forget the end users, as well. As often as it is appropriate to do so, communicate with them about the VoIP project, including why you are doing it and how VoIP will help the organization provide better service in the future.

Outsourcing may scare your employees. Stay aware of how any outside team can breed mistrust at your organization. Get, and stay, ahead of the rumor mill through straightforward, honest communications.

Keeping the Partnership Running Well

The ongoing success of a VoIP project depends on its reliability and quality. Your outsourcing partnership depends on these two attributes, as well. To ensure reliability and quality, apply the same approach to the partnership that you apply to the VoIP deployment itself:

- **Monitoring and management**—As the relationship between the organizations moves forward, three things top the to-do list: communicate, communicate, and communicate. It is not possible to have too much communication between you and your new partner. But at the same time, be careful not to micromanage the project or to manage the provider's business for them. Insist on open communications about what is happening and why. Also, remain open to the flow of innovation and new ideas—outside providers should become a constant source of innovation.

- **Problem isolation and diagnosis**—Talk continuously with your outsourcing provider about what is working and what is not working. Carefully document, analyze, and learn from every problem that crops up.

- **Planning for future growth**—Talk about what the business might need three months from now that may be different from what it needs today. Establish trends with your provider showing their reliability, performance, and quality over time, so you can tune your existing relationship and plan future projects. As you need to grow or change your existing system, you return to the top of the life cycle chart again, doing planning and analysis for the improvements.

The Six Worst Mistakes in Small Business Outsourcing

Michael F. Corbett & Associates, Ltd. publishes this general list of outsourcing mistakes.[3] It is worth passing along:

1   Not clearly defining the desired results and how they'll be measured

2   Not talking to a provider's current and former clients

3   Failing to consider the long-term relationship dynamics

4   Signing a standardized, multiyear contract

5   Not planning up front for how the relationships might end

6   Treating the provider as an outsider

Chapter Summary

For a variety of reasons, a VoIP project may be something that you do not want to undertake yourself. This chapter explained why you might want to consider outsourcing and what parts of the project can be outsourced. A methodology for approaching outsourcing was described, as well as the key questions to ask to help you choose the right outsourcing partner.

The next chapter discusses a requirement for a successful VoIP project—quality of service and tuning.

End Notes

1   "Outsourcing at Southwest Airlines: How America's Leading Firms Use Outsourcing," Michael F. Corbett & Associates, Ltd., http://www.firmbuilder.com/articles/19/42/597/.

2   "Pure VoIP," *Packet Magazine*, monthly online exclusive, February 2002, http://www.cisco.com/warp/public/784/packet/onlineexclusive.html.

3   "A Successful Guide to Small Business Outsourcing," Michael F. Corbett & Associates, Ltd., http://www.firmbuilder.com/articles/19/48/702/.

CHAPTER 5

QUALITY OF SERVICE AND TUNING

Good net, tune away; bad net,
start again from scratch.
A dog is a dog.
—Peter J. Schwaller

This chapter explains how to adjust the devices in your network to improve call quality. It discusses *quality of service* (QoS) and tuning techniques that help make a VoIP deployment successful. It explains what QoS is, when to consider QoS, several different QoS mechanisms and tuning ideas, and how you can configure QoS and make it work. Finally, some practical QoS and tuning recommendations are covered.

The terms QoS and *tuning* are used in the title of this chapter and in the preceding paragraph. Here is what is meant by these two terms:

- **QoS**—Refers to choices about how different *users* or different *application traffic* gets treated on the network. To make changes in your network so that VoIP traffic gets priority over file-transfer traffic, you use QoS techniques.

- **Tuning**—Refers to methods for increasing efficiency or making trade-offs among *resources* or *attributes*. For example, if you make a setup change in a device that decreases delay but uses more RAM, you have made a tuning change.

QoS helps to manage competing users, applications, or traffic that is sharing the same network. In the end, it all comes down to the basic human problems of sharing and fairness.

Sharing a Network

Young children often have to be coaxed and cajoled into relinquishing a toy when it is another child's turn to play with it. Computer users and applications, competing for limited network bandwidth and resources, are not much different. Users share networks more than ever: at home, at work, and while traveling. Whenever many people or devices share a resource, such as a network, that resource can be either overprovisioned or oversubscribed.

Overprovisioning

With *overprovisioning,* more resources are made available than can be consumed. The term describes situations where so much of a resource is available that if every subscriber requested it at the same time, there would still be plenty of it to go around. Overprovisioning requires lots of reserves and is thus usually expensive. The following are some well-known examples of overprovisioning:

- **Food on a cruise**—It seems there is always more than enough food to go around.

- **Congressional parking spaces**—No congressperson goes without a parking space (although they may be prioritized).

- **AOL CD-ROMs**—There may be more than enough for every computer user on the planet.

Overprovisioning is generally rare, but it has probably been the dominant QoS strategy during the history of networking. If the network is slow, add more bandwidth!

Oversubscribing

Oversubscribing is much more common than overprovisioning because most of the time it is cheaper. The term describes situations where a resource has many users (subscribers) who don't all ask for the resource at the same time. Too many concurrent users could consume all of the resource. When too many subscribers request service simultaneously, service may be slow or even unavailable. Some examples of oversubscribing include the following:

- The clown's attention at a 3-year-old child's birthday party

- Batteries, bread, and highway lanes just before a hurricane

- Phone calls on Mother's Day in the U.S.

Oversubscription can occur whenever there is a juncture with many inputs and few outputs—that is, in any situation where a bottleneck or funnel emerges. It also occurs where things quickly go from fast to slow; we have all seen this happen on highways.

In networks, every juncture is a potential bottleneck. With network devices such as routers and switches, the total of all the inputs can greatly exceed the output capacity. High-speed links, such as LANs, frequently merge with low-speed links, such as WANs. Devices at network junctures use techniques such as queuing and prioritization to relieve oversubscription, but queues and patience are finite.

Many more users, much more demand for bandwidth, and new mixes of network traffic make oversubscription a concern for network managers far into the future. The demand for more bandwidth and network connectivity seems unbounded. Most analysts still see 50 to 100 percent annual growth in Internet traffic in many regions of the U.S.[1] Already, most WANs are oversubscribed, and the avalanche of traffic challenges LANs and the network devices connecting them, as well.

Ethernet inventor and industry sage Bob Metcalfe observes that the value of a network increases as the square of the number of users.[2] Users now connecting make the networks they are using more valuable to those who have not connected yet. Increased network resources are obviously needed for VoIP, and more will be required for other multimedia applications.

Performance Requirements

The users of a converged network have conflicting performance requirements and expectations of the network. In particular, most mission-critical business applications and most web transactions use the TCP protocol, whereas multimedia and voice traffic uses the RTP protocol—both on the same IP network. TCP is adaptive, rate based, and connection oriented; it behaves politely when the network is oversubscribed. TCP applications run as fast as they can, but gracefully back down when faced with congestion.

RTP applications often don't get feedback because they are using a connectionless protocol. They send data in one direction with no acknowledgments. When faced with congestion, they don't back off—frames are just dropped, degrading the quality of what is received. Thus, existing TCP business traffic may be starved of bandwidth by ill-mannered multimedia traffic.

Although a VoIP call consumes relatively little bandwidth and uses small packet sizes, voice applications have strict requirements for delay, jitter, and lost data, whereas other applications require high throughput or low response times. What happens when a 64-byte voice packet is stuck behind a large file transfer in a router queue? You would like for the small VoIP packet to move to the head of the queue to avoid the delay. Because networks are shared and can be oversubscribed, mechanisms are needed to protect users and applications from each other and to provide differentiation of service: QoS.

QoS: What and Why

QoS is used to alleviate occasional network oversubscription. When oversubscription becomes noticeable—that is, when the network traffic increases enough that performance declines—you may choose to give some classes of network traffic better treatment than others. The decisions you make will mean that some users or some applications will be treated better, or at least differently, than others.

QoS operation rests on your responses to two broad categories of decisions:

- **How to classify traffic**—What kind of traffic is this? What are the different classes of traffic on the network?

- **How to handle each class of traffic**—How should this class of traffic be treated? How is the handling of this class different from that of other classes of traffic?

An easy way to understand traffic classes is to think of Olympic medals. Some traffic gets gold-medal treatment, other traffic gets silver-medal treatment, yet other traffic gets bronze-medal treatment, while everything else gets "best-effort" treatment. You have probably seen this kind of distinction with hotels, credit cards, and rental cars. You have to make two sets of decisions, though: Who gets gold-medal handling, and what does gold-medal handling mean? And whatever you decide gold-medal handling is, it should be better than silver-medal handling— and demonstrably so. Otherwise, silver-medal service would be good enough for anyone, and there would be no demand for the gold-medal level of service.

Classifying is usually done at the edge of a network; handling is usually done in the middle. Decisions about classifying and handling network traffic are the important business decisions involved in deploying QoS.

Networks with no QoS treat all traffic as best effort—the network devices do their best to deliver frames from senders to their receivers. But all traffic is not created equal. When congestion occurs in a network, should some traffic be given premium treatment? For example, should the VoIP traffic be treated better than payroll data transactions? To introduce a metaphor, QoS changes the playing field; it's no longer level. The flavors of preferred handling that premium traffic can receive are almost as varied as network technologies, such as guaranteed bandwidth, a guaranteed path, low delay, high throughput, low data loss, higher priority during congestion, or some combination of these.

This section began with the statement that QoS is useful in an oversubscribed network. But because QoS inherently treats some traffic poorly, it is not something you want working hard day and night. Ideally, the network will run smoothly without QoS, except in cases of congestion, where QoS helps some traffic to the detriment of other traffic. This brings us to the two guidelines for QoS usage:

- *Only* use QoS to make a good situation better.

- *Never* use QoS in the hope of improving a poor or marginal situation to "good enough."

How do you know that you have a congestion problem? Congestion can be observed when one or more of your performance measurements (delay, jitter, or packet loss) intermittently go bad. That is, most of the time, voice quality is good, because these measurements are in an acceptable range. But every once in a while, during heavy network usage, one or more of these measurements spike upward. The goal of QoS is to smooth out the spikes.

What does congestion on your network look like on a daily, weekly, and monthly basis? Your network administrator probably has graphs showing the frequency, duration, and location of network congestion. For chronic congestion, QoS is not the solution. QoS treats some traffic poorly, and it merely postpones the inevitable failure that occurs when new users and more traffic are added.

Nor are QoS techniques designed to solve static problems that exist when there is no congestion present. For example, if delay or packet loss is consistently high, even when the network is being lightly used, you need to resolve the underlying problems instead of looking for QoS solutions. In Chapter 3, "Planning for VoIP," the section "Working on the Problem Areas" describes the right approaches to chronic congestion and static problems in some detail: adding more bandwidth, upgrading or replacing existing network equipment, laying out your network architecture in a more efficient configuration, reconfiguring or retuning the network, or a combination of these.

Even if your network is a good candidate for QoS, it is still worth exploring the alternatives, particularly cheap bandwidth and a network design with fewer bottlenecks. But, more bandwidth does not always help, especially where delay and jitter are involved, although it does give all of your network traffic more headroom.

Finally, QoS has a few downsides, which are explored in this chapter:

- It is difficult to set up.

- It often involves political decisions, determining who is in each class of traffic and how they get treated. In some situations, QoS is not used for fear of making the wrong political decision—for example, giving priority to the billing department by sacrificing the CEO's traffic. Using QoS for VoIP—a business-critical application—may be politically easy, however.

- QoS roll out and deployment tools must become part of your standard equipment. Traffic generators are discussed later in this chapter, and policy-based network management is discussed in Chapter 6, "Ongoing VoIP Management."

- QoS presents considerable testing challenges. For one thing, QoS works only when congestion occurs. Testing should show how the different traffic classes get handled differently, particularly under high-stress conditions, and needs to demonstrate what happens on the network from end to end.

- Network management tools for QoS are not extremely mature. You would like to see at a glance the answer to questions like these: Is it working? Is it helping? Is it deployed right? What changed? Where?

Having admitted the challenges, it is time to tackle them, and really take advantage of the power that QoS offers.

Classifying Traffic

To be classified, network traffic needs to be segregated. For example, some network applications are easily identified because they use a unique IP port number. By contrast, applications that use dynamic ports are hard to identify solely by looking at port numbers. Of the many ways in which network traffic can be classified, here are some of the most common:

- Protocol (such as TCP, UDP, RTP, ICMP)
- IP header settings, such as the DiffServ/TOS byte
- *Resource Reservation Protocol* (RSVP) signaling
- Port numbers and IP addresses
- RTP header information
- Data content (such as a URL)
- Data rate and flow patterns
- Buffer size
- Routing tags
- Application signature

For some of these methods, classification is accomplished using some implicit characteristic already present in the IP packet, such as its protocol, destination address, or port number. Otherwise, the classification is done explicitly. *Differentiated services* (DiffServ), RSVP, and routing tags are discussed later in this chapter; at any rate, some application or device has to take explicit action to identify traffic to be handled with one of these techniques.

Traffic classification can be done in any of three ways:

- **At the edges of a network**—Devices that classify traffic at the network edge are common today. Edge devices, such as traffic shapers, bandwidth managers, access routers, and firewalls, provide central points of administration. You can secure the edge devices and apply a consistent set of traffic rules at the places through which most traffic passes.

   Classification works best when the traffic goes through devices like these. But beware: These same places can become bottlenecks, compounding performance problems.

- **In the middle of the network**—Traffic classification in the middle of the network is also common, but the devices usually have less knowledge about the traffic. Routers, for example, may classify traffic based on flow rates per connection, queuing conditions, and packet sizes, rather than on content or address.

- **By the network applications themselves**—End users and applications themselves are rarely trusted to classify traffic. If they are given a choice, most users want *their* traffic to receive premium handling. As a result, sophisticated billing methods—that is, ways to charge a premium for traffic given premium handling—are needed for all network users. Thus, applications generally classify their own traffic only when the applications know how to employ the right settings, their users are trusted, and all network devices in the path honor the application settings.

VoIP applications often do their own classification; for example, softphones, IP phones, and VoIP gateways are generally good at explicitly marking their call setup and VoIP conversation traffic.

Handling Traffic

Having identified and classified the traffic, you also need to determine what you are going to do with it, but understand that your decisions will produce side effects when things get bad, such as discarding packets or adding delay to the nonpremium traffic.

For each class of traffic, a series of QoS configuration decisions determines how it is handled at each hop as it traverses a network. Should it be given high, medium, or low priority? Should it get a guaranteed amount of bandwidth or guaranteed latency? During congestion, should it be treated as less likely to be discarded? Does it require a guaranteed route across the network?

For VoIP conversation traffic, focus on its delay sensitivity. You don't want the VoIP datagrams to get stuck in a router queue. You don't want them in competition with transaction-oriented traffic.

QoS configuration changes that enable the appropriate handling for each class of traffic are made to network devices that are at the edges and in the middle of a network. However, the results of the configuration changes are seen by the end users of the applications. This wide separation of cause (configuration changes) and effect (end-to-end behavior) is one of the challenges of setting up QoS successfully.

Network QoS Techniques

The normal behavior of the TCP/IP family of protocols is to give all traffic best-effort delivery service. This works well for the transfer of computer data when the network is moderately loaded. New applications have their own respective requirements for bandwidth, delay, jitter, and packet loss. QoS mechanisms help meet specific application requirements as network load increases, improving on TCP/IP's best-effort delivery.

QoS techniques comprise a mix of classification and handling mechanisms. For the purposes of discussion, these have been grouped into several categories:

- **Link-layer QoS techniques**—Link-layer, or Layer 2, QoS schemes influence the traffic handling on individual data links. For example, ATM has QoS incorporated into its core architecture. In IEEE 802.1p/Q, bytes are inserted into Ethernet frames that indicate each frame's priority. Ethernet switches can use this priority to decide which frames get switched ahead of others. Both of these schemes help at lower layers, but without some correlation to a higher-layer QoS mechanism, they may provide little value to application users, whose traffic needs to be handled consistently across all the data links in a connection. Cisco *Link Fragmentation and Interleaving* (LFI) breaks up large packets so that a small voice packet does not get stuck behind a file-transfer packet on a WAN link.

  Apply link-layer techniques to the "weakest links" in the network. Traffic can't flow across a network faster than the slowest or most congested link in the path.

- **IP QoS techniques**—The Layer 3 QoS schemes, RSVP, DiffServ, and MPLS, work to meet applications' network requirements from end to end. RSVP reserves resources to meet requirements for bandwidth, jitter, and delay for a particular connection through a series of routers. RSVP works best when connections are long (such as those used by streaming video) and when only a few connections at a time require reserved resources. DiffServ marks a relative priority in each IP packet, to be honored by each router that handles the frame. Still needed are ways to ensure the consistent handling of the priorities. *Multiprotocol Label Switching* (MPLS) sets up a virtual circuit through an IP network by prefixing each frame with 4 bytes that tell how to get to the next router in the path. MPLS is getting a lot of attention today from equipment vendors for the core of large networks.

IP QoS schemes treat different classes of traffic differently. They don't necessarily make one class of traffic move faster than another. Rather, they increase the likelihood that traffic in a premium class gets a better guarantee of bandwidth, a better priority within routers, or a better route through a network than traffic in a lower class. APIs are starting to enable applications to do their own prioritizing; for example, recent versions of Windows offer TCP/IP applications an *application program interface* (API) for requesting the QoS they desire. However, these APIs are likely to be little used or ignored because applications cannot necessarily be trusted, and network managers will want to look across the aggregate needs of all the applications on their networks when determining QoS schemes.

- **Queuing techniques**—In addition to QoS at Layers 2 and 3, routers and switches offer ways to prioritize traffic and handle congestion better. Examples of these include the acronyms WFQ, CBWFQ, LLQ, and WRED. *Weighted fair queuing* (WFQ) works to improve the handling of low-volume connections in the midst of high-volume traffic. WFQ can prove beneficial when VoIP traffic is mixed with heavy file transfers. *Class-based weighted fair queuing* (CBWFQ) and *low-latency queuing* (LLQ) work together to give priority to delay-sensitive VoIP traffic. *Weighted random early detection* (WRED) works during congestion to avoid the mass slowdown of all the TCP connections passing through a router. Options like these are quickly effective in a small network, but are hard to administer consistently across many devices.

- **Traffic shapers**—This new category of devices (also known as *bandwidth managers*) stand at the entrance and egress points in a network. These are the first network devices to begin implementing *policies* for the traffic they handle. Although they were initially developed as proprietary solutions, they are evolving into local agents for a broad set of rules implemented by policy servers. (Policy servers are introduced in the section "QoS Management" in Chapter 6.)

The preceding QoS mechanisms are discussed in more detail in the sections that follow.

Link-Layer QoS Techniques

Some data links provide built-in QoS mechanisms. These Layer 2 mechanisms provide ways of classifying and handling traffic for different kinds of links. The most popular Layer 2 QoS mechanisms are discussed in the following sections.

IEEE 802.1p/Q

The Ethernet transmission medium is the LAN standard upon which most IP networks are built today. Ethernet has nearly reached ubiquity—most new computers come equipped with Ethernet card hardware. A couple of IEEE standards, 802.1p and 802.1Q, are used together to specify the built-in QoS mechanism for Ethernet networks. 802.1Q adds a 4-byte tag to each Ethernet *Media Access Control* (MAC) header. Sometimes referred to as LAN QoS, 802.1p defines, within this tag, 3 bits that make up the Priority field. The three Priority bits provide eight different *classes of service* (CoS). Figure 5-1 shows the Priority field in the Ethernet header.

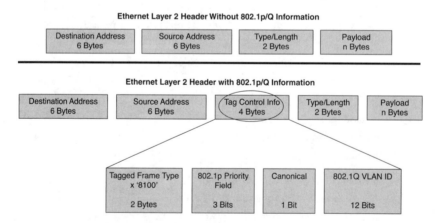

Figure 5-1 *802.1p/Q Fields in the Ethernet Header*

Ethernet switches that support the 802.1p/Q standard can prioritize Ethernet traffic based on the Priority field bit settings. You can run into interoperability problems if you are using older switches that don't understand what to do with these extra bits in the header. It is modern, "802.1p/Q-enabled" *network interface cards* (NICs) that are responsible for setting the Priority field bits. These enabled NICs are found in some IP phones and in softphone computers. Most non-VoIP data traffic sets the Priority field to **000**, which means "best effort," or no prioritization. VoIP RTP call traffic should usually have these 3 bits set to **101** (which is decimal value 5). The call-setup traffic for VoIP uses a Priority field setting of **011** (decimal value 3).

ATM QoS

Asynchronous Transfer Mode (ATM) is another example of a link-layer protocol that provides built-in QoS. Many carrier network backbones use ATM networks because of the services that can be offered. ATM transfers data in 53-byte cells: a 5-byte header and 48-byte payload. An ATM logical connection is set up through the ATM switches, which then negotiate a type of service for the duration of the connection. The *Virtual Path Identifier* (VPI) and *Virtual Channel Identifier* (VCI) fields in the ATM header identify the ATM connection. Figure 5-2 shows the ATM header fields used for QoS with connection identifiers that are used to classify which type of service should be given to the cells in a connection.

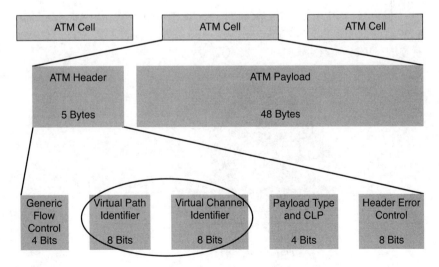

Figure 5-2 *ATM Header Fields with Built-In QoS*

When an ATM connection is established, QoS parameters are negotiated and established. A type of service is requested, with specific QoS parameters. ATM defines QoS parameters, such as *cell delay variation* (CDV), *maximum cell transfer delay* (max CTD), and *cell loss ratio* (CLR). Resources and queues within the ATM switches are reserved to meet the service level requested. You can interpret the terms CDV as jitter and max CTD as latency.

ATM defines four different types of service:

- **Constant bit rate (CBR)**—Data that has a fixed data rate, sent in a steady stream. CBR traffic is usually low bandwidth and sensitive to delay and packet loss. Provides guaranteed delay, jitter, and cell loss.

- **Variable bit rate (VBR)**—Data that is bursty in nature, but is guaranteed a certain level of throughput. Provides guaranteed delay, jitter, and cell loss.

- **Unspecified bit rate (UBR)**—No guarantee of throughput. A "best-effort" service.

- **Available bit rate (ABR)**—A minimum capacity is guaranteed and, depending on network usage, bursts of traffic are allowed that exceed the minimum capacity. Provides guaranteed delay, but no guaranteed jitter and cell loss.

On ATM, VoIP traffic is best served by CBR connections with guaranteed delay, jitter, and cell loss. Figure 5-3 shows an ATM switch with different queues for different service classes.

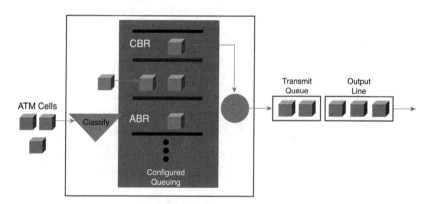

Figure 5-3   ATM Switches with Queues for Four Types of Service

Frame Relay Links

Frame Relay is a data link layer protocol that is often used for WAN connections. In most cases, a Frame Relay link is set up as a permanent virtual connection, which means that a dedicated logical connection is maintained through the underlying network. A built-in form of QoS, the *committed information rate* (CIR) shapes the traffic that is transferred on Frame Relay links. CIR is often expressed in bits per second, and the rates may be different (asymmetric) for each direction of the link. Figure 5-4 shows CIR applied to traffic in different queues.

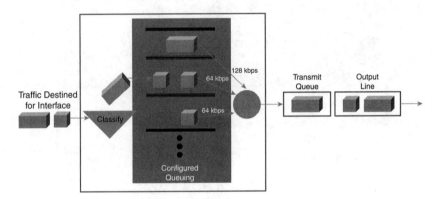

Figure 5-4   *Traffic Is Shaped by the CIR on Frame Relay Links*

If network congestion occurs, traffic that exceeds the CIR on certain links is discarded. For this reason, you should configure the CIR to be slightly above the average traffic volume for the link. As with any network link, a Frame Relay link may be oversubscribed. However, a CIR helps prevent ill-mannered applications from consuming too much bandwidth and thus starving VoIP traffic.

RTP Header Compression

The combined size of the IP, UDP, and RTP headers, 40 bytes, adds a significant amount of overhead to VoIP transmissions. The combined header size can be larger than the VoIP payload size, depending on the codec and the packet delay. This header overhead can consume precious bandwidth on lower-capacity WAN links, especially when you consider that VoIP traffic flows in both directions.

Closer inspection of the contents of the IP, UDP, and RTP headers reveals that many of the field values do not change during the course of a VoIP transmission. Router vendors have taken advantage of this fact to provide a feature known as *RTP header compression* (cRTP). When cRTP is activated, the combined headers are compressed to between 2 and 5 bytes, as shown in Figure 5-5. The bandwidth savings can make room for more VoIP calls on a given link. However, cRTP exacts a trade-off; the compression consumes more CPU and adds delay. Because it incurs some extra CPU utilization and delay, cRTP should be considered only for link speeds of 512 kbps or less.

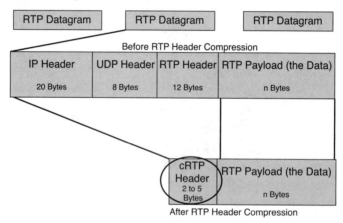

Figure 5-5   *Compression of IP, UDP, and RTP Headers Using cRTP*

Link Fragmentation and Interleaving

LFI is a router technique for alleviating delay on slow links. Packets of all different sizes arrive at routers; some packets may be 64 bytes long, whereas others are 1500 bytes long. VoIP packets are generally the small ones. On a slow link, you don't want a VoIP packet to get stuck behind a 1500-byte packet that is part of a file transfer, because the delay of the VoIP packets can reduce the call quality. Activating LFI in a router means that the router cuts the big packets into fragments, and interleaves smaller packets in between the larger fragments, which are reassembled at the other end. This interleaving avoids excessive delay for any small packet. Figure 5-6 shows how voice packets can be delayed behind larger data packets on a slow link.

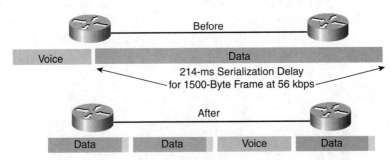

Figure 5-6 *Link Data Flow Before and After LFI (Source: Cisco Systems)*

Consider LFI if you are experiencing high queuing delay due to serialization on slower-speed WAN links. The symptoms of excessive queuing delay are high end-to-end delay or high jitter for VoIP packets. For link speeds greater than 768 kbps, LFI is usually not needed.

IP QoS Techniques

An increasingly popular set of QoS mechanisms is found at Layer 3 in the TCP/IP protocol stack. These techniques—DiffServ, RSVP, and MPLS—are referred to as *IP QoS* because they take advantage of specific features of the IP protocol.

TOS/IP Precedence/DiffServ

There is a 1-byte field in the header of every IP packet that has generally been unused for the past generation. That means every IP packet has a byte that is set to zero—essentially wasted space.

A widely used QoS technique involves setting the bits in this byte to a nonzero value. In the IP version 4 header specification, this field is called the *Type of Service* (TOS) byte. Most TCP/IP stacks have always set the TOS byte to zero, and consequently most network devices have ignored this byte. In recent years, this same byte has been renamed the *Differentiated Services field,* or the *DiffServ byte.*

TOS and IP Precedence were a first attempt to provide IP QoS. Here, 4 of the bits in the TOS byte were designated type of service bits in RFC 1349[3]. These 4 bits create 4 service classes: minimize delay, maximize throughput, maximize reliability, and minimize monetary cost. In addition, RFC 791[4] and RFC 1812[5] define a QoS mechanism known as *IP Precedence*. IP Precedence uses the first 3 bits in the TOS byte. Routers can interpret these 3 bits as 2^3 or 8 different classes of service. Figure 5-7 shows the TOS byte in the IP header.

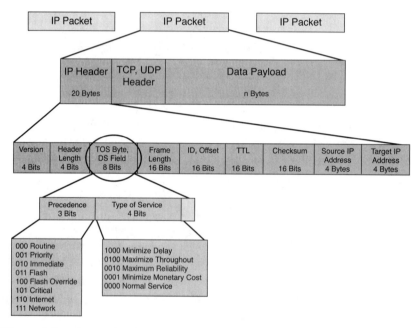

Figure 5-7 *The TOS and IP Precedence Bits, with Their Original Definitions*

DiffServ is the latest attempt to provide QoS using the TOS byte. Defined by RFC 2474[6], DiffServ uses the first 6 bits of the TOS byte, known as the *differentiated services code point* (DSCP). The 6 bits of the DSCP allow for 2^6 or 64 different classes of service. Most routers understand DiffServ, and there is little overhead involved with DiffServ classification because looking at bits in the IP header is something that routers do all the time. Figure 5-8 shows the DiffServ field in the IP header.

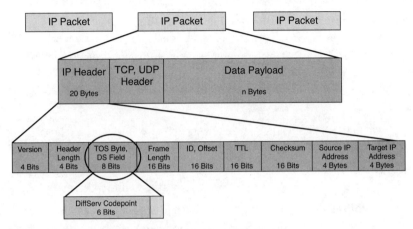

Figure 5-8 *DiffServ Field, Present in Every IP Packet*

Application programs themselves can set the DSCP, but it is rarely done this way. It can also be set by a traffic shaper, which looks at something else in the frame, such as the port number, to decide how to set it. VoIP gateways commonly set this byte as they generate VoIP packets for calls based in the PSTN.

Most IP phones and VoIP gateways set the TOS byte to a nonzero value to denote the priority needed for VoIP. As discussed earlier, in the section "IEEE 802.1p/Q," VoIP call traffic commonly has this byte set to binary 10100000. Sometimes this setting is referred to as 5 because the first 3 bits represent a decimal value of 5. VoIP call-setup traffic generally uses a different value: binary 01100000. The DSCP field creates an efficient scheme for classifying different types of traffic. However, it is only as good as the weakest network link. If a single segment in the path from one codec to the other does not support DSCP handling, the entire path can only be considered best-effort.

Resource Reservation Protocol

RSVP reserves resources to meet requirements for bandwidth, jitter, and delay on a particular network path through a series of routers. Defined in RFC 2205[7], RSVP is sometimes called *integrated services* (IntServ). RSVP sends IP control flows from one end of the network to the other. These IP packets instruct intermediate routers to reserve a portion of their resources (bandwidth, queues, and so on) for forthcoming TCP/IP application traffic.

Applications use RSVP by making additional calls to their underlying TCP/IP stacks. The TCP/IP stacks communicate with the first router on their path, which, in turn, communicates with the other routers on the path. RSVP can work in tandem with other QoS techniques, such as WFQ, to enforce the resource reservations.

Two main RSVP messages are exchanged between routers and hosts:

- **Reservation request (RESV)**—This message is sent from the receiver to the sender along the reverse data path. Each router along the way must accept or reject the reservation request (see Figure 5-9).

- **Path (PATH)**—This message is sent to routers in between the sender and receiver. The path message helps the routers maintain state information in order to send RESV messages.

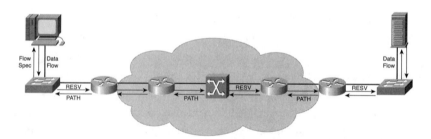

Figure 5-9 *RSVP Messages Flow Between Routers and Hosts*

A drawback of RSVP is that it requires ongoing bandwidth and router resources. A good rule of thumb is that the extra IP flows add approximately 100 bps per connection in extra bandwidth usage and require approximately 1 KB of RAM per router per connection. In addition, it takes several seconds to set up the separate control flows. And RSVP is one of the most challenging QoS techniques to configure correctly.

On the other hand, RSVP can provide a guaranteed level of service for application traffic, which may be especially important for delay-sensitive traffic such as VoIP. Yet RSVP is another end-to-end QoS technique that is easily hindered by the weakest network link. If a single link along the data path does not accept the reservation request, the path is considered best effort. RSVP works best when used within buildings, on a campus, or within a privately owned WAN. It works well when network connections are long in duration (such as streaming video) and when only a few connections at a time require reserved resources. It is probably not the right technique to use for VoIP.

Multiprotocol Label Switching

MPLS is much more than just a QoS technique; it also provides network operators with a way to offer different classes of service. When packets enter an MPLS-aware network, they are "tagged" with a label that can contain a variety of information. MPLS-aware routers, known as *label switching routers* (LSRs), can forward the packet through the network using the label instead of the traditional address fields in the IP header. Different paths through the network, *label-switched paths* (LSPs), can be configured for different label values. Figure 5-10 shows the MPLS tags that are added to the front of an IP packet.

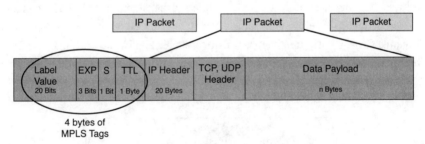

Figure 5-10   *MPLS Label Fields Prefixed to Front of IP Packet*

By using different LSPs, network operators can set up routes for different classes of data traffic from different users. For instance, users who pay for premium network service may be given a less-congested path through the network. MPLS, a handling technique, can be used in tandem with other QoS techniques, such as DiffServ (a classifying technique). The MPLS labels could be assigned based on the bit settings of the DSCP so that the MPLS-enabled network would provide different paths for traffic with different bit settings.

A QoS technique that is better suited for very large network backbones with many routers, MPLS is often used by network carriers and Internet service providers. The complexity of MPLS makes it impractical for most enterprise networks.

Queuing Techniques

Another group of QoS techniques deals with queuing methods within network devices. Queuing techniques generally provide different queue levels and handling for different classes of traffic.

Weighted Fair Queuing

WFQ is a commonly used, flow-based queuing algorithm. Different traffic flows are queued to prevent bandwidth starvation—that is the "fair" part. A flow is composed of all packets with the same source address/port and destination address/port combination. A weight is assigned to flows to grant those flows priority queuing according to some scheme, usually another QoS mechanism. Different queue levels are provided for the weighted flows. Low-bandwidth streams, such as VoIP, are given priority over larger-bandwidth consumers such as file transfers. Figure 5-11 shows different queues using the DSCP field to assign a weight.

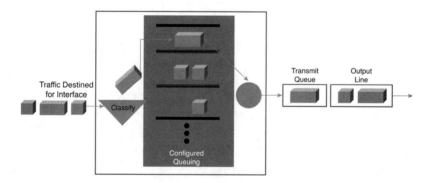

Figure 5-11   *Different Queue Levels Using DSCP to Assign a Weight*

WFQ may use IP Precedence or DiffServ bits to determine the weight of a particular flow. If all weights are equal, then the available bandwidth is divided equally.

Class-Based Weighted Fair Queuing

CBWFQ is an enhancement to the WFQ algorithm that includes user-defined traffic classes. Traffic classes can be defined based on protocol, port, access control, input queues, or DiffServ bits. Each traffic class gets its own queue. Traffic classes can have bandwidth and queue limits assigned to them. The bandwidth is provided to the class when congestion occurs. The queue limit is the maximum number of packets that are allowed in a class-based queue. If the queue fills up, then packets are dropped. Figure 5-12 shows the LLQ reserved for VoIP traffic.

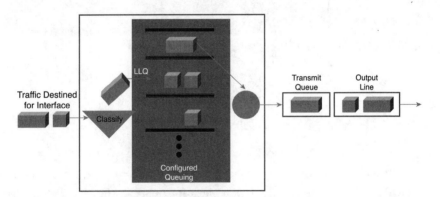

Figure 5-12   *CBWFQ with a Low-Latency Queue for VoIP Traffic*

CBWFQ may be used with a feature called *low-latency queuing* (LLQ). LLQ offers delay-sensitive data, such as VoIP, priority handling over other types of traffic. With LLQ, VoIP traffic gets its own queue, and as packets are diverted to the low-latency queue, they are dequeued and processed ahead of any other queues.

Weighted Random Early Detection

WRED is a little different from other queuing schemes. Instead of trying to deal with congestion after it occurs, WRED tries to detect congestion before it happens and then avoid it. According to Tom Lancaster's Networking Tips, "The problem it solves is called 'tail drop,' which happens when a burst of packets fills up a switch or router's buffer and the last few packets in the burst get dropped because there's no more room in the buffer."[8] Figure 5-13 shows the congestion-avoidance scheme WRED. As a link is becoming congested, WRED randomly selects packets to discard—rather than dropping all that arrive after the queue is 100 percent full.

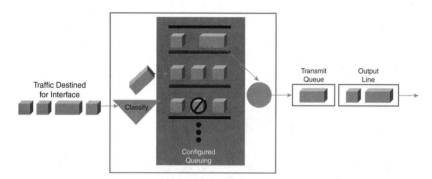

Figure 5-13 *WRED Selects Packets to Discard Before Congestion Occurs*

WRED tries to avoid congestion by randomly discarding selected packets before the queues fill up. Ideally, TCP packets are dropped; when a TCP packet is dropped, the protocol will slow down and retransmit. For UDP or RTP flows that do not retransmit, such as high-throughput video or VoIP, WRED is not as effective. WRED usually relies on IP Precedence bits to provide a weighting scheme to help decide which packets to drop. The higher the priority, the lower a packet's chance of being dropped.

Traffic Shapers

Traffic shapers (sometimes known as bandwidth managers) are devices or software that can classify and prioritize traffic based on a predefined policy. Some operating systems, including Windows XP and Linux, have traffic shapers built in to their TCP/IP stack. Other hardware devices provide traffic shaping and bandwidth management as well. These techniques classify traffic based on common methods and prioritize based on rules that you provide. The goal of traffic shaping is to prescribe the bandwidth consumed by different types of traffic.

Traffic shaping is useful in the following situations:

- **Speed mismatches between networks**—You have a fast network or link, such as a LAN, feeding into a slower-speed WAN link.

- **Oversubscription of links**—You have too many users and not enough bandwidth on a particular link.

- **Traffic patterns are too bursty**—You have traffic that comes in bursts from time to time. Traffic shaping can help smooth out the bursts and provide more consistent bandwidth requirements.

With a traffic shaper, you create rules that give certain kinds of traffic a specified amount of bandwidth. For example, you may give VoIP traffic most of the bandwidth available in a link and give music-download traffic only a small amount of the overall bandwidth. Figure 5-14 shows an example of 18 different classes of traffic before and after traffic shaping. In this case, the streams are classified by port number. After the shaping is applied, each stream receives a specified amount of bandwidth.

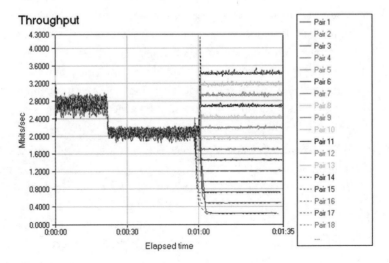

Figure 5-14   *Traffic Shaping Applied to Different Traffic Classes*

Tuning Choices

Tuning is performed to improve efficiency. You tune the radio to get a stronger, clearer signal. If you have an older car, you give it a tune-up to increase the efficiency of the engine. Likewise, you can make tuning choices to improve the efficiency of a network and VoIP deployment.

When tuning your network, consider the trade-offs. Depending on the environment, you may trade increased CPU utilization for less RAM, or more delay for less risk of lost data. Often, tuning involves configuration changes—to the routers, switches, VoIP servers, or IP phones. Default configuration values don't always work well, so you may need to make adjustments to improve efficiency.

TCP/IP Tuning

The TCP/IP protocol stack generally operates with very high efficiency. However, in some cases, tuning can improve performance. Here are some obvious areas you can adjust:

- **TCP window size**—The TCP window size determines the amount of data that can be sent before the sender has to stop and wait for an acknowledgment. If you have a very reliable network—in which the chances for data loss are very small—then increasing the window size can improve throughput. On the other hand, if the network loses data frequently, a larger window size would force more data to be retransmitted when packets get lost, resulting in lower throughput. Most TCP/IP stacks adjust the window size dynamically to optimize performance over a wide range of network conditions.

- **MTU sizes and low latency**—The *maximum transmission unit* (MTU) or maximum frame size on a data network is usually 1500 bytes. This is reasonable for elastic applications, but at an extremely slow speed such as 56 kbps, 1500 bytes takes longer than 200 ms just to put the packet on the wire. To avoid breaking your delay budget for VoIP, you have to set a smaller MTU size to be forwarded through the slower-speed links. Although this costs a small amount of data efficiency, you should not need to change anything other than one router configuration command.

Current Microsoft Windows TCP/IP stacks routinely perform "black hole detection" and adjust their MTU accordingly. (For a detailed discussion of black hole detection, see RFC 2923.[9])

- **Concurrent sessions per URL**—When you type a URL into your web browser, the browser opens TCP/IP connections to retrieve the data. A typical web page may consist of many files of information to retrieve. TCP/IP application writers have to make a tuning choice—open the optimal number of connections to retrieve the data in a relatively small timeframe. The trade-off for concurrent downloads is extra memory and programming complexity. The benefit is faster response time.

VoIP Tuning Trade-Offs

Tuning VoIP implementations entails many possible trade-offs. Often, you are trading off quality (or risk) against some limited resource, such as bandwidth. The following sections describe a few VoIP tuning possibilities, accompanied by their trade-offs.

IP Phone Configuration

Configuring IP phones offers a series of choices. Although most phone vendors do a good job of choosing defaults for configuration parameters, in some cases you need to make configuration changes. Here is an overview of some of the trade-offs:

- **Codec**—Call quality is heavily impacted by the codec you choose. But higher-quality codecs generally require more bandwidth. Codecs, such as G.711, consume many times more bandwidth than G.729. However, the G.711 codec provides a higher MOS given the same network conditions. When choosing a codec, you are inevitably faced with the trade-off of quality versus bandwidth consumption.

- **Silence suppression**—Silence suppression means that when you are not talking, little or no data is sent over the wire. Offered by certain IP phones and softphones, silence suppression can reduce the bandwidth required for a VoIP call by 50 percent or more. However, the resulting speech may sound choppy or clipped, and it may be unnerving for users when they hear total silence during parts of a call. Again, you have to consider the trade-off of quality versus bandwidth consumption.

- **Jitter buffer size**—A jitter buffer can smooth out any variations in packet arrival times that may be introduced by the network. If jitter is a problem on your network, a larger jitter buffer can hide the jitter problem. Some phones can configure the size of their jitter buffers dynamically. Ideally, you would make the jitter buffer as large as the maximum jitter experienced. However, jitter buffers add delay, which can break your delay budget and reduce the call quality. So, you have to consider the trade-off between increased delay and call quality.

- **Speech packet size (delay between packets)**—The speech packet size reflects the size of the payload that is sent in each VoIP packet. The larger the payload, the more voice data that is transferred in a single packet, with a resulting reduction in header overhead. However, if a larger packet gets lost, the impact on the quality is greater than it may have been if smaller packet sizes had been used. You have to consider the trade-off of quality versus bandwidth consumption. Most IP phones have codecs that optimize the speech packet size, so this tuning parameter is best reserved for advanced tuning.

Call Admission Control—H.323 Gatekeeper

Call admission control (CAC) is a tuning technique that can constrain access to a resource. Networks are often oversubscribed, as discussed earlier, and WAN links have a finite amount of bandwidth. Allowing unlimited user access to a finite resource makes everyone unhappy. Admission control schemes try to address this problem. For VoIP deployments, the trade-off is call quality versus allowing all users the opportunity to make a phone call at the exact same time.

- The H.323 standard for multimedia transmissions provides CAC with a device known as a *gatekeeper*. Gatekeepers, as the name implies, control admission of VoIP calls into a network. Assuming that allowing too many calls over a single link degrades the quality of all calls, the gatekeeper's job is to prohibit a new call if the network can't provide adequate bandwidth. To do this, the gatekeeper must keep track of the number of calls in progress and the bandwidth available. You therefore need to consider the number of calls that will be managed by each gatekeeper. If numerous users make phone calls that are rejected by the gatekeeper, you will probably have some dissatisfied users. Figure 5-15 shows a gatekeeper environment.

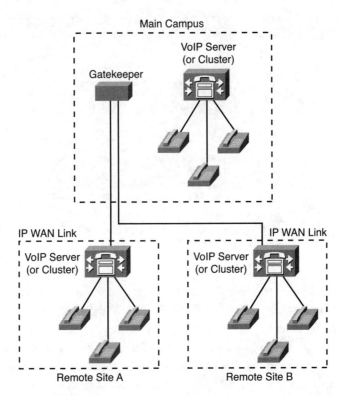

Figure 5-15 *The Gatekeeper Controls How Many VoIP Calls Are Admitted into the Network*

UDP Checksums

By now, you have probably recognized that the complexity of a VoIP deployment rests largely on the sheer number of parameters you can potentially configure. Even a UDP checksum could be considered a VoIP tuning parameter.

The UDP checksum is a field in the UDP header that provides a check for datagram integrity. The datagram sender performs a mathematical computation on the contents of the datagram and stores a value in the UDP Checksum field. Then, the datagram receiver applies a mathematical computation to the UDP Checksum field to detect errors that may have occurred during transmission. Figure 5-16 shows the UDP Checksum field in the UDP header.

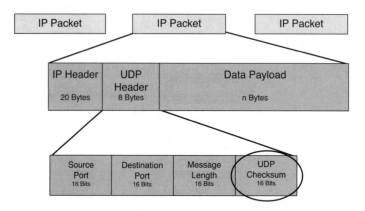

Figure 5-16 *The UDP Checksum Field Is Usually Ignored by the Sending and Receiving Sides for VoIP Call Traffic*

Some IP phones and VoIP gateways set the UDP Checksum value in VoIP datagrams to a value of 0, effectively disabling the data integrity checking that occurs on the receiver side. The reason for doing this with VoIP traffic is to improve the efficiency of RTP header compression and to save the time needed to compute the checksum. With normal UDP Checksum values, the field changes for every datagram. By using a value of 0, which does not change throughout a VoIP call, the cRTP algorithms can better compress the header fields. VoIP accepts the trade-off of a risk of data error versus better compression and slightly reduced delay.

Configuration and Testing

Configuring QoS to do what you need for your network can be a daunting task. You are confronted with many different mechanisms to learn about and, unfortunately, not all vendors implement them exactly the same way. In addition, instead of talking in terms of bit fields and traffic classes, you would probably like to define your QoS configuration in terms that are easier to understand.

Why is it so difficult to set up QoS so that it functions well in a network? The following are some of the reasons:

- **Many QoS schemes and parameters in use today**—This chapter has introduced more than a dozen QoS and tuning techniques. Each has its own terminology, its own parameters, and its own peculiarities, which are new to most network personnel.

- **Lack of knowledge and experience on the part of network IT staff**— Much of QoS is new technology to your team, and there are not many good tips and techniques broadly available. Also, QoS changes are discouraged in many networks, so your team may not have had any opportunity to experiment and gain firsthand knowledge.

- **Many device interconnections and interactions**—Most broad QoS plans involve changes in devices throughout a network, not just in a single router or on a single link. Many network devices and applications may be involved. Mismatches in device setup can occur at any of them. The large "cross-product" of potential problems makes setup particularly error prone.

- **QoS handling is imperceptible under light load**—QoS effects can generally only be observed against heavy traffic—that is, under stress conditions. So, QoS testing requires a congested network

  - To detect its behavior.

  - To see if it is configured right.

  - To show some classes getting improved handling.

  - To see if it still works right after making any change.

  - To see if you are getting the premium handling you paid for.

Configuring network devices one at a time, by hand, is so error prone that it may be out of the question for many large networks. Fortunately, a new set of tools—policy-based network management software—offers the usability needed to make QoS tenable. Policies make it much easier to understand the QoS choices you are making and which devices are affected. These policies are discussed in Chapter 6. But even with better tools, your team still needs solid experience in how QoS behaves both when it is performing correctly and when it is set up incorrectly. Your team needs to test its work, in small settings and in large ones, before applying its changes network-wide.

A QoS Testing Plan

The goal of testing is to make sure something functions as expected, and when it fails, that it fails as expected. Because QoS configuration is very complex and involves the interaction of many different network components, testing is required. You don't want to wait until after you have spent weeks implementing a new QoS scheme to find out that it does not work. QoS and tuning changes pose grand testing challenges. You need reliable, repeatable tests that can be run over and over again each time a parameter is changed slightly.

Testing QoS mechanisms poses unique difficulties. First of all, if QoS schemes go to work only when the network becomes congested, how do you know a scheme is really working unless the network is experiencing congestion? Some network test tools, such as NetIQ's *Chariot*[10], can send broad patterns of application traffic over a network. They can generate enough background traffic to create congestion, to which you can then add the "traffic under test," the traffic streams that the QoS mechanisms are intended to work on. You can do all of this in a reliable, repeatable manner, so that when QoS goes into production, it functions exactly as expected.

For the testing that occurs in a lab rather than on the production network, be certain that the lab traffic accurately represents the production traffic. Otherwise, the values you select will only make sense in the lab and may have either no or undesirable effects in the production network.

Your test plan should take into account two basic approaches to QoS testing:

- **Before and after**—Start with the QoS handling technique deactivated. Run a baseline test, consisting of background traffic and traffic in the class that is to get special handling. Then, activate the QoS handling technique, run the same traffic again, and compare the results against the baseline results. Make sure the background traffic variables have not changed, and that the affected traffic class actually shows the effects of improved handling.

- **Mix of classes**—Start with the QoS handling technique activated. Inject identical traffic with different classifications into the network. The traffic in different classes should be handled differently. Measure the results in terms of the network statistics you are interested in: throughput, response time, delay, lost data, and jitter.

Every time you change any QoS parameter, run another test. Run tests before enabling QoS changes and after making any QoS changes.

The section "Performance Requirements," earlier in this chapter, introduced the network measurements that are most relevant to VoIP performance. For VoIP traffic, the QoS and tuning techniques you apply should result in a higher MOS, by offering lower delay, lower jitter, and fewer lost packets. Keep testing and tuning QoS until you are sure that you have reached your MOS target, even under congested conditions.

QoS and Tuning Recommendations

QoS is a nonnegotiable requirement for a successful VoIP deployment. With that in mind, this section discusses some recommendations for QoS and tuning techniques.

Before you roll out QoS, assess your status. It is important to understand that QoS is not a replacement for VoIP-quality devices and adequate bandwidth. Only use QoS if, after adding all your anticipated VoIP traffic to your existing data network traffic, your network monitoring system is reporting that you are encountering congestion infrequently during the workday, yet your MOS declines unacceptably during those times. The recommended threshold for cumulative congestion per 8-hour day is less than 10 minutes. If you are seeing more congestion than that, go back and upgrade the network: Add more bandwidth, change your architecture, beef up your devices, and so on.

Many different types of QoS and tuning techniques have been discussed in this chapter. The QoS techniques you use will depend a great deal on your network infrastructure and the other application traffic on the network already. Here are some guidelines and recommendations.

Of the IP QoS techniques:

- RSVP is probably the wrong technique to use for VoIP traffic. However, consider applying it to long-running video streams that may be present in your network traffic.

- MPLS is best used by ISPs with large, complex networks. These networks may have dedicated paths through them, tuned for low delay, jitter, and loss—just what VoIP traffic needs. Here, the MPLS technique makes sense— it can give selected traffic dedicated paths through the backbone of a network. In fact, MPLS may be the preferred way for service providers to internally implement premium VoIP service. But you will still need a way to distinguish the VoIP traffic from the other application traffic at the edges of the network, so classifying based on port numbers, RTP headers, the DiffServ field, or packet sizes is still needed.

- Setting the DiffServ bits for VoIP traffic makes a lot of sense. Classify the traffic as close to its origin as possible. Other QoS techniques, such as CBWFQ, can use the DiffServ-marked packets to identify traffic classes. In addition, you need to configure the network devices, particularly the routers, to give traffic with different DiffServ markings different classes of handling. Making a cross-network configuration change for DiffServ requires some planning and good tools; approach it carefully.

Of the link-layer QoS techniques:

- Use IEEE 802.1p/Q on Ethernet networks where the volume of VoIP traffic is likely to grow. Use 802.1p from softphones or IP phones to the switch. Plan to upgrade shared hubs, because they cannot provide the service required for VoIP traffic. Configure 802.1p/Q on the switches and create a separate VLAN for VoIP traffic. Use IP phones or softphone

NICs that can set the 802.1p Priority field to a nonzero value. Configure the switches to provide priority to VoIP traffic that has the 802.1p Priority field set.

- Similarly, use ATM QoS on ATM links where the volume of VoIP traffic is likely to grow. Apply the CBR type of service to VoIP traffic where it is cost effective—because it is normally the most expensive service. Experiment to determine whether the less-expensive types of service are suitable for your deployment.

- On Frame Relay links, use admission control to limit the maximum number of concurrent VoIP calls allowed, then negotiate a CIR with your ISP to guarantee enough bandwidth for those calls.

- Use cRTP to double the VoIP bandwidth on relatively slow links. Use LFI to reduce delay and jitter on those same links. However, place high-horsepower devices at the ends of those links, because the extra processing for cRTP and LFI can consume a lot of CPU and add delay.

In your routers:

- Use CBWFQ and LLQ to give VoIP traffic priority handling. Define the classifying technique, called the *traffic match criteria,* for VoIP using DiffServ bits. Use WRED to improve the handling of marked DiffServ traffic when congestion occurs. If you encounter congestion problems in the LLQ, you have to reserve more bandwidth for VoIP.

- If you have a network with a wide mix of traffic where VoIP is a small percentage, WFQ may help the VoIP traffic compete better with the other traffic. Be sure to test WFQ, though, as you deploy it, to make sure it really achieves the effect you want.

Using traffic shapers:

- If there are clear concentration points in your network, it makes a lot of sense to use traffic shapers. You can have them look at many different attributes of the network traffic, and decide how much bandwidth to give to each different kind of flow. And traffic shaping is probably the easiest QoS method to set up.

- Calculate the maximum number of concurrent calls that can be supported with a good average MOS. Use CAC (gatekeepers) to limit the maximum number of concurrent VoIP calls, and then use a traffic shaper to guarantee enough bandwidth for those calls.

In your IP phone configuration:

- Use the G.711 codec if you have sufficient bandwidth; use G.729 if bandwidth is limited but your overall MOS will still be high enough (that is, your delay, jitter, and packet loss levels are low).

- Don't use silence suppression unless bandwidth is really scarce, you have already chosen a low-speed codec (to conserve bandwidth), and silence suppression will give you enough breathing room to have a good MOS.

- Optimize your jitter buffer usage, depending on how much jitter you observe and how much fixed delay you can afford to add.

Chapter Summary

As mentioned earlier in this chapter, the hardest problems to resolve in a VoIP deployment relate to call quality and reliability. Many problems in these categories can be avoided by using a staged deployment, QoS, and careful tuning. This chapter has provided many QoS and tuning recommendations to help you get your VoIP deployment up and running with good call quality. After a VoIP deployment is up and running well, it becomes your job to keep the call quality and reliability high. Thorough, ongoing VoIP management is the key to keeping a successful VoIP deployment successful.

Chapter 6 covers the core components of a comprehensive VoIP management infrastructure, the parts of the network that need to be managed and monitored, maintaining call quality, and optimizing server performance and availability.

End Notes

1 "Has the Net Stopped Growing?" Jason Krause and David Lake, *New York Times/The Standard,* June 30, 2001.

2 "Metcalfe's Law and Legacy," George Gilder, Forbes ASAP, September 13, 1993, available at http://www.gildertech.com/public/telecosm_series/metcalf.html.

3 RFC 1349, "Type of Service in the Internet Protocol Suite," July 1992, http://www.ietf.org/rfc/rfc1349.txt.

4 RFC 791, "Internet Protocol," September 1981, http://www.ietf.org/rfc/rfc0791.txt.

5 RFC 1812, "Requirements for IP Version 4 Routers," June 1995, http://www.ietf.org/rfc/rfc1812.txt.

6 RFC 2474, "Definition of the Differentiated Services Field (DS Field) in the IPv4 and IPv6 Headers," December 1998, http://www.ietf.org/rfc/rfc2474.txt.

7 RFC 2205, "Resource ReSerVation Protocol (RSVP)," September 1997, http://www.ietf.org/rfc/rfc2205.txt.

8 "Weighted Random Early Detect," Tom Lancaster, SearchNetworking.com *Networking Tips and Newsletters*, March 7, 2002, http://searchnetworking.techtarget.com/tip/0,289483,sid7_gci808666,00.html.

NOTE   You must join SearchNetworking.com to access these tips.

9 RFC 2923, "TCP Problems with Path MTU Discovery," September 2000, http://www.ietf.org/rfc/rfc2923.txt.

10 For more information on Chariot, see the NetIQ Corporation website: http://www.netiq.com/products/chr/.

CHAPTER 6

ONGOING VoIP MANAGEMENT

*Supervision of
VoIP vital infrastructure
yields content users.*
—Chris Lombardo

This chapter discusses VoIP management and explains why it is so important. It begins by addressing the core components of a VoIP management infrastructure. It then outlines what needs to be managed and monitored, and offers advice for maintaining reliability and call quality. It concludes with recommendations for managing your VoIP system.

Understanding VoIP Management

This chapter assumes you are adding VoIP to a reasonably mature data network, and that you are already managing your network components, your users, and their applications. Deploying VoIP means you are adding a new, complex application to your network. It is not the intent of this chapter to reteach network and application management; instead, it discusses how your management goals and tasks will change after VoIP is running on the network.

In the deployment stages of your VoIP project, your goal was to get it right the first time. You needed to make your first group of VoIP phone users happy, with high levels of availability and call quality. But now, in the management stages, your goal is to keep those users happy by keeping availability and call quality acceptably high. What is more, you will be doing this in the face of ongoing changes: more phone users, new network applications, different network components, and daily security intrusions.

Keeping your VoIP system healthy involves carefully managing four things well:

- **Operations**—Smoothly handling the day-to-day changes to the network, applications, and users

- **Availability**—Ensuring high uptime for the overall phone system

- **Call quality**—Making sure that every phone call sounds good

- **Accounting**—Ensuring that the calls are being charged properly, to the right people and departments

Some aspect of security is integral to each of these four topics, so it has not been broken out into its own category. For example, security intimately affects operations. You want tight control over who is permitted to make changes to any VoIP components. Unauthorized access to the phone system or data network must be prevented because it can affect availability and quality through degraded performance. Security also affects accounting. Telephone records contain private information—who called whom, for how long, and when. In addition, Chapter 8, "VoIP Security," is, as the title suggests, completely devoted to VoIP security.

VoIP management encompasses a broad set of tools, techniques, and processes to ensure the reliability and availability of a VoIP implementation. With all the effort required to get VoIP up and running, it is easy for management to be forgotten or postponed. However, good VoIP management practices are not optional in a successful VoIP deployment. There is an ongoing cost associated with VoIP management, so it helps to understand why it is so important, as explained in the following section.

Why VoIP Management Is Essential

VoIP will be a business-critical application on your network—an application that your business depends on for day-to-day operations. Although it is true that some businesses depend on the phone more than others, when you pick up the' phone, you expect to hear a dial tone every time. When you make a call, you expect good quality—always. VoIP management is required to keep a successful VoIP deployment successful.

Deploying VoIP can be a challenge, but after it is up and running, the challenge is not over. A good management system can simplify the day-to-day operations of a VoIP implementation. Consider some of the benefits of VoIP management:

- **Toll-quality telephone calls**—How do you know if the call quality is good? Most phone users will promptly let you know if the quality is poor. The distinction between good and bad is readily measured, using the *mean opinion score* (MOS) as a standard. A good management system can help you recognize performance trends that can lead to lower-quality calls. Management tools can describe precisely what the current quality is—good, acceptable, or poor.

- **High expectations for reliability**—Through years of *Public Switched Telephone Network* (PSTN) usage, people have become accustomed to a high degree of availability from their phone system. In fact, most carriers provide approximately five nines of availability—that is, a dial tone is available 99.999 percent of the time when you pick up a handset. How can you meet these expectations? You need a management system in place to maintain high availability.

- **Avoiding failures altogether**—The best way to achieve low downtime is to avoid failures proactively. Deploy hardware correctly, watch trends, replace failing components before they cause a crash, and upgrade to eliminate bottlenecks before they degrade quality (such as CPUs, bandwidth, routers). It is better to avoid problems entirely than to be very good at finding and fixing them—although good management tools can help you do both.

- **Knowing when failures occur**—With so many components in your VoIP system, when a component fails, it is doubly important to know whether it is a gateway that provides access to the PSTN or a critical server that routes all of your VoIP calls. It is impractical to manually inspect all components for failures. A good management system monitors and detects failures in key components. Once a failure is detected, management tools also can take automated actions, such as notifying IT staff of the problem via pager or e-mail.

- **Pinpointing and diagnosing problems quickly**—Once you know that a failure has occurred, the next step is to locate and then diagnose the problem. Diagnosis can be difficult; you may know that no new phone calls can be made, but you may not know that it is happening because a software application has stopped on a VoIP server. A good management system can help provide quick problem resolution to ensure customer satisfaction.

- **Accomplishing moves, adds, and changes (MACs) smoothly**—They need to be done in a timely manner that is nondisruptive to other users and other network applications, and they must not compromise existing security measures.

- **Maintaining privacy**—In the U.S., it normally takes a search warrant to examine the telephone records of an individual or an enterprise. Who was called, by whom, and when the call was made are all considered private information. In a VoIP system, *call detail record*s (CDRs) containing this information may sit in the database of a VoIP server on your premises. They need to be protected from unauthorized access—only approved individuals or programs should be able to read, delete, or modify this data.

- **Filtering relevant management data**—VoIP servers and devices can generate large amounts of data in log files and CDRs. This information can be very useful, but the sheer volume of data can make it difficult to find what you are looking for. A good management system can quickly filter large amounts of performance data to find the relevant information.

- **Ensuring that regularly scheduled system housekeeping tasks are run consistently**—VoIP systems comprise web servers and database systems, which typically have jobs automatically scheduled to perform backups, data archiving, and database grooming. You don't want to be surprised to find that your backup, at the moment you need it, has failed for the past six months.

- **Planning for future upgrades and purchases**—What is your budget and what is your purchase schedule as the network, users, and applications change over time?

This list focused on VoIP's technical challenges, which is where your IT team is also most focused. But there is probably a management team in your organization that has a focus not on the details of the technology, but rather on the bottom line.

A Look at Downtime Costs

The previous section introduced many areas where VoIP management offers obvious benefits. This section picks one of these areas, availability, and looks at the costs of managing it poorly.

When the phone system is down, the associated costs from lost revenue, lost productivity, and lost time for your IT staff immediately begin to mount. A 2002 TeleChoice study found that the lost revenue per employee per hour can reach more than US$40 (for industries heavily dependent on phone usage) when the phone quality is poor or the system is unavailable.[1] A quick calculation shows that the costs can quickly add up as the number of employees increases. Take, for example, a company with 5000 employees and 5 percent average downtime (over a one-week period):

5000 employees * $40/hour/employee * 0.05

= $10,000 lost revenue/hour

Given an 8-hour workday and 40-hour workweek, this would translate into a cost of US$400,000 for the week. If phone quality is poor or unavailable for a greater percentage than this, the cost is even greater.

A Find/SVP survey conducted in 2000 found that the average network outage among Fortune 1000 companies lasted four hours and cost US$330,000.[2] The same survey showed that "a typical company experienced nine outages per year, resulting in annual losses of almost US$3 million (excluding the cost of lost employee productivity)"—and possibly excluding the cost of lost sales due to unavailable telephone service.

Another cost of downtime is borne by your IT staff. The time it takes to constantly fight fires and deal with problems can take its toll on productivity. You want your staff to be able to focus on making enhancements to your infrastructure rather than constantly putting out fires. A good VoIP management system can pay for itself in the time it saves staff and the productivity enhancements it can provide. The goal is to provide a self-healing system—one that can automatically fix as many problems as possible versus having an IT staff person to resolve every problem.

A similar cost discussion can be developed for other areas that will suffer as a result of poor VoIP management: call quality, privacy, MACs, other network applications, and so on. Rather than creating an extended list of cost justifications for good VoIP management, the next section moves on to one more clear challenge: the inevitable growth in usage that will occur when your VoIP deployment is successful.

Managing Growth

No doubt about it, a VoIP system will change after it is initially deployed. New users may be added and existing users may change locations. Easy moves, adds, and changes are among the key benefits that VoIP can provide over a traditional PBX. But MACs require that procedures be carefully followed. Provisioning needs to be done for each new user: new users need a telephone number and IP address; their calls will generate traffic that requires network bandwidth; their call records will occupy database disk space; and so on. VoIP management helps with provisioning for new users.

In addition, a VoIP management system can let you know if specific servers, gateways, or links reach their capacity. If, for example, you have a WAN link that is fully utilized, you need to delay adding downstream users who may increase call traffic until you have bumped up the available bandwidth.

VoIP systems can really be taxing for IT managers. More users and more network applications continually eat up the consumables: bandwidth, addresses, ports, CPU utilization, RAM, and disk space. As an IT manager, you add more of these consumables to the right places incrementally, as necessary to make system performance acceptable. For example, you may have enough RAM in a router when a VoIP system is first deployed, but as traffic increases over time, call quality may decline unacceptably. If you then double the RAM, performance improves, and you have bought yourself some more time for the traffic volume to grow.

VoIP management also can help establish trends showing network behavior and performance over time, so you can tune your existing infrastructure and plan your spending. As you expand or change your existing system, you return to the top of the IT life cycle chart again, doing planning and analysis for the improvements.

So far you have been provided with a sense of why VoIP management is an integral part of your VoIP project. Next you take a look at what needs to be managed. If you examine the broad range of components that need to interact correctly for VoIP to function, you will see many potential points of failure. The next section addresses which components need to be managed and monitored. The core components of a comprehensive VoIP management infrastructure are introduced, starting with a discussion of operations management.

Managing Operations

Handling the day-to-day changes to the network, applications, and users can be the most difficult part of providing a good VoIP implementation. You are dealing with complex systems with many variables that change frequently and may even be beyond your control. An avalanche of information is available on the state of your VoIP implementation, but filtering out the irrelevant pieces can be a challenge. You need to have good processes in place to control the variables that you can control, and monitor the variables that you can't control. Feedback should be clear and concise. As a rule, good operations management begins with system configuration.

This chapter makes broad slices through the field of network and application management. Under the topic of operations management it covers configuration management, event management, and fault management in depth. These topics address management of changes related to network or VoIP components to indicate a problem or potential problem. Elements of security management are part of operations management, so those are discussed as well.

Configuration Management

Configuration management concerns itself with the setup details (configuration) of the components in a VoIP system. Configuration information can be represented in files, reports, or diagrams. Because the current configuration forms the basis for any changes that are made in a VoIP implementation, it must be carefully managed and fully understood. Reliability and quality problems (and new security holes) are most likely to occur when something is changed, with the fault often located at the place where the change was made. Not all changes work out. In cases where they don't, you need to be able to back them out, returning the network to its previous working configuration. To successfully manage your configurations, you have to

- Make changes and test the changes.

- Track relentlessly what is changed.

- Keep tight control of who is authorized to make the changes.

Configuration management in a network means knowing all the components of the network and how each of them is set up. Each of these topics is discussed in detail in the following sections.

Knowing Your Network Components

Do you know how many routers and switches are in your data network? Do you know which vendors made the routers? What is the current location of the routers? Good configuration management means that all the information you need about your network devices is readily available.

Configuration management in a network starts with knowledge of the components in the network—what they are and what is in them. That knowledge is then enhanced with topology information, such as where the network components are and how they are linked together. After you have fairly complete knowledge of the physical layer, the next step is the logical layer. Each of the VoIP components—IP PBXs, servers, gateways, IP phones—has one or more IP addresses that need to be managed.

You need not reinvent network management, so these topics are treated only briefly. You are likely doing excellent network management already, maintaining complete records of physical and logical layer configuration and topology, but if you are not, the added complexity of VoIP makes this level of network knowledge imperative.

Network Inventory

Your records should include up-to-date documents listing the devices in your network and the hardware and software that comprise them. A network inventory contains information about the devices in your network, such as routers, switches, firewalls, and servers. Although the type and amount of information in a network inventory varies, Table 6-1 provides an example of information that is routinely collected (and extremely useful) from each device in a network inventory.

Table 6-5 *Sample of Information Collected in a Network Inventory*

Device Attribute	Description of Attribute for Network Inventory
Name	The name assigned to this device. Many times this name is the DNS name.
Location	The physical location of the device, often a room number in a building.
Network address(es)	The IP address of the device. Some devices may have multiple IP addresses.
Role	The role or function of the device. For example, this is a router acting as a gateway to the PSTN, or a router acting as a firewall.
Vendor	The vendor of the device. This is useful information when considering upgrades or new equipment purchases.
Model, serial number	The vendor's model and serial number for the device.
OS revision	The operating system and its version number, currently running on the device.
Memory, disk space	The amount and type of physical memory in the device. Some devices have multiple types of memory—RAM and ROM (sometimes called *Flash*). Include the capacity of any disks, as well.
CPU type and speed	The processor type—RISC, Intel, and so on—and its operating speed.
Installed modules	The hardware cards or modules installed in this device. Modules may provide different functions, such as WAN links or gateway functionality.

A variety of tools can help you to create and maintain an up-to-date network inventory. Most tools discover network components by using the *Simple Network Management Protocol* (SNMP) to query *Management Information Bases* (MIBs) on the network devices. The devices respond to the SNMP requests with the information that was requested. You can either scan a range of IP addresses for devices or provide a starting router that offers its routing table information to initiate a discovery of devices in the network.

Network Topology

After you have compiled or updated a network inventory, a network topology diagram is useful to graphically present the information. Where are the network devices you have just cataloged? What are the links among them? A network topology diagram shows the network devices—routers, firewalls, switches—and how they are interconnected. (See Figure 6-1.) The different addresses and subnets are shown with each associated router interface.

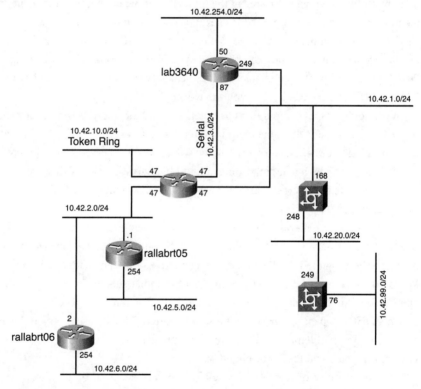

Figure 6-1   *Excerpt from a Network Topology Diagram*

A network topology diagram provides a quick, high-level overview of how the network is connected. Network topology diagrams often show WAN link information, such as link type, provider, and bandwidth. In VoIP implementations, you may want to add the locations of key VoIP servers and IP PBXs to the topology diagram. Excellent tools are available, such as Microsoft Visio (http://www.microsoft.com/office/visio/), to help you discover and diagram your network.

Network Addresses

Knowledge of your equipment and topology is important; you need to know exactly what is physically deployed in the network to find and fix problems quickly. But the real magic occurs at the logical layer, where every component in the network has one or more IP addresses. For good operations management, you need accurate documentation of the ties between each IP address and the actual physical box that is its home. And because most VoIP networks rely on DNS and DHCP to keep IP phones in contact with critical servers, you need to monitor the DNS and DHCP services used in your network.

DNS provides a mapping from a name to an IP address. For example, www.netiq.com is a DNS name that maps to the IP address of the web server that runs the NetIQ website. You most likely already have a DNS server in your network that provides a mapping from names to IP addresses. The DNS server that lets you navigate the Internet and your own network also enables each VoIP phone to locate its VoIP server readily.

IP phones are generally DHCP-enabled. The DHCP server provides an IP address when a network host, in this case an IP phone, becomes active on the network. By using the DHCP service, you can move IP phones with relative ease. When you relocate an IP phone (by moving it to another subnet, for example), the DNS server for that subnet should be able to find it, unless you disabled the phone's DHCP capability and gave it a static address. In that case, you will have a configuration problem after the move. For similar reasons, if your DNS server goes down, you could lose your phone service.

The availability of the DNS and DHCP servers needs to be monitored. In addition, if it is possible with your current budget and if you have not already done so, you should reconsider your current DNS server redundancy plan. The software company Men & Mice, which specializes in DNS testing, conducted a survey in 2001 and found that around 250 large companies' websites "are still at risk of virtually shutting down if the single network segment housing their DNS servers fails."[3]

Maintaining Control over Critical Files

The hardware components in your VoIP system are probably running advanced software programs that control their operation. The active management of this critical software is part of day-to-day operations management.

The critical software files to be managed are the executable program files that control how the devices operate and how they convey their health, and their essential configuration and data files, which control how the software is set up to do its job. These files are spread across many computers and devices in the network, often installed in remote locations.

The management of these files is explored soon in more depth in this chapter, but first consider these recommendations (which are just commonsense preventative-maintenance steps):

- Tightly control who can access these files

- Back up frequently

Configuration and Data Files

Many of the devices in a VoIP system run on off-the-shelf PC hardware with commonly available operating systems. One analysis puts a darker spin on this fact by noting that "much of the VoIP gear on the market is based on commodity operating systems and commonly hacked software."[4] You are probably familiar with the critical data files that these VoIP devices are using—files with extensions .ini, .dat, and .sys, as well as Registry files. Critical VoIP configuration and data files also extend to applications: database index files, CDRs, and call routing files. Other network components have equally critical files, such as router and firewall configuration information. This discussion focuses on the most important protection measures, as follows:

- **Access control**—Because configuration and data files really are critical to the successful operation of your VoIP telephone system, you need clear policies about who can read and change them. You want to make sure that no unexpected changes are made. Some of the files contain personal information; for example, CDRs contain information about who called whom and how long the call lasted. Personal information needs assured privacy.

In particular, apply strict change control to VoIP servers. Use access control to designate who can make changes and restrict the changes they can make.

- **Remote control**—The ability to manage computers and their critical files remotely is a necessity, to avoid having to visit them each time something is amiss. Write and enforce policies that describe what can be remotely accessed, and what permissions are required to obtain remote access. Record all occasions when sanctioned remote access took place, and make sure you are alerted when a nonsanctioned access occurs.

- **Backups**—You must be able to restore critical files if a failure occurs, or if you want to back out a change. Keeping a backup copy of these files is good configuration management. If the device should crash for some reason, a backup of the configuration enables you to restore it quickly. Backup configuration files also can be useful for planning configuration changes. The changes can be applied and tested offline, before being rolled out in a production network.

  The obvious recommendation is to do frequent backups. Store some of the backups offsite. If a backup job fails, it should alert your staff.

- **Intrusion prevention**—Viruses or other, similar invading programs may affect or damage your critical files. Where appropriate, run a vulnerability assessment on the target computers, and install, run, and update antivirus software on a scheduled basis.

Call Routing

A clear-cut example of critical data files that you must protect are *call routing tables,* which describe dial plans and how each telephone call is routed as local, long-distance, and international calls are made. Routing tables control long-distance access, for example; you don't want people using the IP phone in the lobby of your offices to make calls to Nepal. Call routing tables also describe how incoming calls are forwarded. They are typically stored in a database and configured through an IP PBX or VoIP server.

Call routing files are an example of configuration files that are particularly fragile. Few tools are available for managing them well, and their configuration is something of a black art. Routing calls to the proper destinations can require very complex setup. VoIP servers must be configured to map the phone numbers dialed to their destinations, which may be an IP phone, or a phone in the PSTN.

The fragility of call routing files highlights the points previously made: maintain tight control over who can access these files, and back them up frequently. If an invalid change is made, you can back it out by reverting to the last good backup copy.

Program Files

The executable files for the operating system, and for relevant VoIP applications and management agents, are also critical to the operations of each computer. The same types of management requirements discussed in the previous section apply to executable and configuration files:

- **Access control**—Access control deals with who has access to the physical keys, who can log on to the computer, and what changes they can make. Maintain strict control over who can read or modify executable and configuration files, as discussed above. However, you also need to maintain access control to determine who can execute the files and who can replace them. You also want to know each time anyone else accesses these files remotely.

- **Remote control**—As with configuration files, you want to manage operating system and VoIP program files remotely. You also want to manage and monitor the applications remotely. Any given application may hang, run amuck, or consume the last of its available disk space. Less severely, application performance may simply degrade. In each case, you want remote-control access to the VoIP applications and program files—or you want your management software to take care of some of the problems when personnel are unavailable.

  Install management software on all VoIP servers. But, look for management agents that are vendor-certified and consume few resources. You don't want a management program to create VoIP server performance problems by using large amounts of CPU time and memory.

- **Security**—The VoIP software components are critical to your business, and you need to protect them with your highest level of security. Secure computing begins with physical security; where possible, the computers and network devices should be kept under lock and key. Access control, as discussed previously, is the next step.

  The section "Software Reliability and Features" in Chapter 3, "Planning for VoIP," discusses working from clean computers. Install the operating systems and necessary applications from scratch. Then, run a vulnerability assessment and load latest antivirus software. Enable intrusion-detection instrumentation wherever possible to prevent (or at least detect) unwanted security intrusions.

  To avoid running into constraints on memory or other resources, and to avoid introducing unnecessary software vulnerabilities, keep the footprint of the operating system and applications as small as possible. Turn off unneeded services, and lock down the options on major applications such as web servers and database servers.

- **Update control**—As time passes, software applications usually need version updates and patches. Keep careful records of server software versions and patches to reduce compatibility problems.

  Establish a methodology and use automation tools to apply patches and roll out new software versions. You don't want to visit each computer or device each time there is a new version or patch for the operating system, one of its critical applications, or one of its management agents. Tools such as Microsoft's SMS enable you to distribute software updates from a central console, to selected computers, on a scheduled basis.

Event Management

Modern operating systems keep a record of most of the events they see. They take note when key programs are started and stopped. They track application errors and suspect traffic arriving at the computer. Many computers and network devices also keep logs of these events, which are usually specific to a certain operating system, application, or network component. You can see the evidence of these events on your own computer; for example, open Windows Event Viewer or dump a UNIX syslog. (See Figure 6-2.)

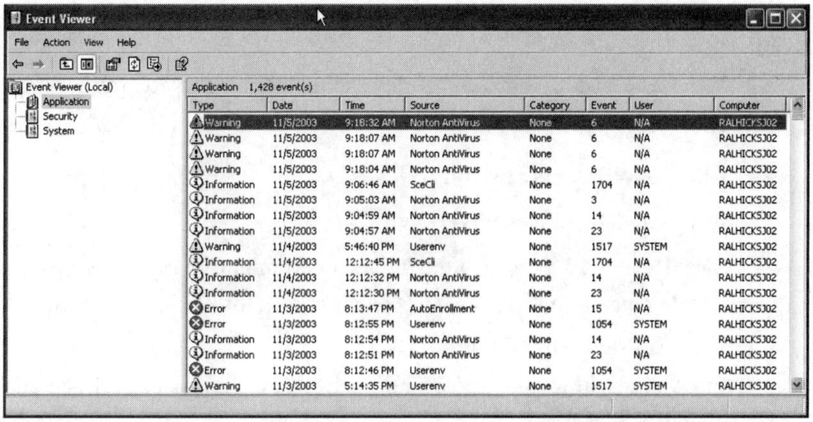

Figure 6-2 *Application Event Information In Event Viewer*

In their simplest form, events come in three varieties: Error, Warning, and Information. You are probably aware of the significance of these on each system you are working with. When a failure occurs, when performance declines, or when intruders attack any part of a computer network, it is likely that telltale signs are left behind, written as events to the logs of computers near the problem.

Your goals for successful event management are to develop policies that describe which events are important for the health of your organization's network and to define what actions should be taken for each event. Appropriate actions include paging an administrator, sending e-mail, or calling someone, but, as much as possible, you would like the management system itself to execute the right corrective action automatically, in a timely manner.

In a VoIP system, many events are generated every second, every hour, every day. The sheer volume of events that are logged can make for a tremendous management task. Event management focuses on filtering the large amount of event information to find the important, relevant events and respond appropriately. You define rules for action when events of different severity occur.

The following are some of the types of events and the places where they are recorded:

- Windows: system log, security log, application log, web browser log
- UNIX syslogs
- Application-specific event and log files
- Intrusion detection events
- SNMP events, which are often traps sent for monitored systems, covering a wide range of events, such as "performance threshold exceeded," "out of disk space," and so on
- Firewall log files, showing events such as connections established and connections refused

Managing all of these events and event logs is obviously not a job for a human to tackle alone. For one thing, trying to check every log fairly often is incredibly time-consuming. For another thing, you would like to see these events as they occur, rather than going back to each system after a problem and dumping its system logs. Clues to what is happening in a computer network are widely available—they are just spread out all over the place. Good event management means that you have the events from different systems correlated to isolate failures or detect broad attacks. And you have the log data consolidated and synchronized so that you can see what is happening and where. Most important, good event management generates automated responses to certain events, corresponding to the response policies you have established in your organization.

Event correlation in any large organization is a huge data-processing task, well beyond the capabilities of humans. It requires consolidating copious amounts of event data, eliminating redundancy in the data, discovering patterns in the events, and then initiating actions to respond to what is discovered. Despite the daunting nature and size of the task, some people continue to perform event correlation manually.

IT systems in a large organization can accumulate more than a terabyte of event data over a seven-day period. In addition, that data must be kept online for some period if the intent is to perform any forensics after a security intrusion has been detected.

When you can centralize event recording and handling, you also gain the ability to correlate events across an organization. For example, suppose someone attempting to crack a password at the VoIP server moves from workstation to workstation to avoid detection. Under normal circumstances, this method would not raise any alarms, because the only way to notice the moving intruder would be to look at event logs on a computer-by-computer basis. However, event correlation systems can see "the big picture" by gathering events from all of these locations. They can correlate these actions and detect a pattern that raises an alert, and then initiate an automated response, such as disabling a user ID for some period of time.

Even after extensive data reduction, the task of correlation and pattern matching requires a strong analysis engine. In particular, you want the pattern analysis to identify points of failure across the networks, systems, and applications. Look for applications that are designed to perform the analytical and alerting tasks described here.

Finally, it makes sense to forward the summarized event to a central management console, where it can be consolidated with other events appearing across a broader range of components, including hardware.

Fault Management

Achieving high availability for your VoIP system can be viewed as a process of reducing downtime. The best way to avoid downtime is to avoid problems altogether, a core management process covered in more detail in the next section. In a network with real hardware and software, unexpected failures do inevitably occur, however. To reduce downtime, you want to find and isolate the failure quickly, and then minimize its impact by fixing it quickly. Finding and fixing problems quickly is part of your day-to-day operations.

When applications and networks consisted of terminals accessing mainframes, problem determination was much easier. Now, with a mix of protocols, applications, and dispersed intelligence, your job is much more difficult. If a user is unable to get a dial tone, is the server or the network at fault? You need to make this top-level diagnosis quickly, because you often have different teams who specialize in either network or application troubleshooting.

In which place is the source of the problem most likely located—that is, where should your team look first when doing fault isolation? The following are a few considerations:

- Places where the most recent changes were made

- Places where there have previously been failures

- Places where the monitoring trends show escalating trouble

In the diagnosis of a VoIP problem, it is important to know the network path between the phones. There could be many devices in between the two endpoints of a phone call. Each device and link in the path represents a potential point of failure. If you have good records from your network inventory and topology diagram, fault isolation is easier. But nowadays, tools are available that map a logical path between two phones. Once the path is mapped, each device and link along the path can be monitored to isolate the problem. Figure 6-3 shows the path between two devices on the network.

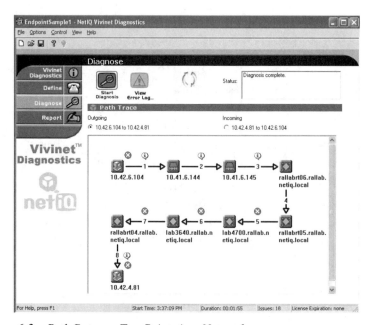

Figure 6-3   *Path Between Two Points in a Network*

Best-practice fault management means applying the principles of incident tracking. Tracking an incident means that someone owns the problem at every step, and that the current status of the problem is always visible. With proper tracking, every incident should have the following:

- **An author**—The person who found it
- **An owner**—The person who is currently responsible for it
- **A status indication**—Open, assigned, under investigation, or resolved
- **A resolution code**—To identify problem areas and trends
- **A severity**—An indication by the author of how bad the problem appears
- **A priority**—A ranking by the owner, who prioritizes it among all of the owner's other problems
- **A sizing**—An estimate of the effort required to find and fix it
- **A schedule**—An estimate by the owner of when the problem should be fixed
- **A problem description**—A detailed description of the problem and re-creation scenarios

Often problems are reported using information that is based on their symptoms. When the same symptoms are seen again, you can go back and see what the fix was the last time this occurred. You will determine either that the problem has recurred or that the symptoms have been caused by something new. A really excellent system can capture the symptoms and the solutions, in order of likelihood for your location, making it straightforward to debug a problem given its problem description.

Often, when a severe system-wide failure or security attack occurs, you need to drop everything. Immediately, you must act to reduce the depth and breadth of the damage. Firefighting like this is a poor way to spend your IT budget.

But, in a larger sense, all firefighting is costly, because everything that is productive and proactive stops, sometimes throughout the entire organization. In lieu of making forward progress, you try to reduce the amount that you fall back. Schedules slip, people become stressed out and lose sleep, more accidents occur, morale declines—rotten conditions prevail. Lots of collateral damage occurs as a result of a severe failure or attack, including, potentially, your reputation or the reputation of the whole organization.

Develop a firefighting plan. Establish a set of processes to be followed when a system-wide failure does occur. Plan ahead for fighting fires, to reduce the chaos when they arrive. Hold "fire drills" by simulating problems that your team must handle. Everyone on the team should have clear assignments, and should be able to tell when one step is complete so that they can move to the next step. Let every incident become a lesson on how to prevent or reduce the size of the next fire. If necessary, change your management policies so that certain types of fire don't happen again.

Maintaining High Availability

VoIP management is absolutely essential if you are committed to reducing downtime. (The other side of keeping availability high.) Availability is defined as follows:

Availability = 1 – (Total downtime)/(Total elapsed time)

where:

Total downtime = (Mean time to repair) * Number of problems

To reduce downtime, focus on both aspects of the right side of this equation. You want fewer problems—and when you do have problems, you want to minimize the time required to find and fix them.

The section "Understanding Reliability" in Chapter 3 discussed the main reasons for downtime or system unavailability. You may remember that user errors and processes, software applications, and technology all contribute to downtime.

A good VoIP management system helps to reduce availability incidents cause by user errors and process problems. In addition, when a software application problem occurs, a VoIP management system can potentially restart the application to correct the problem immediately.

The following are the three areas to consider when approaching the management of VoIP availability:

- **Prevention**—The best way to reduce the problems you encounter is to avoid the problems altogether—before they occur, before they lower the availability.

Here is where good processes, careful management, and vigilant monitoring come into play. To avoid problems, you need to see them coming long before they occur. By analogy, you like to see something turn warm before it turns hot. This means going deeper than basic event management; you monitor specific things important to VoIP, such as computer temperatures, internal counters, failed logins, and so on, and proactively respond as the relative "temperature" increases.

- **Detection**—If a problem does occur, its location and cause need to be isolated quickly. To make sure that the *mean time to repair* (MTTR) is short, your team needs to be efficient at isolating, diagnosing, and repairing the problem. Techniques for reducing the MTTR were discussed in the previous section, as part of day-to-day operations management.

- **Reaction**—Reacting well means providing a short-term fix, plus doing the long-term things needed to avoid the problem in the future—or, at least, to lessen its effect or speed the isolation and repair time if it does recur.

A 1999 University of Michigan survey showed that router failure causes about 23 percent of IP network downtime.[5] As mentioned at the beginning of this chapter, this text is written with the assumption that you are already managing your existing network components well, so it does not digress into router management. Even more important for VoIP availability are the new boxes, in particular, the VoIP servers.

Monitoring VoIP Servers

No single definition covers all so-called VoIP servers. A single "VoIP server" may encompass such varied functions as IP PBX, PSTN gateway, call manager, application server, and accounting hub—or these functions may be distributed among multiple computers.

VoIP servers are such crucial components in a VoIP system that they must be monitored continuously. Most VoIP servers run off-the-shelf software on off-the-shelf hardware, and therein lies the problem. The software and hardware were not necessarily designed for five nines of availability. Yet keeping VoIP servers running well is at the core of maintaining high availability.

Monitoring a VoIP server means watching the hardware, the operating system, and the major applications running on the server. The hardware boxes used today are frequently Intel-based systems or Sun SPARC systems. The operating systems may include Windows, Linux, or Solaris. Applications include web servers, databases, and file transfer services.

What exactly needs to be monitored on VoIP servers? The list is long. Table 6-2 looks at some of the key elements.

Table 6-6 *Examples of Elements to Be Monitored on a VoIP Server*

Monitored Element	Description of This Element
Hardware	The box temperature, cooling fan operation, disk errors, and network interface errors.
Phone calls	The number attempted, number completed, currently active, in progress, busy attempts.
Performance thresholds	For delay, jitter, lost packets.
CPU	The maximum CPU utilization threshold exceeded per application and across the entire system. Consider user and kernel modes.
Memory	The memory usage maximum, per application and across the entire system. Physical and virtual memory. Page file maximum. Paging rate.
Model, serial number	The vendor's model and serial number for the device.
Disk	The disk utilization percentage. Free disk space minimum. Disk operation maximum time, for reads and writes. Backup status. Disk failures or error reports in an event log.
Applications	The status of software applications necessary for successful operation.
Database	The blocked access—time and number of incidents. CPU, memory, and disk usage for database operations. Lock and connection utilization.
Network	The network interface usage. Bandwidth utilization.
Security	Intrusion detections. Invalid or failed login attempts. Denial-of-service attacks.

Exercise care when monitoring critical servers. You don't want the monitoring to affect the performance of the server's main functions. In addition, you don't want the action of monitoring to adversely skew the statistics that you are trying to monitor.

There is a trade-off involved with real-time monitoring. To get real-time information about the status of the server, you want to collect the monitored statistics from the server, but not so frequently that the collection affects performance. You want to optimize the data collection so that batches are sent back to management consoles at different intervals. However, you never want the monitored information that is collected to consume a noticeable portion of your bandwidth.

It is difficult to achieve "true" real-time monitoring. Instead, depend upon thresholds and events. Set thresholds that, when exceeded by the collected statistics, trigger early warnings. Configure event generation to alert you when something specific occurs. Monitored elements work economically when they incorporate thresholds that determine when an event is logged. Define policies and actions for handling important events.

Most management systems allow for some degree of automation. For example, if a critical VoIP server software application goes down, an event can be generated. One automated response action could be to alert the IT administrator. An even better response (at least your IT administrator thinks so) is to log the failure, automatically restart the application, and then notify the IT staff about the problem.

But, how is the monitored information gathered? Because most VoIP servers run on standard operating systems, information can be gathered via standard *application programming interfaces* (APIs). Here are several sources for system information that is valuable for monitoring the health of VoIP servers:

- **Log files**—These provide an audit trail of what is happening in a system. Applications and the operating system itself may write to log files when events occur. Log files are also an excellent source of early warning information. For example, Windows disk management services can log warnings before hard drive failures have a chance to wreak havoc.

- **Performance counters**—Applications and the operating system periodically publish performance information and key statistics.

- **SNMP**—SNMP is the standard way of gathering information published in device MIBs (collections of device configuration and utilization data). It is possible to set up SNMP monitoring so that it keeps very busy collecting and reporting information. Unfortunately, this can result in high CPU utilization and additional network flows, which may perturb the system you are trying to monitor.

- **Operating system APIs**—Powerful, low-level APIs enable direct access to operating system information. These APIs let a management application take action and restart services or kick off other responses to events.

Security intrusions can often be identified using data from a mix of monitored data sources. For example, an event can be raised if the number of failed server logon attempts, as recorded in a security event log, exceeds a threshold. An unexpected spike in CPU utilization at the web server can indicate a virus attack, such as the Code Red virus. The sooner you know there is a problem, the more easily you can prevent it from spreading and taking your system down.

VoIP servers may be deployed in clusters to provide redundancy and scalability. Within the cluster, different servers perform different roles. Monitor these servers individually and as a single entity.

NetIQ's Vivinet Manager (http://www.netiq.com/products/vm/) is an example of a software system that is designed to monitor the wide range of elements described above (and call quality and call setup) and to automatically respond when failures occur or thresholds are crossed.

Servers are not the only significant VoIP components to monitor, though. Monitor and manage your PSTN gateway function, as well. Many calls will pass through it to the PSTN. Increased CPU utilization, increased memory usage, and an increased percentage of PSTN lines in use could signal a capacity problem. Gateways can be viewed as a single point of failure: They are your connection to the PSTN, and they usually have many interfaces for incoming and outgoing traffic.

Application Management

Despite its complexity and capabilities, most software today is more fragile than people would like it to be. As a result, combining applications inside a computer increases the likelihood that the software may interact unexpectedly. A typical VoIP server runs many software applications to support VoIP calls. For example, VoIP servers use database applications to store everything from phone numbers to phone IP addresses. If lookups on this information are slow or blocked, VoIP calls cannot be completed. In addition, the database software on which VoIP applications and servers rely is complex and can consume large amounts of server resources: CPU, memory, and disk space.

Applications can be greedy at times, quickly consuming scarce resources. You should therefore consider monitoring the CPU usage of certain applications. Automated management tools let you set thresholds, with event generation when an application uses too much CPU. An appropriate response may be to stop the application or kill the thread it is running under.

Continuous monitoring is required for VoIP servers to maintain high availability—five nines is the goal. With good management, this goal can be attained. Now it is time to look at another core component of VoIP management infrastructure—managing call quality.

Maintaining Call Quality

A VoIP management system should help to ensure that a high level of call quality is maintained. One survey of 250 IT executives by Network World found that VoIP quality-of-service assurances were the number one VoIP drawback.[6] In an odd twist, call quality is a source of enormous stress in a VoIP deployment because it is a nonissue in the PSTN—it is something you just don't worry about. Before beginning a VoIP deployment, many consider it an unknown factor.

Two broad areas affect call quality:

- **Problems at the VoIP server**—Overloading, constraint of a key resource, or failure of a critical component

- **Problems in the network**—Configuration errors, congestion, attacks

By using the planning guidelines discussed in Chapter 3, you should not experience poor call quality on an initial deployment. However, things will no doubt change as new users and applications are added to the network. Good management practices can ensure that call quality is not an issue as the network traffic and number of users increase. Monitoring VoIP components is a way to help ensure that the experience for end users remains good.

Determining the Call Quality

The first step in managing call quality is to determine what level of quality your users are experiencing. Call quality is measured in terms of a MOS. MOS was discussed in great detail in Chapter 3, but as a brief refresher, remember that the scale ranges from 1.0 to 5.0, where 1.0 is very poor and 5.0 is excellent. A MOS of 4.0 or better is considered toll quality. A MOS below 3.6 could be considered poor and would not be good enough for most business-quality phone calls.

How do you know what the MOS would be for calls on your network? Management tools can monitor network performance statistics and calculate a MOS based on these statistics. Following are some guidelines for monitoring call quality:

- **Monitor continuously**—It is important to monitor 24 hours a day, 7 days a week. By doing so, you can establish network baselines for quality and spot trends in the call quality. Trends can help you determine if the quality is declining over time and, if so, the severity of the decline.

- **Monitor different areas of the network**—Monitor network links where the VoIP traffic flows. WAN links for branch offices are especially important areas for monitoring call quality because of their limited bandwidth and variable usage patterns.

- **Monitor actively**—If you have management agents that can actively simulate calls to monitor their quality, you can monitor even while no users are making calls on the network. Active monitoring lets you be proactive and spot potential call quality problems before your users experience them.

- **Monitor passively**—Most IP PBX systems can provide some quality statistics for the calls they control. These statistics are usually available in CDRs, which report measurements from already-completed calls. With passive monitoring, you know the quality after the fact, which does not help prevent quality problems, but may help with problem diagnosis and resolution.

Management tools generally enable you to set call-quality thresholds. When the call quality drops below the threshold, an action can be taken to alert the appropriate staff or perform other automated tasks. And these tools often offer reporting capabilities. Reports that reveal call-quality metrics over time are useful when looking for trends. Call-quality trends can help you to spot problems before they affect end users. Figure 6-4 shows call-quality trends over time.

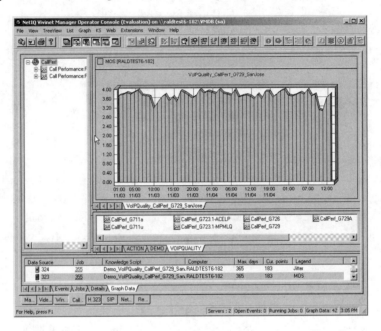

Figure 6-4 *MOS Changes Among a Set of Locations, Across Four Days*

Chapter 3 showed that call quality equals network performance. If the network performance is bad, then the call quality will be poor. A good VoIP management strategy includes network performance management.

Managing Network Performance

Network performance issues are quite often the culprit behind call-quality and availability issues. By defining and then monitoring performance metrics for the network, network performance management helps to avoid problems, or at least reduce their duration. Monitoring needs to occur on a continual basis to ensure good network performance.

Performance management not only ensures good call quality, but also measures how VoIP traffic affects the other applications running on the network. Most business applications that use TCP have performance requirements much different from VoIP. For example, TCP applications usually require low network response time and high throughput. Does the response time increase dramatically as VoIP traffic is added to the network? Does the throughput drop when the application begins competing with VoIP calls? These are the kinds of questions that network performance management can help answer.

For VoIP, the key network performance metrics are delay, jitter, and lost packets. The MOS is directly affected when any of these statistics increases. Although many network components may be active between two IP phones, the overall network performance is only as good as the weakest links. Network performance management therefore should look at the key performance metrics for the entire path to see the level of quality that your users are experiencing.

A network performance management plan includes service-level management and QoS management. The following sections examine what is involved with each.

Service-Level Management

Users need to be as happy with the level of service being delivered as the IT team. *Service level agreements* (SLAs) provide a quality target for the actual performance you are delivering.

To create a VoIP SLA, you define a VoIP performance target, using the best information you have available. Start by taking baseline measurements, to make sure that the performance levels you seek are actually achievable. Historical performance data also can serve as a baseline of normal operating characteristics and use of network elements and end systems. For example, you might define an SLA that says the MOS should be above 3.9 for 98 percent of the core business hours.

Finally, collect the key performance metrics and compare them with the SLA. Performance data gathered on an ongoing basis provides good input to help effectively plan for infrastructure growth. And because an SLA is often put in place to manage a service provider, you need to define what levels of service are acceptable, what happens when the agreement is not met, and how the service will be managed.

SLAs for VoIP are usually structured around the key VoIP performance metrics: availability and MOS. The MOS is determined by the following (and the codec being used):

- **Delay**—VoIP traffic is intolerant of delay. Long delays can make phone calls sound like walkie-talkie conversations. SLAs for delay are usually specified as a maximum allowable time, in milliseconds, for packet delivery.

- **Jitter**—Variations in packet arrival time can cause packets to be discarded and VoIP call quality to suffer. SLAs for jitter are usually specified in maximum allowable milliseconds of variability in delay, among packets transmitted from the same source.

- **Lost packets**—If lost, VoIP packets are not retransmitted. Lost packets thus result in missing syllables or words in a call. SLAs for lost packets are usually specified as a maximum allowable percentage of all packets sent.

Chapter 7, "Establishing VoIP SLAs," discusses SLAs in greater depth.

QoS Management

Another aspect of managing call quality involves the management of QoS. The goal of QoS management is to make sure that QoS is configured correctly and continues to work correctly.

Chapter 5, "Quality of Service and Tuning," discussed the complexities of QoS configuration. Implementing and configuring QoS to do exactly what you need for your network can be a daunting task. There are the many different QoS mechanisms to understand and, unfortunately, not all vendors implement them exactly the same way. In addition, instead of talking in terms of bit fields and traffic classes, you probably want to define your QoS configuration in terms that are familiar to your enterprise—such as gold, silver, and bronze levels of service. *Policy-based network management,* touched on briefly in Chapter 5, can provide help with network QoS configuration.

A range of tools offers big usability improvements for the complex network configuration challenges. Policy-based network management lets you capture broad descriptions or policies for what should occur in a network, including classifying and handling network traffic. New software components turn these policies into configuration instructions and deliver them to groups of network devices at the same time, in a coordinated manner. Figure 6-5 shows QoS policies being applied to network devices. QoS policies are interpreted by a policy server, which distributes configuration instructions to the devices in a network.

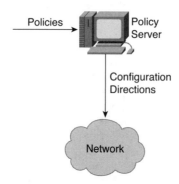

Figure 6-5 *Policy Server Interprets QoS Policies and Distributes Configuration Instructions to Network Devices*

With policy-based network management, you create a set of rules, called *policies,* that describe the behavior you want to see. For example, policies might describe which users and which applications are vital for your organization, such as VoIP, e-mail, ERP, and payroll applications. If congestion occurs, the network should give preferred treatment to traffic from these applications.

Policies that reflect QoS decisions cause configuration updates to be made in the network to implement the desired classification and handling of traffic. The policy server provides a central location for making automated, orchestrated device configuration changes to implement the policies you create.

Although applied policies lead to configuration changes in the middle of the network, the goal of these changes is to solve actual business problems by improving the end user's experience. Planning is critical. When developing policies, start by listing the problems you are actually trying to solve. Follow this with a list of possible solutions and their associated costs and risks. Determine who decides what solutions to implement, in what timeframe, and who writes the policies to guide the implementation.

Start your policy writing with a simple set of priorities: high, medium, and low. Decide which applications should be treated with high priority and which should be treated with medium priority, and then treat everything else as low-priority or best-effort traffic. Make the high-medium-low decisions for your mission-critical data applications. Then do the same for your voice and video applications, and decide how they should interact with your data applications. Avoid complex planning for day-of-the-week or time-of-day policies.

Policy-based network management is still evolving. Hardware and software from different manufacturers don't necessarily interoperate well, so it is hard to predict the effects of policies that result in QoS configuration changes. You will find that extensive testing and tuning are needed to understand the cause-and-effect relationships involved when deploying QoS. However, policy-based management should be a part of an overall plan to manage network performance and call quality. Its greatest benefit is that it helps to fit QoS into a larger, more cohesive, network performance management scheme.

Planning for Future Growth

One of the chief benefits of a VoIP management system is the ability to effectively manage growth, in terms of users and applications. Whenever you add new users or applications, you should ask how call quality and availability are likely to be affected. Will the call quality and availability decline as additional users and applications are added? Proper management means that such declines are not inescapable.

Additional users and applications inevitably consume more network bandwidth and VoIP server resources. As more network bandwidth is consumed, you move from being overprovisioned (having plenty of resources) to being oversubscribed (having too few resources), a condition that can easily reduce call quality. As more VoIP server resources are consumed, servers can reach the limit of their processing capacity, which will also affect call quality and availability.

These management components will help you prepare for future growth. As you establish trends showing availability and call quality over time, you can tune your existing infrastructure and plan for future investments. With less IT time being spent checking error logs and tuning minute elements of your QoS solution, you will be able to focus more on real improvements to tighten and organize your VoIP system and management solutions.

As your VoIP system grows, more calls are placed on your IP network. Your system may grow from a single department to an entire site. The more users and sites that are in your VoIP network, the more important it becomes that the calls are being charged properly, to the right people and departments. You need to have good accounting and billing management to provide tracking and proper charges for the traffic as it grows.

Accounting and Billing

Somewhere in your VoIP server (or in some other component in your VoIP system) an application is collecting CDRs. A CDR includes information on who originated or received each call, where each call went (intra-office or international), and how long the call lasted. These details about each call are usually written into a database by a VoIP server application.

CDRs are used primarily for billing, although they are also useful for monitoring and troubleshooting. Typical accounting practices demand that every call and attempted call be charged to the proper entity, whether it is a person, department, or company. The charges agreed to by the billing and the billed parties may include a portion of the costs of the network resources they consumed and a portion of the cost of the network management.

For enterprises, the phone bill (chargeback) may be part of each department's budget; each department's portion of the total phone cost may be based on the number of people in the department or on the number and duration of calls. For service providers, billing is obviously much more important—they need to demonstrate when and where every call was made, and to whom it should be billed.

CDRs may provide information about delay, lost data, and jitter for each VoIP call that is logged. You can gain access to this data by using database queries; however, some of the sophisticated VoIP performance management/monitoring tools now available can generate reports from this data and also let you know at a basic level whether excessive data loss, collisions, or bottlenecks are causing call quality to deteriorate.

These CDRs should be treated as private data. CDRs are an example of the critical files discussed in the earlier section "Maintaining Control over Critical Files." Because they contain private information, they should be protected with physical security measures, and should be accessed only by authorized individuals. This is almost certain to become an increasingly important issue, because legislation in the U.S. now requires government and medical agencies to maintain strict control over their sensitive data.

Chapter Summary

A lot of territory has been covered here, even after starting from the assumption that you already have excellent systems for managing your networks, users, and applications. Here are some highlights of the VoIP management recommendations introduced in this chapter:

- Maintain an up-to-date network inventory and topology diagram.

- Secure and back up critical files in your system, and establish strong access control policies on who can see, modify, or delete them.

- Provide redundancy for key existing services, such as DNS and DHCP, and monitor them continually.

- Provide redundancy to eliminate bottlenecks and single points of failure.

  For example, use highly reliable hardware, use high-speed CPUs, and supply lots of memory for the computers serving in the roles of IP PBX, VoIP server, or PSTN gateway.

- Implement a change control system to track configuration changes.

- Implement incident management to assist in isolating, fixing, and tracking problems.

- Deploy an IP address management plan, particularly as the number of IP phones increases.

- Monitor the operation of the hardware components within your VoIP equipment. Closely watch CPU, memory, and disk utilization.

- Monitor the software applications at the heart of your VoIP equipment.

- Monitor call quality across your entire range of components and locations.

- Monitor the completion of VoIP calls, such as how many calls are blocked or how many experience call setup problems.

- Set thresholds so that events are generated when performance declines and automated responses are taken when failures occur.

- Coordinate policy-based management within your overall performance management strategy.

- Connect the monitoring and event generation back into your central management console.

The idea of SLAs was briefly introduced in this chapter, and will be explored in more detail in the next chapter. Issues such as typical SLAs for VoIP, what metrics should an SLA be based upon, and what penalties should be built in to your SLA will be addressed, as well as what you need to look for in an SLA from your service provider.

End Notes

1   TeleChoice survey 2002, http://www.telechoice.com.

2   Margeson, Bill, "Identifying Vulnerabilities in Networked Systems," *Serverworld Online*, February 2002, http:// www.serverworldmagazine.com/monthly/2002/02/vulnerabilities.shtml.

3   Cowley, Stacy, "Survey: Sites Still Open to DNS Outages," CNN.com website, October 11, 2001, http://europe.cnn.com/2001/TECH/internet/ 10/05/dns.outages.idg/.

4   Hochmuth, Phil, "Is VoIP Vulnerable," *Network World*, June 24, 2002, http://www.nwfusion.com/news/2002/0624voip.html.

5   Gilmer, G. Hudson, "Examining the Cost of Poor Quality in IP Networks," Avici Systems, 2001, http://www.avici.com/technology/ whitepapers/reliability_series/cost_of_poor_quality.pdf (p.5).

6   Hochmuth, Phil, "Quality Question Remains for VoIP," *Network World,* October 7, 2002, http://www.nwfusion.com/news/2002/ 1007convergence.html.

ESTABLISHING
VoIP SLAs

Uptime and bandwidth:
ISP sells and you buy.
Trust, but verify.
—Chris Selvaggi

This chapter explains the service-level agreements that are needed for a VoIP implementation. SLAs have become a common means of defining how network performance is measured and guaranteed by service providers. The concept of SLA management was introduced in Chapter 6, "Ongoing VoIP Management," as part of network performance management. This chapter goes into more detail and discusses some typical SLAs for VoIP, the metrics these SLAs are based on, and how to implement a VoIP SLA—within your organization or with a service provider.

An SLA is exactly what the name implies—an agreement between two parties about the delivery of a certain level of service. Why should you consider implementing an SLA? Because you are depending on a service provider, such as an ISP, to deliver a service, such as WAN access, that meets certain quality expectations. And when the delivered service does not meet those expectations, it costs you—both time and money. An SLA can help you recover some of the cost incurred during a period of degraded or unavailable service. Equally, an SLA can represent a promise you make to VoIP phone users for a guaranteed level of quality and availability. But in either case, to create an effective SLA, you need to consider what you want to measure when evaluating the service and what expectations you and your network's users have for the network service provided.

Determining What to Measure in a VoIP SLA

In a VoIP deployment, you want your phone users to be as happy with the level of service being delivered as they were with the PSTN. SLAs provide a target for the actual performance your VoIP system delivers. In a sense, an SLA is quite a simple matter: You define performance and availability goals and then monitor the system to see how well you are meeting them. But just as a VoIP SLA can include a huge variety of performance metrics to be monitored, so can it be defined in many different ways.

What kind of SLA is best for you? It depends. First of all, do you need an internal or external SLA, or both? Consider the definitions:

- **Internal SLA**—An SLA within your enterprise. It typically describes the mutual expectations between users of the system and another internal organization, such as your IT group.

- **External SLA**—An SLA between your company or organization and a third-party service provider. The service provider may be an ISP, carrier, or other VoIP outsourcer.

The type of SLA you need is determined by business requirements and user expectations. You may end up with both types of SLAs, or you may develop only one. However, key components of both types of SLAs are the metrics that will be collected and evaluated. The metrics you emphasize should be based on your overall business goals.

The key SLA metrics can be categorized into four main groups:

- Availability
- Call-setup performance
- Call quality
- Incident tracking

Each of these categories contains several submetrics. The sections that follow cover each group of metrics in more detail.

Availability

As discussed in previous chapters, today's PSTN users expect to hear a dial tone 99.999 percent of the time when they pick up a phone. This expectation makes availability important in any VoIP SLA. But what exactly does the term *availability* include? To begin with, you want to hear a dial tone when you pick up the phone; to state the case simply, *no dial tone* equates to being unavailable. Next, when you dial a phone number, you expect the call to go through; *no ringing* or a network *busy signal* equates to being unavailable. Finally, while you are talking, you expect to be able to complete the call without being disconnected; *abnormal call termination* equates to being unavailable.

In addition to directly measuring downtime, here are some of the submetrics to monitor and include in an SLA that tracks availability:

- **IP PBX availability**—Is the IP PBX (or equivalent server) active and functioning properly? If not, how long was it down due to hardware, software, or network problems? Was the IP PBX unavailable while patches or updates were applied? If multiple IP PBXs are involved, this metric captures the availability statistics of all of them.

- **Network availability**—VoIP calls depend on the IP network. Is network connectivity available? If not, how long has the outage persisted? Was the network unavailable during router updates or configuration changes? You probably already have some SLAs in place for network availability. Consider updating them for VoIP by making them more stringent.

- **Network service availability**—Many IP phones and VoIP servers rely on critical network services to perform call routing. Are the DNS and DHCP servers available? Are these network services running? If DNS and DHCP are unavailable, users may not be able to make any calls.

- **Call-completion percentage**—This metric is sometimes referred to as the *answer seizure rate* in the telephony community. It represents the percentage of attempted calls that were successfully completed. A low call-completion percentage generally points to declining availability.

- **Abnormal disconnections**—These refer to calls that were not ended by one of the talkers. How many calls that were in progress were abnormally terminated? Where did these disconnections occur? A high number of dropped calls may point to declining availability.

- **Line busy**—How many times did a caller receive a busy signal? Was the line really busy, or was the busy signal an indicator of oversubscribed gateway ports? The key metric here is the number of busy call attempts caused by oversubscription of resources.

Because availability metrics are so basic to the health of your entire system—and to users' satisfaction levels—they are the first group of statistics to put in a VoIP SLA. Next, you need to think about what happens when availability is good, but performance problems plague calls during setup.

Call-Setup Performance

When you make a VoIP call, a complex series of events has to occur in sequence, and without errors. The first set of events, the call-setup phase, takes care of getting a dial tone, dialing the phone number, and getting a result, either ringing at the desired location or a busy signal. Several different protocols are used for call-setup in various VoIP implementations, and all could experience poor performance. Call-setup protocols such as H.323, SIP, SCCP, MGCP, and Megaco operate principally using the TCP protocol, sending a large number of different flows between the IP phones and VoIP server to establish a call between two parties. Call setup can involve many network flows. Figure 7-1 shows the simplest example of call setup using SIP between two IP phones.[1]

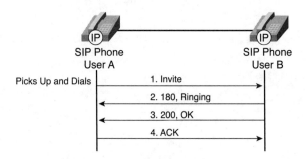

Figure 7-1   *Simple Example of Call Setup Using SIP*

Poor call-setup performance can affect the user's initial perception of the call. If the normal sequence of tones and responses is not provided quickly enough, users may get impatient and hang up. Call setup can be divided into two subphases:

- **Dial tone response time**—The amount of time that elapses from the moment you pick up the phone until you hear a dial tone. If the delay is long enough, users may think the system is unavailable. Today, most IP phones generate a dial tone almost instantaneously, so this metric may not be a major issue for your systems. However, it is still vitally important. A good upper bound to use is two to three seconds. Any additional delay would not be acceptable to most users.

- **Call-setup response time**—The amount of delay between the time you dial the phone number and the time you hear ringing or get a busy signal (sometimes referred to as *post-dial delay*). How much delay is too much for this metric? It depends on the users and their expectations. But if the delay becomes too long, some users may get frustrated and hang up, thinking the call cannot go through. A good upper bound for call-setup response time is 2.5 seconds.[2] This matches the average call-setup response time in the PSTN.

You should also pay close attention to call-setup response times for calls between the VoIP system and the PSTN. There is extra work involved in routing IP calls over analog lines, and gateway signaling protocols, such as MGCP and Megaco, are added to the mix. Translations between signaling protocols at the gateway may add additional delays to the call-setup time.

Call-setup metrics must be considered in any VoIP SLA. Next, you need to take into account what happens when availability is good and call-setup completes quickly, but the call quality is poor.

Call Quality

Users have well-established expectations for a VoIP system: It ought to sound as good as the PSTN. As a result, call quality is a key component of a VoIP SLA.

The *mean opinion score* (MOS) is the standard metric for user perception of call quality. The SLA for all calls should be drafted in terms of the MOS scale, from 1.0 to 5.0. A MOS of 4.0 or higher is considered toll quality or equivalent to the PSTN. A MOS of 4.0 should be considered good, 3.6 and above is acceptable, and anything below 3.6 should not be considered acceptable for business-quality calls.

Figure 7-2 shows user satisfaction with different MOS values.

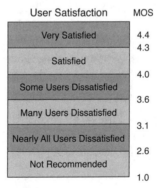

Figure 7-2   User Satisfaction Shown on a MOS Scale

When you incorporate the MOS into your SLA, you create an additional requirement: You need tools that can monitor the performance of calls on your network and calculate a MOS from what is measured. Chapter 3, "Planning for VoIP," discussed the network-performance metrics used to calculate MOS:

- **Delay**—VoIP traffic is intolerant of excessive delay. Long delays can make phone calls sound like walkie-talkie conversations. SLAs for delay are usually specified as a maximum allowable in milliseconds for packet delivery. The widely accepted limit for end-to-end delay is 150 ms; if your delay exceeds 150 ms in a single direction, it is likely that the MOS will decline.

- **Jitter**—Variations in packet arrival times can cause packets to be discarded and VoIP call quality to suffer. SLAs for jitter are usually specified in maximum allowable milliseconds of variability in delay among packets transmitted from the same source. A good number for the maximum allowable jitter is 40 ms.

- **Lost packets**—If lost, VoIP packets are not retransmitted. Lost packets thus result in clipped syllables or even missing words in a call. SLAs for lost packets are usually specified as a maximum allowable percentage lost of all packets sent. A packet loss percentage of less than 0.50 percent is recommended for good-quality VoIP.

A fourth component of the MOS, the codec, is usually a fixed parameter per call—so it is not measured in real time. Chapter 2, "Building a Business Case for VoIP," includes a table that shows standard quality impairments for each codec.

There is no need to spell out separate SLA metrics for each of these measurements; the call-quality portion of your SLA should simply specify the MOS. However, you may choose to set up monitoring thresholds for these metrics, to trigger early warnings that quality is declining. For example, you may set a threshold that is crossed whenever end-to-end delay rises above 150 ms. Although the measured MOS may not yet have declined, a delay above 150 ms signals a potential reduction in call quality.

Incident Tracking

If any of the availability, call-setup, or call-quality SLA metrics decline, you will want to determine why. Whenever an SLA metric deteriorates and crosses a threshold, the incident-tracking metrics come into play. Incidents often occur because of an outage or severe degradation that requires repairs. Scheduled changes and ongoing maintenance are also tracked as incidents. Several metrics are usually part of an SLA to deal solely with incident tracking:

- **Mean time to repair (MTTR)**—When an SLA value is violated, how long does it take for the provider to fix a problem, make an upgrade, or perform required maintenance? The time it takes to resolve each incident is averaged to get the MTTR. The MTTR is probably the most common SLA metric that deals with incident tracking. For this metric, lower numbers are better.

- **Mean time between failures (MTBF)**—Do failures occur frequently or only rarely? This metric defines the average time between failure incidents. The MTBF gives an indication of how often failures are occurring and can help identify potential availability problems. Proper monitoring of the MTBF also can inform you if failures are starting to occur more often. For this metric, higher numbers are better.

When tracking downtime or low call quality, set thresholds proportional to the SLA metrics and configure events or alerts to be sent when these thresholds are crossed. Tie the events into your fault-management and event-response systems. Early warnings may prevent SLA violations for the crucial VoIP network metrics and help you to avoid triggering violations of incident-tracking metrics.

A good VoIP SLA should include incident-tracking metrics to give you an expectation for how rapidly your service provider will respond when service levels are not being met. In turn, incident-tracking metrics help to guarantee the high availability, call-setup performance, and call quality already specified in the SLA.

Implementing VoIP SLAs

Armed with a good understanding of the SLA metrics that are important for VoIP, you can begin actually implementing the right SLAs for your enterprise. Like many topics covered in this book, it is best to view this as a staged process. Working through the five stages discussed in this section, listed next, will bring you the results you are seeking—a trouble-free VoIP system, transparent to your end users:

1   Define who is responsible for each role in the overall task of SLA implementation.

2   Identify the right VoIP service levels for your enterprise.

3   Negotiate the SLA itself.

4   Begin measurements, to determine when the SLA is being met and when it is not. You want this stage to be automatic, so you will choose among the tools that are available to make this painless.

5   Manage and enforce the SLA.

Define Responsibilities

The implementation of an SLA should be segmented into several roles. Most of the following roles apply more readily to external SLAs—those negotiated with a third-party provider. However, each implicit task must also be completed by someone when an internal SLA is being developed, and must also remain someone's responsibility once the SLA is in force. The following series of questions illustrates the types of roles that need to be assumed:

• Who defines the SLA? Who decides which metrics are important for the organization?

• Who writes the contract and guides it through the negotiations? Who determines the penalties?

• Who manages the network, its equipment, and the related computer hardware and software? These are the items against which the service covered by the SLA is being measured. Who is responsible for maintaining them?

- Who takes the measurements for the metrics specified in the SLA? Who assures the quality of the measurements as they are taken?

- Who manages the SLA? Who specifies the thresholds for the metrics and gets notified when they have been crossed?

- Who responds to and resolves incidents when a managed threshold or an SLA metric is crossed?

- Who does the SLA-related accounting? Who measures the percentage of compliance and presents it to the provider or service recipient at the end of each week or month?

- Who enforces compliance with the SLA? This involves determining penalties and collecting them.

- Who decides when it is time to get a new provider, if compliance with the SLA becomes an issue?

In a small organization, many of these roles may be handled by the same person. But, in larger organizations, these responsibilities are probably divided among several people who need to communicate well with one another.

Identify Service Levels for VoIP and Other Applications

Before beginning your SLA contract negotiations, determine what you are going to measure and what the target SLA values should be. Although the VoIP SLA metrics discussed earlier in "Determining What to Measure in a VoIP SLA" are all important to varying degrees, your own SLA should comprise the metrics that are most meaningful to your business. A good piece of advice to take to heart follows: "Creat[e] SLAs that are based on the quality of end-user application experience, rather than IT metrics which customers cannot or do not want to understand."[3] VoIP is an example of a network application whose value is driven nearly 100 percent by the perceptions—positive or negative—of ordinary users.

For VoIP, the relevant metrics for an SLA are the metrics discussed previously: availability, call quality, call-setup performance, and incident-resolution time. The first three are end-user, end-to-end measurements—they are what counts. You could alternatively measure only their lower-layer constituents, such as delay and packet loss, but it is best to consider those metrics principally for diagnostic purposes, to reduce the "find and fix" time. You also should include measurements related to problem repair, such as MTTR and incident management: how problems are identified, submitted, and passed among the team.

Having added VoIP to the network, do you now need to add SLAs for your other business-critical applications, which you may not have been monitoring before? These include e-mail, groupware, e-commerce, and industry-specific business programs. Maybe you should have had a response-time SLA for your ERP applications, but you were not aware of much dissatisfaction before you deployed VoIP. Adding VoIP traffic to a system near its capacity may significantly increase the response time of other business-critical applications. Application performance is something you now really need to pay attention to.

To establish the target SLA metric for your most important applications, begin by establishing performance baselines. These let you know what is actually possible and provide a starting point. You know that at the time you take the baseline, here is where MOS, response time, or throughput stands. You obviously should not write an SLA to support 100 VoIP calls with a minimum MOS of 3.9 if there is clearly not enough bandwidth or other resources to support 100 calls with that level of quality.

Start your VoIP call-quality baseline with the results provided by the VoIP-readiness assessment discussed in Chapter 3. Work from the last assessment you did—the one where the MOS met your standards and was conducted after you had done all the necessary upgrades and eliminated any bottlenecks or other problems that were identified. It is similarly straightforward to get baselines for the network performance of other applications, such as response time, throughput, or packet loss. Don't go overboard; be sure to measure what is important to end users for each application. For example, for a database application, focus on the response time for queries or updates rather than on throughput.

Likewise, create your availability baseline using the best numbers you have to describe your current availability statistics. Without making any significant changes to the network or the users, this gives you a place to start, a place where users know what to expect.

If you plan to monitor application response time, avoid insisting that all requests be met with a response time of 1 second or less. That is unrealistically strict. Instead, it would be better to state, for example, that 95 percent of requests must have no more than a 1-second response time and 5 percent may have a response time of between 1 second and 5 seconds.

Starting from these baselines—the expected and observable behavior—create some SLA targets. SLA targets are values representing performance that is so bad that it is no longer acceptable. For example, if your VoIP baseline MOS is 4.15 today, you might create an SLA target that reads something like this:

MOS of 4.0 or above 85 percent of the time; 3.9 or above 95 percent of the time; and 3.8 or above 100 percent of the time; measured on 10 concurrent calls with the G.711 codec, between Raleigh and Houston.

Negotiate the SLA

The intention of an SLA is to spell out which services are to be provided, how the services will perform, and what should happen if their performance does not meet the expected service levels. But a certain amount of negotiation, compromise, and perhaps even controversy will undoubtedly enter into any SLA you implement. One author made the analogy that "SLAs are nothing more than insurance policies. Just as life insurance doesn't guarantee life, SLAs don't guarantee levels of service. They provide you with compensation in case something goes wrong."[4]

You should anticipate some give-and-take in the relationships affected by a VoIP SLA. Here is a top ten list of topics to be addressed in your VoIP SLA negotiations:

1   **Specify the SLA metrics and their target values.**

   The earlier section "Identify Service Levels for VoIP and Other Applications" describes this topic in detail. The measurements that affect the end-user experience are important to your organization and should be included in your VoIP SLA: availability, call quality, and call-setup performance. You also may want to include metrics for other applications so that their performance does not degrade because of the addition of VoIP, as well as a metric for incident rates and their rates of resolution.

2   **Describe how the SLA metrics are measured and who measures them.**

   The earlier section "Define Responsibilities" identifies the wide range of roles and responsibilities associated with creating and enforcing a VoIP SLA. Do you take SLA compliance measurements in your organization, or are they taken by a third party or the service provider? If the provider takes the measurements, how do you, the customer, verify them? Tools for taking measurements are described in the next section, "Deploy Tools to Measure SLAs." The SLA should describe in detail how the measurements are to be taken. It should specify the locations to be monitored. And the SLA should spell out how measurements and compliance should be handled if an end-to-end metric involves multiple ISPs.

The SLA should also explicitly describe what time periods are covered. The following quotation appeared in an ISP offering brochure: "A high-end VoIP carrier will offer 99.99% availability, which does not include scheduled maintenance windows where the carrier may take down the network to upgrade equipment; clean or switch fibres *or perform any other work that could lead to network downtime*."[5] [Italics added.] Wow! A lot of time may elapse in these periods that are not included in the availability agreement; what time periods are covered in your SLAs, and how are they measured?

3   Describe the SLA reports and their schedule.

Your service provider should demonstrate its compliance with the SLA by sending you monthly or even weekly reports. In your negotiations, make sure the contract specifies what metrics and what parts of the network will be included in the reports. It should also say how often you will get reports.

4   Allow requests to review SLA compliance information on demand.

The SLA should establish a procedure for requesting SLA compliance information on demand. This type of data can be helpful for trouble-shooting. For example, if you are experiencing a delay problem, information from your ISP may help you narrow the problem down to a WAN link that you don't control.

5   Specify the turnaround times for change requests, by severity.

As you gain more experience with your VoIP system, you will make changes. For example, as you add new locations and new users, you may want to add more locations to be monitored as part of the SLA. This may require a change request to your service provider. What is the expected turnaround time for the change request? It is also reasonable to include a prioritization scheme in the SLA's timetable for such requests. A slow or overburdened link may be one of your highest-severity items and should be expedited accordingly.

6   Specify support-personnel and help-desk staffing levels.

The last thing that you want is to be placed on hold indefinitely when there is an SLA-related fire to put out. Get it in writing: How many people are available to support your VoIP system when incidents occur? What is their skill level? What hours do they work?

7   Schedule periodic reviews and adjustments to contract provisions.

Your initial VoIP deployment will no doubt change over time: new users, new locations, new applications, new hardware, more bandwidth, mergers, and so on. These may cause your SLA requirements to change. Don't let your SLA requirements get too far out of date. Schedule regular reviews with your service provider.

8   Describe the rewards for great compliance and penalties for noncompliance.

What penalties should you build in to your SLA? And if an unsatisfactory situation drags on, how long do the penalties build up before you call it quits?

CommWeb.com points out that, "It's easy for service providers to promise 99.999 percent uptime—especially when the penalty for not delivering is a meager day or two worth of credit. Obviously, penalties of this sort are no compensation for the potential loss in revenue when a company's web site is down or critical applications aren't performing."[6] Your provider must have a strong motive for complying with the SLA you have negotiated. That motive may be either positive (a bonus or additional business) or negative (a substantial monetary penalty).

Your best safeguard when entering into an SLA is a "system of rewards and penalties for compliance and noncompliance," notes Mandy Andress of *InfoWorld*. "An unenforceable SLA serves little purpose. It is well and good to say that all requests should have a 1-second response time, but if the group responsible for system performance does not incur any penalties for slower response times or reap any rewards for faster response times, then they have no real incentive to comply."[8]

9   Discuss transition assistance for services, should the service provider fail or suffer a setback.

Put together a plan that gets you through the difficulty if something catastrophic happens with your service provider. This type of situation has unfortunately become more common in recent years. Aside from bankruptcies, service providers face the same scary threats that you do; floods, tornadoes, malicious attacks by network intruders, and other unpleasant possibilities that need to be anticipated and planned for.

10 Create a procedure for terminating an SLA contract.

If you will pardon the analogy, sometimes the relationship with the service provider just does not work out, and an amicable divorce makes sense. Write the "prenuptial" agreement before the marriage, not after the relationship starts to go bad.

Is it reasonable to expect your service provider to agree to all of the types of stipulations just outlined? Figure 7-3 shows the results of a 2001 survey in *Network Computing*, asking service providers and outsourcers what is covered in their SLA contracts.[7]

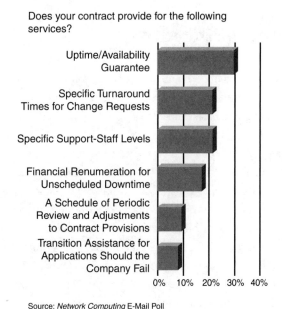

Source: *Network Computing* E-Mail Poll

Figure 7-3   *Survey Results from* Network Computing, *Showing Provisions Covered in SLA Contracts*

Most boilerplate SLA contracts are probably not good enough for you. They can have lots of holes and exceptions. For example, if a carrier's subcarrier goes down, who is responsible? Depending on the size of your deployment and its geographical scope, there may be a chain of subcarriers and subcomponents to take into account; determine who is ultimately responsible. Make sure you fully negotiate the contract details with everyone potentially involved.

Additionally, consider letting SLA contract quality guide your choice of service provider. You are now armed with a top ten list of things to include in the negotiations. "If you are choosing between two otherwise-equivalent service providers, if one has a better SLA does that make a difference? And is that more important than past brand experience, than price?"[9] A 2002 survey of enterprises with SLAs found that "not only were SLAs important, but the enterprises were willing to pay a significant premium for verified quality and guaranteed service...."[9]

Deploy Tools to Measure SLAs

After you have deployed your VoIP system, determined the expected performance, and negotiated your SLA contract, you need to watch the metrics specified in your contract. This means that the performance values must be monitored on an ongoing basis, and events must be triggered when the target SLA value is about to be crossed.

Monitoring SLA compliance can be done by the service provider, by a team in your enterprise, by a third party, or by some combination of these. In any case, the provider will surely be motivated to allow for some comprehensive monitoring of its offerings. And for you, monitoring is even more important. "Enterprises want to outsource their networks, service offerings and have proof that they're getting what they're paying for," notes Laura Spear, VP of marketing at Trinagy. "That means they need tools to provide proof and credibility back to their customers."[11] Figure 7-4 shows the results of a survey in *Network Computing* that describes how SLA performance measurements are received.[7]

How do you receive SLA performance measurements?

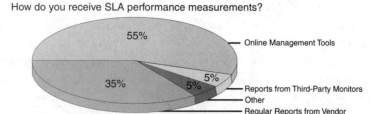

Source: *Network Computing* E-Mail Poll

Figure 7-4   *Survey Results from* Network Computing, *Showing how SLA Performance Measurements Are Received*

Although one reason to perform consistent SLA monitoring is to check SLA compliance, a more important reason is to avoid SLA infractions altogether. This means determining how much early warning you need to deal with developing problems. Although you would like to know what is going on at any given moment, the closer you get to "real-time monitoring," the greater the amount of data that is collected and the greater the amount of network traffic this is generated in reporting it. A better method is to set useful thresholds.

For a given SLA measurement, set a pair of thresholds that are stricter than the SLA target. When the second threshold is triggered, take immediate action so that the SLA level is not reached. You want to force action to be taken before an SLA violation, not when the SLA metric has been crossed and it is too late. Consider this the good-to-bad threshold; when it is crossed, initiate the incident/ fault-management processes discussed in previous chapters.

When setting thresholds, create two threshold crossings: crossing on the way down (going from good to bad), and crossing on the way back up again (going from bad to good—indicating that the incident has been resolved). And make sure you allow for some gap between these threshold-crossing values—you don't want a flurry of alarms to besiege your e-mail inbox if the value you are measuring is fluctuating back and forth across this boundary.

Reading up from the bottom of Figure 7-5, you first encounter the SLA target; if the measured MOS crosses below the line, an SLA violation occurs. Above that is the threshold where, as the MOS declines, you decide that it has gone from good to bad, and you trigger the event and actions necessary to avoid a further decline. You would like to reset that event when the problem is truly fixed, so the top line is the threshold that is crossed on the way back up; as the MOS improves after having crossed below the "Good to Bad Threshold," it can be declared good again when it crosses above the "Bad to Good Threshold."

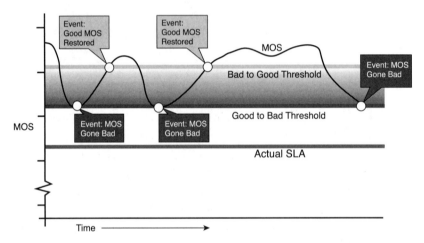

Figure 7-5   *Example of a Fixed SLA Target for the MOS, Along with a Pair of Thresholds Preceding It*

As you become more adept at working with your SLA thresholds, you may consider implementing thresholds that are not just fixed lines or numeric targets. Thresholds can be intelligent, responding to changes in overall behavior, the time of day, or the number of users.

A wide range of SLA monitoring tools is available to help you monitor your VoIP SLAs. Sterling Research summarizes the different choices available to you:

Some companies offer a limited tool set because they have decided to focus primarily on the monitoring aspect of SLA compliance. Others offer a range of tools that treat SLA compliance as an end-to-end process. One tool is initially used to establish baseline performance for a particular service; the next is used to monitor the service on a day-to-day basis; and—finally—simulation tools are used to spin what-if scenarios that calculate the impact on service performance if changes are made to the environment.[10]

Manage SLA Compliance and Enforcement

Suppose it is the end of the month. You review your VoIP SLA reports and see that one of the SLAs has been violated: That is, too much time has been spent outside the SLA target. What transaction now needs to occur between you and the service provider?

First, don't get in this situation. Overcommunicate with the team that is fulfilling the SLA responsibilities described in the earlier section "Define Responsibilities." All members of the team should be well informed all along the way. You don't ever really want to get into the enforcement or penalty stage of an SLA contract. Avoiding disputes and legal actions altogether is almost always cheaper and less stressful than pursuing them.

Jared Huizenga of Sage Research believes that enterprises are currently trying to develop "a more proactive SLA" with their providers. In a "proactive" SLA, providers "have to spot, correct, and recompense customers for any problems before customers inform the service providers of the problems." Huizenga also believes that most enterprises that enter into an SLA with their providers "want to be able to actually monitor, at their own site, compliance" and "receive an automatic credit" if a compliance issue arises.[11]

As discussed previously, your SLA contract should establish a system of rewards and penalties for compliance. These are the incentives for the SLA provider to perform well. Rewards for excellent SLA compliance may include things like cash bonuses. The penalties for SLA infractions can include automatic credit or reimbursement of your charges, withholding of payment, or cancellation of the contract. Penalties must be stiff enough to have real meaning for a larger provider. A *Network Computing* survey showed that 67 percent of respondents expected "financial remedies" from their provider if the SLA was breached, as shown in Figure 7-6.[7]

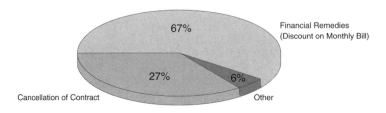

What legal remedies do you expect from an SLA if the vendor fails to deliver expected service levels?

67%

Financial Remedies
(Discount on Monthly Bill)

27%

6%

Cancellation of Contract

Other

Source: *Network Computing* E-Mail Poll

Figure 7-6   *Survey Results from* Network Computing, *Showing Expected Legal Remedies for SLA Noncompliance*

When expectations are not met, any changes for the better should come from the provider. They need to determine how to improve their quality and their processes so that expectations are consistently met in the future.

SLAs should be reviewed regularly. An annual review is specified in many contracts. Because of the rapid pace of technology development, user expectations may change frequently—this is especially true of expectations for availability and the response time of business transactions. This means that SLAs must be periodically updated to reflect these changes. Otherwise, SLAs can quickly become outdated, demanding service levels far below existing technological capabilities.

Contract cancellation may be the most effective penalty to levy in cases of SLA noncompliance. David Kaufman, of Brix Networks, argues that the proactive testing and monitoring with SLA thresholds described previously in this chapter is appealing to service providers for that very reason. "Having the advance warning that something is beginning to go wrong with a[n] SLA is really vital because, if there's an SLA outage, you have a one-in-three chance that you've lost that customer," he says.[11]

Chapter Summary

This chapter explained how to establish VoIP SLAs. The first step in this process is to determine what metrics to measure in a VoIP SLA. There are several key metrics that are unique to VoIP. The next step is to implement the SLA. Implementation involves defining responsibilities, identifying service levels, negotiating the agreement, deploying tools, and managing SLA compliance. Once you have SLAs in place for VoIP, there is another very important topic to consider—VoIP security. VoIP security is covered in the next chapter.

End Notes

1   This picture taken from http://www.vovida.org/document/ Vocal_Technology_Overview/Technology_Overview7a.html.

2   This value was taken from a discussion in http://www.cs.columbia.edu/ ~hgs/papers/Eyer0004_Predicting.pdf.

3   "Policy-Based SLA Compliance for Hosted Applications: Identifying the Weakest Link in Next Generation Services," Response Networks, Inc. brochure, http://www.cisco.com/warp/public/765/emea/aip_asp/ documents/Pulsar_xSP.pdf (p. 1).

4   Stanley, Shally Bansal, "Strengthen Service-Level Agreements," *Network World*, May 6, 2002, http://www.nwfusion.com/careers/2002/ 0506man.html.

5   "VoIP–The Gateway for Smarter Communications," a Light Paper by KPNQwest, 2002.

6   "The Price of 99.999 Uptime," CommWeb.com, June 1, 2001, http:// www.commweb.com/article/COM20010601S0008.

7   "E-Poll Results: Web Hosting," *Network Computing*, September 3, 2001, http://www.networkcomputing.com/1218/1218f15.html.

8   Andress, Mandy, "Internal SLAs Benefit the Entire Company," *InfoWorld*, April 27, 2001, http://www.infoworld.com/articles/tc/xml/01/ 04/30/010430tcintersla.xml.

9   "Business-to-Business Research," reprinted by Sage Research with permission of *Quirk's Marketing Research Review*, April 2002, http://www.sageresearch.com/Quirks.pdf (p.3).

10 Alunni, Samuel M., "Enterprise-Class Service Level Agreements," *Sterling Research Market View*, July 1, 1998.

11 Garifo, Chris, "No Downtime," *XChange*, May 15, 2001, http://www.xchangemag.com/articles/152back.html.

CHAPTER 8

VoIP
SECURITY

Assuming still time,
security is dandy.
Else give whatever.
—Mark McCorry

This chapter explains the various considerations for security in a VoIP deployment. It is a tough set of problems to deal with, there is no doubt, but don't let that scare you away. There are three stages in dealing with the problems—prevention, detection, and reaction—and these are discussed in detail. Specific problem areas related to VoIP security are covered in depth, followed by the best recommendations known today.

Network Security Is Tough!

Information and knowledge comprise most of what is valuable in today's organizations. This valuable data is stored on computers and flows across networks. Security is used to avoid theft or damage to something valuable.

People experience physical security in everyday life. For example, they lock the doors of homes, cars, and banks. Although they know that they are vulnerable—because there are only a limited number of possible keys out there—they also know there are risks and costs. Even if someone had all the keys, it would take them a long time to try them all out. If someone were to smash a locked window, it would make a loud noise that other people might hear.

What is different about computers is that they operate on a superhuman scale. They can repeat intricate instructions tirelessly. They can operate at fast or slow speeds beyond human perception. They work without the concept of pain or boredom. They can be connected and networked into elaborate systems. Their overall capability and complexity are beyond our intuitive grasp, even beyond our physical perception.

Bruce Schneier, in his well-written book *Secrets and Lies: Digital Security in a Networked World*, describes three advantages that computer criminals have over those dealing solely with physical security: automation, action at a distance, and technique propagation.[1]

Automation

Dull, repetitive, trivial actions can be automated and run for extended periods across a large number of computers. Computer programs can do repetitive things very fast, such as trying all the password combinations. It may take one termite a long time to fell a mighty tree, but millions of them working relentlessly can dispose of it rapidly.

At the other extreme, computers also can repeat things very slowly to avoid detection. The accumulation of tiny "nicks" can add up to something over time. To extend the previous analogy, homeowners are often surprised to discover that termites have slowly eaten away the underpinnings of the home they built only 10 years ago.

Action at a Distance

In the past, to rob a bank, you had to physically go there with your gang to commit the deed. Crimes are usually solved because of physical evidence: The perpetrators voices were heard or recorded, their pictures were taken, they left something behind, and so on.

Computer criminals are often anonymous because they don't need to be physically present at the crime location. No one gets to see their face or know their identities or those of their collaborators.

Computer networks let you commit crimes from afar, without having to physically show up. On the Internet, anyone in any location can take a crack at the security of your system. Moreover, a particularly good location is a country with weak security laws.

Technique Propagation

A perpetrator's success or failure in physically robbing a bank depends on how smart, thorough, and lucky he or she is. Bank robbers need personal mastery of a wide set of criminal techniques, as well as meticulous execution.

However, only one intelligent, agile mind is needed to come up with a new computer-security-cracking technique—and only once. From there, everyone can use it. Any one person, anywhere, who cracks any security mechanism can post the solution to the web. Then, anyone else anywhere, no matter how low his or her skill level, can try the newest technique or run the tools that automate it. New techniques regularly spread worldwide in seconds; old techniques never disappear.

In fact, one type of invader is known as a *script kiddy,* an amateur who downloads cracker programs from the web and runs them in anonymity, with *no* knowledge of their operation or effects. They can run crippling attacks at the push of a button.

System Complexity

In addition to counteracting these advantages of computer criminals, those implementing security measures have to deal with the complexity of computer systems. Every computer and network device has its own unique hardware, software, and data. Each has unexpected vulnerabilities, failure modes, and interactions. Connecting the computers and devices together into a complex system increases the potential problems combinatorially, often beyond the grasp of human defenders.

Computer security is a tough challenge—and it will continue to get tougher. VoIP equipment is based on computer and data networks; by adopting VoIP, you are adopting all the security problems inherent in computer systems. However, with proper planning and attention to security details, you can prevent, detect, and react to security problems in an efficient manner. The next section looks at approaches you can take to make these problems more manageable.

Three Stages in Managing Security

An *intrusion* occurs when someone attempts to break into or misuse a system. The word *misuse* is broad, and can refer to a whole range of actions, from stealing confidential data to something as minor as using your e-mail system for spam. The smallest element of intrusion detection data is referred to as an *event.* An event is an auditable occurrence on the network.

The challenges in securing a computer network can be viewed in three stages:

- **Prevention**—To avoid intrusions, if possible

- **Detection**—To know as soon as possible when an intrusion attempt occurs

- **Reaction**—To respond to an intrusion, and to prevent and detect it in the future

Any approach to securing networks, computers, and the data they contain must address each of these three stages. And the work that is needed through all three stages is continuous. According to Matthew Kovar, director of the Yankee Group's Security Solutions & Services research and consulting practice, "Security vulnerabilities and threats, like diseases, are dynamic and can mutate or combine with each other to make a more severe impact with far greater detrimental effects to IT systems. Drugs are countermeasures that are put in place and include solutions such as anti-virus, firewalls, intrusion detection, content screening, and virtual private networks."[2] However, Kovar warns, "Security professionals, like medical professionals, must interact with a patient continuously to monitor and diagnose in real time the security health of an organization."[2]

Prevention

Preventing security breaches altogether is the right place to start—and it is where the most money is spent in today's IT security marketplace. It is an ongoing battle. You can usually prevent the attacks that are well understood or for which patches or fixes exist, but you often can't prevent ones that the systems' architects never envisioned.

There is always something new on the horizon. New attacks can occur because of newly found vulnerabilities that are latent in old software: for example, a hole that has been in a product for years, but that has just been discovered or exploited. New attacks also can occur when new software is installed or when peculiar interactions occur between existing software and hardware.

It is well known that insiders cause most security breaches. So, the first step in securing your system is to know your users well. You should have strong validation for each user: Are they really who they say they are? You should also have strong access controls in place for each user: what objects is each user allowed to read, write, modify, create, or delete? Is the data they manipulate properly authenticated? Are the access controls consistent across all systems? When users change roles or jobs (or leave the area), are the access controls updated appropriately? Are changes to the validation, authentication, and access control audited?

The next step is defending against known vulnerabilities. There are software-based tools that do *vulnerability assessments* (VAs). They examine your hardware and software, and let you know how to remove the vulnerabilities used in active invasions. They don't necessarily stop invasions; they help you patch the security holes used by invaders. They ask, for example, "What ports are open?" "What files should be encrypted?" "What exploitable applications are running?" VA rules are frequently updated, as new (initially vulnerable) software is shipped or as new vulnerabilities are discovered in existing software and hardware.

Another common threat is software viruses. *Antivirus* (AV) detection tools watch for the byte sequences that indicate a computer virus has attached itself to a file. These tools also need to be updated and run frequently. It is startling to observe that computers that are not checked frequently with VA and AV tools become more vulnerable to outside attack simply because time passes.

A third type of preventative measure is firewalls. Firewalls work to block invasions at the point where the invading traffic enters a local network. Firewalls not only can inspect incoming and outgoing network traffic, but can also log unusual activity as it occurs.

David Freeman has noted that "the security war can seem like an infinite standoff; for every new defense researchers devise, invaders develop countermeasures, leading to countermeasures, and so on."[3] But he added, "Fortunately, defenders don't have to make it impossible to break into networks; they only have to make getting in so difficult, or so fraught with risk of being tracked down, that the bad guys think twice."

Detection

Despite the preventive steps you take, intrusions that involve new techniques usually succeed. With hackers, spies, and saboteurs continually finding new ways to break into networks and computers, chances are it is only a matter of time before they get in. Therefore, a principle emphasized during SANS (*System Administration, Networking, and Security*) Institute training is that "prevention is ideal, but detection is a must."[4] Not only is detection a must, but detection *must* be achieved in real time—not several hours or days after the intrusion has occurred.

An *intrusion detection system* (IDS) is designed to detect intrusion attempts as they occur. Intrusion detection systems can be broken into several categories:[5]

- **Host-based intrusion detection system (HIDS)**—Work to detect attacks originating within individual computers. They can detect intrusions in two ways:

  - By monitoring the actions within a computer, such as file accesses or login attempts. This frequently involves identifying attacks as they occur, by the sequence and timing of bytes or system calls (the *attack signature*) or by correlating information in event logs.

  - By using heuristic techniques to prevent or detect attacks as they occur.

- **System integrity verifier (SIV)**—Monitor system files to detect when an intruder changes them—potentially leaving behind a back door to be exploited later. An SIV may watch other components as well, such as the Windows Registry, to find well-known signatures. It may also detect when a normal user somehow acquires root/administrator-level privileges.

- **Network intrusion detection system (NIDS)**—Monitor packets on the network, to discover when someone tries to break into a system or cause a *denial-of-service* (DoS) attack. An example is a system that watches for large numbers of TCP connection requests to many different ports on a target computer, to discover whether someone is attempting a TCP port scan. A NIDS may run either on the target computer, which watches its own traffic (usually integrated with the TCP/IP stack and services themselves), or on an independent computer promiscuously watching all network traffic (in hubs, routers, and switches).

- **Log file monitor (LFM)**—Observe the log files generated by network services. Like NIDS, these systems look for patterns in the log files that suggest an intruder is attacking. One example is a program that analyzes web server log files, looking for intruders who try to exploit well-known security holes.

- **Deception system**—Contain pseudo-services that emulate well-known holes to trap intruders. Some deception systems (also known as decoys, lures, fly-traps, or honeypots[6]) are simple tricks, such as renaming the administrator account on Windows, and then setting up a dummy account with no rights—but extensive auditing.

Reaction

When an intrusion is detected, how does your team react? You would like your team to take a systematic approach—clear steps to be followed when a security breach occurs—to stop the intrusion or stop its spread, repair any damage, catch the perpetrator, and avoid it in the future.

Reacting should be more effective than simply tearing your hair. Software tools offer short-term responses—things you do immediately—and longer-term, more thoughtful responses. The goal of these actions is to stop the intrusion, reduce the damage it causes, and quarantine it (to prevent further spread).

An alarm may be the simplest short-term response: notify an administrator that an intrusion is occurring. Beep, play a WAV file, send an e-mail message, or page the system administrator. Write event details to the local operating system's event log. Perhaps an even better alarm is to forward a trap to a system management console, such as NetIQ Application Manager, Microsoft Operations Manager, or HP OpenView.

Modern detection systems have rules that automate the short-term reaction to a breach. In addition to alarms, they can launch programs or run scripts to handle the event. For instance, these systems can stop an offending process or session on a local computer. Or, they can direct a firewall to filter out packets from the IP address of the intruder. They might stop the offending TCP sessions by forging TCP RST packets to force their connections to terminate.

You also want your system to collect detailed information about the intrusion. The better the quality of the data about an intrusion, the better the quality of the reaction. Log the attack, saving the attack information (time stamp, intruder IP address, victim IP address/port, protocol information). Save a trace file of the raw packets for later analysis.

Over the longer term, you want to prevent a repeat intrusion. One way is to catch those who initiated the intrusion, with the hope that the legal system will prevent them from causing future damage. Who did what to whom? Determining this usually requires a process called *forensics*—a thorough examination of the available evidence. The material you collect when you detect an intrusion may need to be turned over to law enforcement.

You also want to review what occurred, to improve your team's prevention and detection processes for "the next time." Such a review asks the following:

- What procedures need to change?
- What software needs to be updated?

- What policies need to be strengthened?

- What rules and actions need to be improved?

- What went well (it can't all be bad news)?

- Finally, there is a much longer-term cycle related to overall systems management. What are the historical trends? How often do intrusions occur? What damage do they do? What does it cost to prevent or detect intrusions? Are the staff and budget adequate?

The background information on general network and computer security has been covered. It is now time for a look at some of the specific problem areas associated with VoIP security.

Problem Areas for VoIP Security

Security concerns exist whenever you have something that others consider valuable or something that others want to disrupt. If the cost of obtaining something is low relative to the value, then more than likely it needs to be secured. A thief is more likely to steal a car with the doors unlocked and the keys in the ignition than a car with the doors locked and an active car alarm system. When the security system is active, the potential risk to the thief is probably above the value of stealing the car.

In a VoIP deployment, you have something of value: phone service and information. In addition, you have something that others may want to disrupt— your phone service is a business-critical application. For VoIP security, you want to identify vulnerable areas, and then make the cost to the attacker higher than the value. It is not possible to list all of the problem areas in this chapter, but broad classifications are provided so that you can think about where to look for problems.

When thinking about VoIP security, it helps to begin with what you are trying to accomplish. What are you trying to avoid, prevent, protect, or secure? Here are some examples:

- You want to avoid disruptions to your VoIP phone service.

- You want to prevent unauthorized calls.

- You want to protect sensitive phone conversations and records.

- You want to secure VoIP servers and other network devices.

The next area to think about is what others (attackers) are trying to accomplish. What are people after? Who might the hackers be: internal employees, corrupt administrators, external terrorists, script kiddies? Here are some examples:

- They want to disrupt your business by disrupting the IP network or causing phone outages.

- They want to obtain long-distance phone calls free (that is, at your cost).

- They want to hear confidential, proprietary, or insider information.

- They want to hack into VoIP servers to redirect calls or obtain call details.

There are many different reasons why hackers do what they do. Sometimes there is a financial component. If someone can make unauthorized calls on your network, they can save money. Sometimes there is a personal aspect. A disgruntled employee or competitor may seek to damage your company through disruption of key business services. In many cases, the potential attackers could be end users, internal or external invaders, and possibly corrupt administrators. Or, as a colleague noted, some people are just sick jerks who find satisfaction in making trouble for others.

The next sections present some of the potential security problem areas for a VoIP implementation. These are areas that you want to make sure to secure.

Toll Fraud

Financial motive can be strong incentive to hackers who are looking for free phone calls. VoIP presents unique problems, because VoIP phones operate over your IP network.

Easy Access

With the traditional PSTN, someone had to have physical access to a phone in your company to make phone calls. Because VoIP can make it easy to perform "action at a distance," a freeloader doesn't necessarily need to be physically present to use a VoIP phone.

Where are the vulnerable points in a VoIP deployment? Consider a few of these access points:

- **Network access points**—Any place in your network where an IP device can plug in. Because IP phones generally use DHCP to request an IP address, consider locking down by hardware address those phones that can receive an address.

- **Wireless access points**—Many enterprises have wireless access points liberally available around their campus. Can IP devices roam freely onto your network through these access points? Authentication is needed to make sure only authorized users are allowed access.

- **Remote access points**—You may have set up remote access for your users, as more people work on the road and from home. How do your users log in to your network remotely? Is it through a *virtual private network* (VPN)? Do you have user authentication in place, to ensure that hackers can't get onto your network remotely?

Network access needs to be secure. You want to avoid situations where someone can plug a phone into the network and make a call—with the charges going to your VoIP system.

VoIP Server Configuration

Arguably, the most important components in a VoIP system are the VoIP servers that handle call processing. If a hacker can get into your VoIP servers, there are several areas where toll fraud can occur:

- Account fraud can happen when someone makes calls without proper billing. In a VoIP system, *call detail records* (CDRs) are frequently stored in a relational database system. Often, the database system is an off-the-shelf application, with its inherent security vulnerabilities. Access to the CDRs could allow a hacker to change the billing information to gain free calls.

- Some VoIP servers have a feature that lets unknown phones download a generic configuration to get them started. You want to disable this feature for your day-to-day operations. Unauthorized access to VoIP server configuration lets a hacker enable this feature and use an unknown phone to make calls.

- An incorrectly configured call routing plan could allow the IP phone in your lobby to make international phone calls. Routing plan configurations are usually configured on the VoIP server and stored in a database. Access by a hacker can allow calls from certain locations to any other location.

Softphones

IP phones come in software and hardware versions. The hardware IP phones are considered by some to be more secure, because they typically run embedded operating systems. Softphones present a unique challenge, in that someone can potentially install a software phone on any computer on your data network. Now there is web server software that is integral to both IP phones and softphones. Web servers that are running with your phones offer many vulnerabilities and access points to potential hackers.

You may be careful to lock down the hardware IP phones, but you must consider softphones, as well. A hacker could install a softphone on any exposed computer and obtain free calls. In addition, softphones have all the vulnerabilities associated with off-the-shelf operating systems and web servers, including exposure to viruses and worms.

The financial appeal of free phone calls provides some incentive to hackers. However, there is another, bigger problem area for VoIP security: the private, confidential, and proprietary phone call information that is now traveling on your data network in a VoIP implementation.

Accessing Private Information

Keeping sensitive information private has long been a security issue for data networks. Web browsers use special encryption protocols to keep private the credit card numbers that you type into online order forms. Corporations use VPNs to provide secure network communications. The security issues are similar when you add voice conversations to your data network. Voice conversations now flow on the data network with your web and e-mail traffic.

A VoIP system has many pieces of information that need to be protected. The conversation itself, voice mail, call activity records, and phone lists are some examples of the kinds of information you must keep private.

Overhearing Conversations

What if you could listen in on the CFO's conversations the week before quarterly results are announced? How about listening to your lead engineers discuss a new proprietary technology? How valuable is that information to you or your competitors? You can see that one incentive to hack into a VoIP network is to overhear conversations. A VoIP conversation is only as secure as the network that it is carried on.

In a VoIP system, voice data is transferred between phones by using the RTP protocol. The RTP header of each packet has a standard format; anyone can tell how the payload is encoded by looking at RTP's Payload Type field. (See Figure 8-1.) VoIP payloads use standard codecs such as G.711 and G.729. RTP streams can be captured, reconstructed, and replayed. In fact, on the Internet, a tool known as *Voice Over Misconfigured Internet Telephones* (VOMIT) is available that can take a capture of an RTP stream and construct a WAV file that can be replayed on a Windows computer.[7] So, as you can imagine, you don't want people capturing your VoIP conversations and playing them back or distributing them to others.

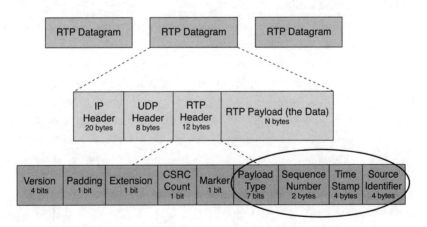

Figure 8-1   *RTP Header with Payload and Sequence Information*

Consider this scary thought. With an analog phone system, if a hacker taps an analog line, he gets access to a single call. In a VoIP system, if a hacker taps into a data segment, he can see all the packets flowing in either direction. (See Figure 8-2.) Depending on the bandwidth of the network link, there might be dozens or hundreds of voice calls in progress at the same time. IP taps can be difficult to notice because unauthorized devices can capture packets unnoticed. When deploying VoIP, your goal is to prevent the unauthorized interception and decoding of conversations.

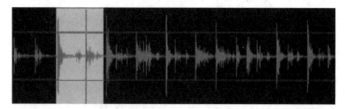

Figure 8-2 *VoIP Phone Conversations Are Easy to Reconstruct if You Can Capture the RTP Frames (Image Taken from http:// www.sonicspot.com/soundwave97/soundwave97.html)*

VoIP is also vulnerable to the use of rogue servers and spoofing. If a hacker sets up a rogue VoIP server or gateway, calls could potentially be diverted and captured. In addition, a hacker could masquerade as a valid IP phone and intercept calls that were intended for the real phone.

Unified messaging offers much appeal to VoIP users. The idea of accessing messages anywhere, anytime, is leading to many deployments of this feature. However, unified messaging is not without security problems. Unified messaging integrates closely with your e-mail servers. Voice mail is stored as sound files on your e-mail server and can be accessed as e-mail messages. A hacker who can break into your e-mail server can obtain not only private e-mail information, but also private voice mail information.

While phone conversations are some of the most sensitive information on your network, there is call detail information in the VoIP system that is just as sensitive and should be kept private as well.

Call Detail and Phone List Information

CDRs are logged as calls occur. The CDRs contain information about who made calls, where they called, and how long the calls lasted. The CDRs contain information similar to what you see on a typical phone bill. In the wrong hands, this information could show competitors (for example, what customers you are calling and how often). The CDRs are stored in standard databases on VoIP servers, so they face the vulnerabilities associated with these database systems.

Most IP phones contain built-in web servers for simple management services. A hacker who cracks the IP phone's web server can potentially get access to such information as recently called phone numbers and address book information.

Where is your company phone list stored? Is it secure? Telemarketers love to get new phone lists to call for various solicitations. A new trend that is starting is fax spammers. After obtaining a list of fax numbers, automated faxes are sent out at an annoying rate. There is lots of private information pertaining to your phone system that you need to protect.

Another problem that you must deal with is that of hackers who don't want your information but who do want to disrupt or damage your enterprise.

Disrupting, Corrupting, and Doing Damage

Perhaps the most disconcerting area of data network and VoIP security is the fact that there are attackers out there who want to disrupt, corrupt, or flat-out damage your organization. You see this often in the Internet, where a DoS attack is launched against certain websites. If a website provides online ordering of merchandise, and a hacker can prevent real customers from accessing the site, the site owner loses money. DoS attacks can be *distributed* (DDoS) in a way that many different computers over a network are participating in the attack.

Denying Service

Imagine the problems that may arise if a DoS attack is launched against your VoIP phone service. Phone service disruptions can have huge costs because of the business-critical nature of the phone system. In attempts to deny your phone service, an attacker usually focuses on crashing or inhibiting phones, VoIP servers, or the network—all in an attempt to create problems with availability, call setup, and call quality.

A DoS attack usually consists of a flood of spurious connection attempts. The attacker sends to the server a connection request, but never responds to the acknowledgment of the request. A good example for VoIP is an attack that bombards a call-processing server with many invalid session initiation or call-setup requests. The VoIP server may become so busy trying to respond to the invalid requests that it cannot process the valid call setup requests. In the worst case, the DoS attack creates an availability outage of the service.

Another common way to reduce system availability is with computer viruses or worms. Viruses take advantage of vulnerabilities in applications or operating systems. Because most VoIP servers run on off-the-shelf operating systems with off-the-shelf applications, virus writers can potentially disrupt VoIP service with a strategically placed virus. Traditional *private branch exchange* (PBX) systems have not had this problem because they are closed systems, so there just are not a lot of viruses out there on these systems.

Call Hijacking

Hijacking is generally thought of in terms of cars or airplanes, but it applies to other situations as well. Someone takes control of something and uses it for his or her purposes or redirects it to another location. In a VoIP system, a potential for hijacking calls can cause security concern. There are several ways in which this can happen:

- **Rogue VoIP server or gateway**—If a hacker can get access to phone configurations, calls can be redirected to rogue VoIP servers or gateways.

- **Call-forwarding control**—Some IP phones have vulnerabilities that allow call-forwarding settings to be manipulated remotely. A hacker could potentially use this to forward all calls to another location. In some cases, the user may not even be aware that the call was forwarded to someone else.

- **Controlling a conversation**—Although technically challenging, a hacker could take control of a VoIP conversation. The RTP packets that comprise the conversation each contain a sequence number. If a higher sequence number is sent to a phone during a conversation, the previous sequence numbers are discarded. A hacker could play out their own conversation on the receiving phone.

- **Message integrity**—How do you ensure that the message received is the same as the message sent? Redirected calls could potentially pass through a hacker's control and the packets could be altered or manipulated to control the call.

Annoyances

Nearly everyone has faced the telemarketers: Those annoying calls that always seem to occur when we are just sitting down for dinner. How does VoIP deal with these kinds of calls? You would like to have features such as call screening and anonymous call rejection in place to help protect your users.

What about prank calls? Sometimes people make calls to have fun or joke with others. With unified messaging in VoIP implementations, voice mail is more closely tied to e-mail. Just as software developers have rushed to address the issues of e-mail spam, there will likely follow software that deals specifically with prank voice mails that may show up in your e-mail.

Change Management

Who can change the equipment configurations in your VoIP system? Router configurations are especially sensitive. Some routers have built-in wiretap features. If a hacker were to enable this feature, packets could be redirected to another server. What about QoS changes and policy? Someone could make changes so that he or she receives higher priority than other users during periods of high usage.

Change control is especially important for VoIP servers. The installation of any applications on these critical computers should be carefully controlled. For example, installing a new application may create shared drives—which are notorious for being susceptible to virus propagation. In addition, you don't want everyone to have the ability to change private account or billing information for your phone system.

VoIP Security Recommendations

Keeping your VoIP system secure is essential to maintain five nines of reliability, to have quick call setup, and to have consistently high call quality. You also must maintain the privacy of information related to users and their phone calls, and avoid corruption or damage to the overall system.

Start with the physical security of the facilities and the computers and networks inside them. Next, make changes to your network and its core equipment. There will be numerous IP phones and softphones in your VoIP deployment; they need to be secured, because they are potential portals for attack. To keep conversations private, the VoIP traffic must be encrypted. Encryption must be implemented carefully so that delay and jitter don't increase unacceptably. Finally, VoIP is complex, and affects almost everything you know about data networking. Its success calls for the very best practices in management processes, skills, and tools.

Secure Your Central Facilities

When you think about securing your facilities you should think about three areas: 1) the physical aspects of security, 2) hardening the key servers, and 3) providing for authentication and authorization of users. Strong security begins with physical barriers to prevent easy access for hackers.

Maintain Strong Physical Security

Maintaining physical security means controlling the comings and goings of people and equipment and providing protection against the elements and natural disasters. Physical security is important for keeping your computers and data secure—if an experienced hacker can just walk up to a computer, it can be compromised in a matter of minutes. This section covers securing the datacenter, the network and VoIP equipment, and the environment around the equipment.

Secure the Datacenter

The crucial VoIP components—servers, gateways, IP PBXs, databases, and routers—should be confined to a locked room. Protect the room, as needed, with electronic card access, so that you can record who enters and leaves the room.

Most enterprises maintain datacenters, where they keep their important servers, databases, network equipment, and management systems. They enforce strict control over who can enter the datacenters, using badges, cards, keys, or a keypad system, as well as log books and human security. Physical access to the datacenter or server room should be limited to a select set of trustworthy administrators. Maintenance people should not be allowed to enter unaccompanied. It may also make sense to install motion-sensor alarms or surveillance cameras in these rooms.

If you don't have a datacenter, this might seem like overkill. Small organizations often tend to have their servers in hallways, reception areas, or other publicly accessible spaces. Not only does this expose them to malicious attacks, it increases the risk of accidents from spilled coffee, people tripping over cables, and curious children.

Secure the Equipment

Lock computer CPU cases and ensure that the keys are protected. Make copies of the case keys and keep them in a restricted location outside the datacenter. Most desktop and tower cases have locking lugs that you can use to keep an intruder from opening the case.

The server room should be arranged in a way that people outside the room cannot see the keyboards, so that they can't see user or administrator passwords as they are typed. There should be no evidence of passwords near the systems or under the keyboards. Documentation concerning LAN settings or network equipment settings should not be visible. Avoid keeping confidential information on notes stuck to the edge of your displays. Keep important user IDs and passwords in a restricted location.

Secure the Environment Around the Equipment

Network cabling, hubs, switches, routers, and even the external WAN interface are vulnerable points in a network. An attacker who can attach to your network can steal data in transit or mount attacks against computers on your network, or on other networks! If at all possible, keep hubs and switches behind locked doors or in locked cabinets, run cabling through walls and ceilings to make it harder to tap, and ensure that your external data connection points are kept locked.

Don't let security concerns override the environmental requirements of your hardware. For instance, locking a server in a closet prevents malicious users from accessing it, but if the closet is not adequately ventilated, the computer will overheat and fail, rendering your security concerns pointless. Provide temperature and humidity controls to avoid any equipment damage.

Install uninterruptible power supplies on the servers, and connect them with the operating system. They can keep the servers alive or initiate a staged automatic server shutdown when there is a power outage.

Any unused modem or NIC connection should be disabled or removed.

Harden the Servers

A computer's exposure to outside threats begins the moment it is booted up and hooked to a network. It is the job of the IT team to see that the computer is as clean, invulnerable, and manageable as possible from the first day. The sections that follow describe some methods that you can use to limit your server's vulnerability to attacks.

Manage Your Storage Intelligently

On crucial hard drives, employ RAID technology or disk mirroring. And, of course, make regular backups of the data and the configuration settings for each critical computer. Keep the backed up files in a restricted, offsite location, so that you are not wiped out by a storm or a fire.

Create a Secure Build Image

Use a secure build image to install the software on all computers related to your VoIP system: VoIP servers, DNS and DHCP servers, database servers, web servers, gateways, and so on. Never install a virgin operating system and its applications on a computer and boot it up in the network. Each computer should contain four security components: vulnerability-assessment software, antivirus software, a personal firewall, and HIDS software.

Start with a computer with a hard disk that has been wiped clean. Install the latest version of the operating system that you support. Next, apply the latest patches to the operating system. These appear to change on a daily or weekly basis—consider using a service to keep up to date. Then, install your organization's applications and their latest patches.

Next, run a vulnerability assessment against that system, set at the highest level of "pickiness." The assessment may report hundreds of potential holes in the system, usually ranked in importance from critical to low. Spend the time to research and close the vulnerabilities it finds. This may take several days, but it is a good investment—you will be replicating these fixes across many computers, with the intention of avoiding identifiable intrusions. Leave the vulnerability agent on the computer so that it can be updated and run remotely. NetIQ's Security Analyzer (http://www.netiq.com/products/sa/) is well suited for this job; it can analyze a variety of operating systems.

Install a personal, or host-based, firewall on the server computer. Ensure that the firewall is initially set in its most secure position. One at a time, open any ports or change any other defaults you know will be needed.

An IDS watches traffic patterns for known attack patterns, and stops them or creates an alert when they occur. A HIDS is recommended for critical servers. Given the high target value of a VoIP server and the lag time involved in validating an application or operating system security patch for production use, a HIDS provides early attack mitigation. Install a HIDS on the mail servers if they are being used to store voice mail, in addition to installing e-mail content filtering.

Get the latest antivirus software for the operating system, and make sure it is up to date. Ensure that no viruses have been introduced during your build and, again, leave an antivirus agent on the computer so that it can be updated and run remotely by an authorized administrator.

This is now the hardened "gold standard," the computer image to clone when creating VoIP servers, DNS servers, database servers, and so on. Replicate this base image with each new installation.

Secure the System and Application Software

After computers are placed into the production environment, protect them from undesirable booting. Modify the BIOS boot sequence in each computer. Set the hard drive to boot up first, with the floppy and CD/DVD drives thereafter. This makes it harder for an attacker to remove passwords and account data from system disks. On mission-critical servers, floppy and CD/DVD drives could be disabled or even removed to provide the highest level of physical security. Implement strong passwords for accessing the BIOS. If possible, modify the BIOS settings so that the combination of keys to press to access the BIOS is not displayed during the bootup sequence.

Turn off all unneeded services, disable any features on the servers that are not in use, and do not run any applications that are not needed on the server, such as an e-mail client or a web server. NetIQ Security Manager has a useful function that enables you to specify exactly which processes and applications are allowed to run on a computer. It enforces those rules, and it ensures that no other applications can be started.

VoIP servers may run multiple services that can be distributed across multiple devices to increase scalability and manageability. You can use the ability to run different applications on different computers to increase the level of security. For instance, call-processing managers typically support call control, web configuration, IP phone browsing services, conference calling, and device configuration services. By running these services on separate computers, you can harden each of them and avoid potential interaction among the applications. Also make sure that the services use user or service accounts with only the privileges that are absolutely necessary to run normally. A compromised service should not provide root or administrative access.

Use Windows' Capabilities

A fast-typing attacker might get to your computer and share its disk drives with no passwords in under 10 seconds, but not if the computer is locked. There is a simple security feature that is free on Windows computers: lock the computer as you walk away from it. To do this, press **Ctrl-Alt-Delete** and then press **K** (which is the shortcut for the Lock button). Get in the habit of locking your computer whenever you are away from it.

Use the *Encrypting File System* (EFS) to encrypt sensitive folders on your computer. EFS is available for Windows 2000 and Windows XP Professional.

The SYSKEY program is used to enable strong encryption of account password data. It uses a 128-bit key to encrypt the password data in the Registry *Security Account Manager* (SAM) database. Once enabled, this key is required by the computer every time it is started, so that the password data is accessible for authentication purposes. Use the Windows SYSKEY utility to secure the local accounts database, local copies of EFS encryption keys, and other valuables that you don't want attackers to have.

Beware of Shared Drives

Shared drives are convenient and easy—they are easy to set up and let you quickly copy files from one computer to another. However, a shared drive without proper access control gives a computer virus a mechanism for propagating itself to other computers. Human viruses are spread through the air and by physical contact. Computer viruses are spread through unsecured shared drives and by e-mail attachments. The best advice is to avoid using shared drives if at all possible. They may be necessary in some cases, but try to limit access to read-only or make sure that only authenticated users are granted full access.

Authenticate and Authorize

This section starts by defining three terms that many people find confusing:

- **Authentication**—Are you who you say you are? How do the communicating parties authenticate each other? Is the party who answered the call the intended destination?

- **Authorization**—Okay, you are authenticated, but what are you allowed to do?

- **Non-repudiation**—Once someone accepts a call, is there anything in place that prohibits that person from then denying receipt of the connection? If he or she says "I didn't get that call," can your systems prove that wrong?

Insiders cause most security problems. Despite the obvious focus on external attacks, studies show that "about 70% of the security risk is internal—either by accident or maliciousness," says Marius Swart, GM of security solutions at Internet Solutions.[8] "However," Swart adds, "a thorough analysis of potential threats can substantially reduce risk of a security breach."

Minding the users and administrators within the enterprise is an essential part of analyzing threats and developing a security plan. Creating a thorough plan means establishing or revising your security policies, and then putting processes in place to enforce those policies. Sophisticated software that is designed to coordinate and enforce security policies system-wide should be a part of any attempt to reduce internal security threats.

For example, your security policies should describe how new users are handled as they join an organization: How are they identified and what can they access? When users change roles or jobs (or leave the area), are the access controls updated? How are contractors or temporary workers handled when their work and contracts end?

Just as important are the policies that are applied to the members of the security team. For example, it does not make sense for a single team member to have full access to all the resources in an organization. Identify the administrators and the functions they are allowed to do. Each team member should have an appropriate range of control, with all actions subject to ongoing auditing.

To secure your VoIP system is to know your users and administrators well, and to incorporate that knowledge into the way the system operates. Strong authentication of each user and administrator should be performed, to be certain that they really are who they say they are.

Stringent access controls should be enforced, especially for the IT administrative team. Access policies must be clearly and consistently applied: What objects is each administrator allowed to read, write, modify, create, or delete? Is the data that they manipulate properly authenticated? Are the access controls consistent across all systems? Are changes to the validation, authentication, and access control audited? How is data integrity checked?

Carefully monitored processes are needed to implement a thorough set of policies like these. For example, NetIQ's Directory Security Administrator (http://www.netiq.com/products/sm/) provides a central view of objects, such as files, folders, and printers, across an enterprise. It shows the objects in the directory structure and displays their associated permissions. Administrators can easily identify the assigned rights and privileges of each object, and make changes to *access control lists* (ACLs) as necessary.

Limit administration access to IP PBXs among the IT staff. Allow only selected members to have access to the core operating system on a VoIP server, gateway, or database. Similarly, protect routers, switches, and gateways. Restrict *Simple Network Management Protocol* (SNMP) and Telnet access to these devices, so that they can only be used by authorized administrators.

Strengthen Your Data Network

Data network security is probably already part of your security plan. There are several ways that a data network can be further strengthened for VoIP. Consider keeping voice traffic separated from other types of network traffic, carefully deploying firewalls and NIDSs, and implementing solid policy management practices.

Separate VoIP Traffic

You want to avoid competition and disruption among different types of traffic wherever possible. In particular, you would like to keep the key VoIP components well isolated, and you would like to keep the VoIP traffic separate from the other data traffic. For increased strength, enforce the separations at multiple layers:

- **At Layer 2, isolate IP PBXs and VoIP servers on their own virtual LAN (VLAN)**—The core VoIP components interact frequently with one another and their databases, but they don't necessarily need to see the rest of the traffic on the same LAN. Putting them on a separate VLAN should isolate them from lots of other traffic on the enterprise LANs, especially chatty protocols, multicasts, broadcasts, and some level of DoS attack.

- **Put chatty protocols on their own VLAN**—Network protocols such as DECnet, IPX, and NetBIOS should have nothing to do with your VoIP protocols. Don't allow chatty protocols like these (and their vulnerabilities) on the same network with VoIP traffic, which is sensitive to delay and jitter.

- **Isolate voice traffic onto a separate VLAN**—Many IP phones contain a data port that allows for computers to be plugged into the phone. Switches can be configured so that the voice and data traffic are carried on separate VLANs. Be sure to put wireless LAN devices on their own VLAN, which helps ensure that users are not orphaned as they move from access point to access point. Don't depend entirely on VLANs for VoIP security, but consider them a good way to keep traffic separated without two physical networks.[9]

- **Use switches instead of hubs**—Switched networks are more secure than shared hubs and can help prevent hackers from just plugging in a device and capturing data. Again, if your organization is deploying VoIP, eliminate all of your hubs.

- **Separate IP PBXs, VoIP servers, and gateways on the LAN by putting the devices in different Windows domains from other servers**—The core VoIP components should have different permissions and different users (that is, authorized administrators) from all the other computers on your network. If they need to be in a Windows domain, give them their own.

- **Use private IP addressing inside your enterprise: 10.0.0.0/8, 172.16.0.0/12–172.31.0.0/12, and 192.168.0.0/16**—One way to reduce external DoS attacks is to use private IP addressing for the VoIP devices. Using IP addresses in the private address ranges 10.0.0.0/8, 172.16.0.0/12–172.31.0.0/12, and 192.168.0.0/16 prohibits Internet-based attacks, because private addresses are not routable on the Internet.

Deploy Firewalls and NIDSs

Firewalls block undesirable traffic. A firewall is analogous to a checkpoint on a highway—it looks at each car and decides whether it will let the car pass through or whether it will turn it back. It may reject green and yellow cars, but let cars of all other colors pass through. It may reject cars from North Carolina with fewer than two occupants, but let all others through. If there were plenty of time, inspectors could look deeply into each car, say, rejecting those that are not carrying a valid vehicle registration.

Admittedly, this is a simple analogy, but it describes roughly how a firewall operates—it looks at frames one at a time and decides which ones it will allow through. The firewall does this based on policies that you have defined; the policies capture the reasoning behind the rules you are having the firewall enforce.

Some firewalls can remember information they have seen in recent frames from the same source, to help them make smarter decisions. To continue the analogy, suppose there was a checkpoint that allowed only 10 cars per day to pass from North Carolina into Virginia. A count would have to be kept, allowing the first 10 cars to pass freely, but rejecting all others until the next day. Firewalls that can remember information about what they have seen, and dig deeply into frames for context, are said to do *stateful inspection.*

Streaming voice traffic generally flows on dynamically assigned, even UDP port numbers greater than 16,384. The ports to be used in a phone conversation are specified in the call setup flows (that is, in the H.323 or SIP transactions). To tie a port number to a conversation, a firewall needs to look for the port numbers inside the call-setup frames. Without stateful inspection, a firewall would have to open a wide range of UDP ports (which does not help when it is trying to block undesirable traffic).

Firewalls generally add some delay, because they hold each frame while they are looking at it, deciding what to do. In contrast, NIDSs usually don't add delay. Rather than looking a frame at a time, they look across a broad collection of frames flowing in either direction, looking for patterns that signify an attack. The pattern of packets and their flows for many network attacks have been identified; these are known as *attack signatures.*

NIDSs generally reside in switches. They have a lot more to do than firewalls, so they are generally used to detect attacks, not prevent them. They raise events when they detect attack signatures. A technique known as *NIDS shunning* can block traffic from sources that have generated traffic that matches one of its attack signatures. Once an attack signature is detected on a LAN segment, shunning can be used to dynamically change the Layer 3 filtering configuration of a network device to drop all additional traffic from the source on that segment. Resets can be used to tear down a TCP session that triggers an attack signature. NIDS shunning could be used to block UDP flood attacks sourced from the data segment against the voice segment. Deploy this carefully, though; like any automatic detection system, you want to beware of false positives.

You probably need both firewalls and NIDSs in the portions of the network under your control. Research their capabilities with respect to recognizing and protecting VoIP traffic, both the call setup and the actual call flows. Also, examine how much delay and jitter a firewall adds to the VoIP traffic that it passes. Firewalls and NIDSs are improving all the time, but, unfortunately, so is the sophistication of VoIP traffic attacks.

Implement Policy Management

Keeping a consistent, viable configuration of all the elements in a network can be tough. There are many protocols, many types of devices and software, many details to master, and too few hours in each day. In addition, static configuration is no longer adequate—network configuration may need to change throughout a day, week, or month. Some applications need specialized handling depending on when they are run. For example, the payroll department needs assured response time twice a month; the CEO's broadcast each Thursday afternoon should receive adequate bandwidth.

Policy servers are designed to remove you from network configuration details. Consider them a tremendous usability improvement over manual configuration. Rather than mastering every device and its possible interactions, you describe the rules and criteria—for the devices, applications, and users of your network. You also can write policies that take effect at certain times of the day or days of the week, so that the policy server is essentially doing custom configuration on the fly.

You create and change policies at a user-friendly GUI called a *policy console*—the exact look and feel will vary among different vendors. A policy console is connected to a policy server; they may reside together in the same computer. The policy server stores policies in a repository, a structured database for holding the information about each policy. Creating and changing policies should look like other administrative tasks you already have, such as creating and changing the user profiles for the users of a file server.

Now the real work occurs. The policy server software converts its policies into actions to be taken at specified times or under certain conditions. Those actions must be conveyed as configuration instructions to real devices in the network, such as switches, routers, and firewalls. To do this, the policy server pushes instructions to *policy agents,* which translate these into local device-specific configuration commands. For new and up-to-date network devices, the policy client software may reside within the network devices themselves. For older devices, it will probably reside outboard, in a *configuration proxy*—a computer running policy client software, which knows how to issue device-specific configuration commands. The proxy may issue commands using SNMP, for example, rather than the new protocols designed specifically for policy management. Vulnerabilities often present themselves when equipment is not configured consistently. Figure 8-3 illustrates policy servers delivering configuration directions throughout a complex network.

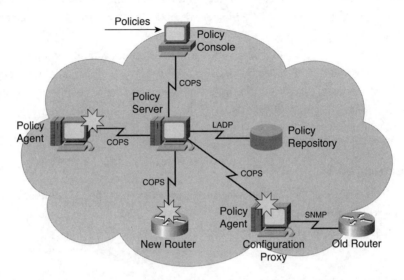

Figure 8-3 *Policy Servers Can Deliver Consistent Network Configuration*

The policy console, the policy server, and policy clients communicate with one another by using a high-level protocol called *Common Open Policy Service* (COPS). COPS is an emerging IETF standard that uses TCP to communicate policy information. Although policy-based network management offers tremendous usability and productivity improvements, expect it to take several years before COPS is supported in all the network devices you use. Configuration proxies will be used in the interim to extend the useful life of the devices you are using today.

The policy repository uses a standard directory structure to store its information. This is important for usability and security reasons. Suppose you were to define a policy that enables members of the sales team to get high-priority access to a certain application. You want to use your existing user access definition in the policy for "the members of the sales team." You don't want to re-enter the IP addresses for everyone on the team, or change the policy when someone new joins.

You want your policy repository to tie to your existing enterprise directories, to improve the consistency of the administration. Recent policy repositories are compatible with the *Directory-Enabled Networks* (DEN) schema, so they interface well with the directory services of the major vendors, such as Microsoft Active Directory, Novell NDS, Siemens X.500 Directory, and Sun Directory Services.

Because the policy server works from the same central administrative directory as the rest of your network management, you can maintain a uniform level of security. Software that remotely accesses the repository uses the *Lightweight Directory Access Protocol* (LDAP) for the communication.

Secure the IP Phones

Don't overlook the security of the IP phones. Incorrect phone configurations create vulnerabilities that can enable hackers to take control of the phone, redirect calls, or possibly overhear conversations.

Set Up the Phones Securely

The sections that follow describe some precautions that you can take to ensure that phones are set up securely.

Manage Phone Passwords Carefully

Some IP phones are shipped from their manufacturer with no administrative password—that is, their password is set to null. Null passwords allow easy access for attackers, who can then gain both remote and local administrative access to the phone. Find and change all default passwords. Change them again as soon as someone changes departments or leaves the organization. Follow good password procedures, as always, using complex strings that are not readily guessable or calculable. Where passwords are used, they should be aged and changed frequently.

Pay Special Attention to Phones Containing Web, Telnet, or FTP Servers

The march of miniaturization continues. Many IP phones and softphones now have web, Telnet, and FTP servers in them. The web server is there to let you use a web browser to update the phone's configuration information. These internal web servers can also be helpful for gathering diagnostic and debugging information.

However, a web server is susceptible to every known web-based attack—and there are a lot of them. Some phones require no authentication to get to their web pages. Those who can get through can cause damage by, for example, manipulating the call-setup signaling, rebooting the phone, or getting information about calls made from the phone.

Lock down the phone and its internal servers. Check with its manufacturer for details, and keep an eye on the ongoing network forums for information on vulnerabilities and their fixes.

Maintain Vulnerability Assessment, Antivirus, and Firewall Software on Softphone Computers

Softphones are not as resilient as their IP phone counterparts. Softphones run in regular computers, so they are more susceptible to attacks because of the wide variety of ways they can be attacked. These include operating system vulnerabilities, application vulnerabilities, service vulnerabilities, worms, viruses, and so on. IP phones often run custom operating systems with limited service support and are less likely to have vulnerabilities. Softphones are vulnerable to any attack against a network segment, not just an attack against its host computer. The Code-Red and Nimda invasions, for instance, bogged down softphone user systems and the segments they resided in to such a point that they were unusable. No amount of QoS will prioritize voice traffic over data traffic if the end-user computer that is placing the call is unusable.

Limit the Functions Available in Publicly Available Phones

Which VoIP phones are more vulnerable: those in the lobby of a public building that anyone can get to, or those in a windowless office or closet, where an attacker can hook in a laptop and let it silently process passwords or invasions for hours on end? Both are significant security problems, now that the phone is a portal into your IP network.

So, treat every internal phone as if it were in a dark corner, where any nefarious employee might try to tap into it. Apply this treatment across all of your VoIP phones. Treat the phone in the lobby even more tightly. If it is to be used only for room-to-room calls within the building, make sure the call routing tables are specifically configured so that toll, long-distance, and international calls are disallowed.

Allow Limited Administrative Access

The ability to manage phones and their configuration remotely is a necessity. You don't want someone to have to travel to the phone whenever something is wrong. Create security policies that describe what can be remotely accessed and what permissions are required to obtain remote access. If Telnet is not the mechanism used for remote access, disable the Telnet server that may be running on the phone. Record all occasions when sanctioned remote access takes place, and make sure you are alerted when a nonsanctioned access occurs.

Identify Users

Authenticating users and their devices can reduce the attacks against the VoIP network. The primary way to authenticate IP phones is with their MAC address. If a phone with an unknown MAC address attempts to download a network configuration from the VoIP server, then that IP phone will not receive a configuration. Some IP phones support simple user authentication, forcing a user to "log in" to a phone. By providing either a valid password or *personal identification number* (PIN), the attacker is granted access to the phone and a custom configuration.

User authentication occurs after successful device authentication. User authentication was originally designed for shared office spaces, and may be an inconvenience for the everyday office worker. Some VoIP systems also support legacy features, such as requiring a user to enter an access code before placing calls to restricted locations. Typically, these codes are fixed, changed infrequently, and sent over the IP network in the clear.

User authentication reduces attacks in which a device spoofs a MAC address and attempts to assume the identity of its target. Requiring user authentication also provides some level of nonrepudiation, because if both parties are successfully authenticated, you have some level of certainty that you can trust the party on the other side of the call. Of course, if the user walks away from the desk without logging out, all bets are off. Enabling call control logging on the VoIP server to provide records of placed calls also aids in nonrepudiation. Some softphones provide Windows-based authentication, whereas others use a combination of username and password/PIN. A combination of username and password/PIN may also be used to identify the user to the VoIP server. This feature lets users access their custom configuration settings after successfully authenticating.

Some voice-mail systems support two-step handshake authentication. Users undergo strong authentication if they want to change their custom settings (for example, their greeting message) or listen to voice mail.

Encrypt VoIP Traffic

VoIP packets are vulnerable to snooping. All it takes to intrude is one IP packet monitor sniffing somewhere on the network, watching for VoIP packets and storing them on a hard drive for playback later on. Sniffers are available as free software from most any techie software repository. Many come with source code that can be easily modified for tapping.

The only way to avoid this simple form of wiretapping is to encrypt the audio portion of the call. On-the-fly encryption and decryption takes time, though, which adds to the end-to-end delay. Add too much delay, and the *mean opinion score* (MOS) for the call declines. Many VoIP gateways have some form of encryption available or coming soon, but it is rarely used. Even though encryption is a component of the H.323v2 standard, it is likely to be one of the last features implemented.

End-to-end encryption and decryption are strongly recommended for VoIP calls. In particular, do not send unencrypted IP voice over an unmanaged or public network. Unfortunately, many encryption devices are still too slow. If an encryption device is used to pass VoIP traffic over a public network, it is likely that the voice quality will be unacceptable, especially as the number of VoIP users grows. This is another case where MOS testing is important in device selection and calibration.

A VPN lets you connect from one computer to another over any network. To the two computers, the network connection appears private and secure. Although you often see VPNs used from site to site through VPN gateways, they also can be used from computer to computer across a LAN. VPN technology has matured rapidly during the past few years, particularly with the adoption of a group of standards known as *IPSec* (IP Security).

IPSec technologies offer to VPNs various levels of the following:

- Authentication, verifying the identity of the two computers
- Assurance that the data has not been modified
- Assurance that the data cannot be observed by anyone capturing network packets

The most cost-effective way to do VoIP encryption and decryption is to use an IPSec VPN. IPSec is widely implemented; many vendors support it and it interoperates well among devices. Its encryption algorithms are state-of-the-art and strong, and they have been widely tested. Because IPSec is standardized, there is a broad body of literature available to explain its operation to your support staff.

Modern software tools, such as NetIQ's Chariot, can show you how VPN settings affect performance for different traffic types. Such tools also can identify network configuration errors or limitations of your service provider. Most importantly, they can demonstrate capacity limits: how many of your users can connect to your VPN, where each user gets good MOS for their voice calls and reasonable performance for their other applications.

There is an excellent software-based IPSec stack that is shipped as part of Windows 2000 and Windows XP. However, consider testing to ensure that the IPSec stack doesn't add too much delay. You may find that the horsepower of a dedicated hardware VPN server is what is needed. You may not want to do this alone—there are still many things that can go wrong when using VPNs in heterogeneous networks. Consider using a VPN service to worry about the hard stuff, but be sure to track its performance and audit its security.

Tighten Your Processes

Good processes can prevent many security problems. Evaluate your processes in the context of security to see where education is needed and how problems can be prevented in the future.

Create a Well-Educated Security Team

Good computer and network security has rarely been taught in schools. The reason for this omission is evident: Students armed with state-of-the-art knowledge about the ins and outs of security usually find the time to experiment on the very tempting system in front of them, the school's. Also, both the state-of-the-art and the state-of-what's-easy-to-do knowledge advance quickly in information security. So, in an area of extreme importance, most IT professionals and most students, at every level of education, are seriously undereducated. What they have learned, they have usually learned on their own, on the street (well, probably "on the net").

The stakes are different for someone whose job now focuses on his or her knowledge of security. As an employer, it is important to have thorough, in-depth, ongoing education for your security team.

Those who know system security well often have learned their trade from the other side of the fence, as an intruder. That is a valuable skill, but it does not necessarily translate to the classic roles of the defender in managing computer security: prevention, detection, and reaction.[1] Members of the team need to master the processes in each of these areas.

It is important to understand user psychology. Most breaches are enabled by lapses in human engineering. Use insight into intruders to think ahead of them. What knowledge does your team need to prevent new attacks, to defend against their damage, and to react as they occur?

Intruders take advantage of vulnerabilities. Educate your team on solid processes that avoid vulnerabilities. Send them to classes, buy them books, and give them a time and place to experiment. You should insist on courses such as "Windows: Designing Security" and "Windows: Network Security Design" for those seeking or renewing their MCSE certification.

The SANS Institute maintains an excellent web page, describing the top 20 Internet vulnerabilities.[10] Microsoft offers "The Ten Immutable Laws of Security."[11] Pass these lists to your security team.

The education should not stop. Look at the weekly trade magazines; there is constant focus on the security problems with the pertinent technologies, such as VoIP, encryption, VPNs, and viruses.

Also, educate your employees on security issues. Conduct random security "fire drills," gauging employee reaction to security situations. An uneducated employee may be your worst security back door.

Perform Postmortems

Whenever a security incident occurs, take some time after the fact to go back and review it. How did the intrusion occur? How could it have been prevented? How could it have been detected earlier, before it did too much damage? How could the users and the security team react better, to reduce the damage? What roles were not covered well, and which were?

Log data is a primary input for postmortems and for the forensic analysis of incidents. Log every action and anomaly observed in the network or systems as they occur. Use a reporting tool to correlate and reduce the log data, and to generate reports from it. Log all available fields; what you consider unimportant today may be the most important field tomorrow. Export all logs to a secure server and back them up. Hackers may attempt to modify logs to cover their tracks, so their export and storage is critical. Never modify logs from their original format; modified logs may not be legally admissible.

Postmortems are a rich source for plans and actions in your organization. Write down the observations, and turn the lessons into something manageable, such as a Top 5 or a Top 10 list. The key is that it is *your* list, not one from Microsoft or from a magazine. Factor the list back into budgets, job descriptions, and employee feedback reviews. Use it as a mechanism to make improvements and to move your team forward—not to blame them.

Exploit Vendor Resources

Stay attuned with your network equipment, operating system, and application vendors. They are extremely motivated to avoid the poor reputation of shipping vulnerable products. Many vendors offer subscription email lists for security alerts and information updates.

Stay Up to Date with Your Network Equipment Vendors

The major vendors of VoIP equipment know how important security is to the success of VoIP. They generally have on their development staff a team that consists of the collectors of security "stuff." This team finds active security holes and takes reports from the field about vulnerabilities or attacks. It, in turn, builds defenses against the attacks or closes the vulnerabilities.

Your equipment vendor is a rich source of information about its specific products. Stay up to date with the latest security alerts and product patches. Also, stay current with information available on the public forums—your peers may find and fix security problems before the vendor does.

A good starting place for information focused on VoIP security is the Cisco SAFE Blueprint (http://www.cisco.com/go/safe/). See the section "IP Telephony Security."

Stay Up to Date with Your Software Vendors

The VoIP servers and IP PBXs from vendors such as 3Com, Alcatel, Avaya, Cisco, Nortel, and others generally run on off-the-shelf server computers. Their specialized VoIP applications run on standard operating systems such as Windows, Linux, and UNIX. The products have standard TCP/IP stacks, with vulnerabilities that have been widely studied, so they are susceptible to DoS or hacker attacks. Many VoIP servers also include web-based administration clients or configuration tools built on Microsoft *Internet Information Server* (IIS) and Apache web server—platforms that are being frequently patched for security holes and bugs.

Inside many of the key VoIP servers lies an Intel-family computer running a version of Microsoft Windows. When was the last time a virus took out your pre-VoIP phone system? If you migrate to a VoIP solution that is dependent on Windows, you may come to learn a whole new meaning for the word *convergence*. When the next Nimda or Code-Red invades your e-mail and web servers, your VoIP phone system could fall victim as well.

Many VoIP components ship with strong dependencies on Microsoft's web server. These bundled solutions introduce yet another challenge for an IT staff: the problem of third-party patching. Although you can download a patch for the latest IIS hole and apply it to your web servers, your procedures must change when you don't have the same kind of administrative access to a turnkey appliance or a switch blade. "On traditional PBXs, although they had PC processors in them, they were not necessarily as susceptible to viruses," noted Kevin Wetzel, manager of global network services for chemical manufacturer H.B. Fuller.[12] "People are writing NT viruses, not PBX viruses, so it's a trade-off," says Wetzel.

Microsoft has increased its focus on Windows security as a key to its ongoing success. In 2002, Bill Gates initiated an intense focus by Microsoft on "trustworthy software."[13] Microsoft's three-pronged approach is aimed at the right places, but as 2002 has stretched into 2004, most readers will argue there is still a long way to go:

1   Making Microsoft's software less vulnerable to attacks

2   Making online transactions private and under the control of the users

3   Making their software easier to use and more reliable

Microsoft has a dedicated area of its website where the members of your security team should start their search for information (http://www.microsoft.com/security/) and another area that has detailed technical information for IT professionals (http://www.microsoft.com/technet/security/). Microsoft's Security Toolkit CD is free. It takes a few weeks to arrive, so go to http://www.microsoft.com/security/mstpp.asp and put your order in today. Another free offering is the Product Security Notification (http://www.microsoft.com/technet/security/bulletin/notify.asp), an e-mail notification service that Microsoft uses to send information to subscribers about the security of Microsoft products. Anyone can subscribe to the service and unsubscribe at any time.

Insist on Best Practices IT Production Management

VoIP management was discussed in detail in Chapter 6, "Ongoing VoIP Management," which included extensive coverage of these key elements:

- Change management
- Event management
- Access management
- Network management

VoIP will probably be the most mission-critical application on your data network for the foreseeable future. There may be some management tools and processes that you know you need to get around to some day. With VoIP, that day has arrived; you will find that high-quality, production-level management is imperative to keep your VoIP users happy.

Don't rely on traditional PBX administrators to manage VoIP. VoIP is a whole new can of worms for them, requiring broad systems and network management skills. PBX administrators often have a limited knowledge of computer security, if any. VoIP security in an organization is mission-critical, and should be handled by qualified professionals.

Chapter Summary

VoIP security presents many challenges, which have been discussed in this chapter. Many of the recommendations to meet these challenges have been covered here as well. Security issues are hot topics for computers and computer networks. There is no reason to think that this will change in the near future. Don't let the abundance of security issues scare you away from a VoIP deployment. Careful planning, awareness, and proper management can go a long way toward preventing, detecting, and reacting to security problems before they can impact your business.

Conclusion

This book included the steps you can follow to "take charge" of your VoIP project. Consider the high-level points again:

- **Chapter 1, "VoIP Basics."** First, you need to know the technology and key components.

- **Chapter 2, "Building a Business Case for VoIP.** Make smart decisions on the financial and business justification.

- **Chapter 3, "Planning for VoIP."** Prior to deployment, put in the up-front work that makes the deployment a breeze.

- **Chapter 4, "Do It Yourself or Outsource?."** Make the decision whether or not to work with excellent partners to get the job done.

- **Chapter 5, "Quality of Service and Tuning."** You need QoS for VoIP. Understand the key mechanisms and when to use them.

- **Chapter 6, "Ongoing VoIP Management."** After VoIP is deployed, make it run well.

- **Chapter 7, "Establishing VoIP SLAs."** The service level metrics that you should consider and how to make sure that they are being met.

- **Chapter 8, "VoIP Security."** Don't leave out security planning and management.

There are VoIP projects that go out of control and VoIP projects that go smoothly. By following classic IT project management and applying proper planning and process control, a lot of the risk can be removed from VoIP deployments.

End Notes

1   Schneier, Bruce, *Secrets and Lies: Digital Security in a Networked World* (Hoboken, NJ: John Wiley & Sons, 2000).

2   Kovar, Matthew, "Network Security Industry Must Undergo Fundamental Paradigm Shift in Order to Evolve," Yankee Group news release, July 16, 2001, http://about.reuters.com/newsreleases/art_16-7-2001_id659.asp.

3   Freeman, David, "Information Warfare," *MIT Technology Review* 104, no. 9, pp. 61–67, November 2001, http://www.technologyreview.com/articles/freedman1101.asp.

4   Thompson, Todd, "Where Did All My Bandwidth Go?" SANS Institute Reading Room, June 18, 2001, http://www.giac.org/practical/gsec/Todd_Thompson_GSEC.pdf (p.1).

5   Graham, Robert, "FAQ: Network Intrusion Detection Systems," http://www.robertgraham.com/pubs/network-intrusion-detection.html.

6   The Honey Project, "What a Honeynet Is," in *Know Your Enemy: Revealing the Security Tools, Tactics, and Motives of the Blackhat Community* (Boston: Addison-Wesley, 2001).

7   "vomit–Voice over Misconfigured Internet Telephones," a software program by Niels Provos. Web page: http://vomit.xtdnet.nl/.

8   Swart, Marius, "The Enemy Within: Don't Overlook Internal Security," *ITWeb*, July 18, 2001, http://www.itweb.co.za/sections/techforum/2001/0107180819.asp.

9   Taylor, David, "Are there Vulnerabilities in VLAN Implementations?" SANS Institute resources, July 12, 2000, http://www.sans.org/newlook/resources/IDFAQ/vlan.php.

10 SANS Institute, "The SANS Top 20 Internet Security Vulnerabilities" SANS Institute resources, http://www.sans.org/top20/.

11 "The Ten Immutable Laws of Security," Microsoft Corporation, http://www.microsoft.com/technet/columns/security/10imlaws.asp.

12 Hochmuth, Phil, "Is VoIP Vulnerable?" *Network World*, June 24, 2002, http://www.nwfusion.com/news/2002/0624voip.html.

13 Gates, Bill, e-mail of January 15, 2002, "Subject: Trustworthy computing," http://news.com.com/2009-1001-817210.html?legacy=cnet.

INDEX

Numerics

P

packets, 16
  IP, header format, 18
  security vulnerabilities, 269–270
packet-switched connections, 13
packetization delay, 87
PAMS (Perceptual Analysis Measurement System), 81
partnership with VoIP integrator
  developing, 136–137
  maintaining, 137
PBXs, (private branch exchanges), 8, 23–25, 127
PCM (pulse code modulation), 6, 85
performance
  QoS
    best practices, 174–176
    identifying need for, 146
    IP mechanisms, 157–161
    link-layer mechanisms, 152–156
    managing, 209–211
    overprovisioning, 143
    oversubscribing, 143–144
    queuing, 162–164
    selecting metrics, 145–147
    testing, 171–172
    traffic classification, 145–149
    traffic shapers, 165
  requirements for voice
  applications, 144
  SLAs
    availability metric, 217–218
    call quality metric, 220–221
    call setup performance metric, 218–220
    implementing, 223–230
    incident tracking, 222
    managing, 208–209
    measurement tools, 230, 233–234
    selecting metrics, 216–217
  TCP/IP, tuning, 166–167
  tuning, 128, 167–170
  voice quality, MOS, 220
  VoIP tuning, 167–170
performing
  data network upgrades, 104–105, 124–125
    changing network design, 107
    eliminating equipment gaps, 108
    obtaining more bandwidth, 105–106
    postmortems, 271–272
    QoS tuning, 108
    replacing equipment, 106
  VoIP readiness assessment, 93
    bandwidth modeling, 99–102
    call-quality assessment, 97–99
    configuration assessment, 93–95
    utilization assessment, 95–97
PESQ (Perceptual Evaluation of Speech Quality), 80
phone tag, 39
physical security, 254–256
pilot deployments, 125–126
  building, 109–110
    evaluating systems, 111–113
    solving echo problems, 113–114
    transcoding, 115

response time, 78

returns, estimating in VoIP
deployment, 53, 55

RFCs (Request For Comments), 12

ROI (return on investment), xvii

    analyzing, 43–44

    calculating, 48–55

    ensuring profitability, 56–57

    evaluating, 30

    investments, estimating, 50–53

    measuring benefits of VoIP, 31–32

        business risks, 43

        convergence, 41–42

        cost investment, 42

        cost savings, 32–37

        hard benefits, 32

        new features, 39–40

        productivity savings, 37–38

        soft benefits, 32

routers, 25

RSVP (Resource Reservation
Protocol), 159–161

RTP (Real-time Transport
Protocol), 78

    header compression, 105, 155–156

    header fields, 21–22

    lost data, 91–93

    multiplexing, 106

R-value, calculating, 82–85

S

scalability

    cost savings of VoIP network
expansion, 36

    growth management, 184–185

planning for future growth,
211–212

Schneier, Bruce, 238

SCP (Session Control Point), 10

script kiddies, 240

security, 238

    detecting breaches, 243

    events, 240

    forensics, 244

    hackers versus physical intruders,
238–240

    intrusion detection, 242

    intrusions, 240

    prevention, 241–242

    reacting to intrusions, 244–245

    recommended practices, securing
central facilities, 254–258, 260

    vulnerabilities of VoIP

        annoyances, 253

        call hijacking, 252

        confidentiality, 248–251

        data network, 261–264

        DoS attacks, 252

        IP phones, 266–269

        packets, 269–270

        toll fraud, 246–248

        *undefined processes,
270–274*

selecting

    codecs, 85–87

    integrators, criteria, 132–135

    metrics for SLAs, 216–217

        availability, 217–218

        call quality, 220–221

        *call setup performance,
218–220*

    MSPs, criteria, 130–132

T